BTEC First

Travel and Tourism

Christine King • Andy Kerr
Malcolm Jefferies • Dennis Brombley

www.heinemann.co.uk
✓ Free online support
✓ Useful weblinks
✓ 24 hour online ordering

01865 888058

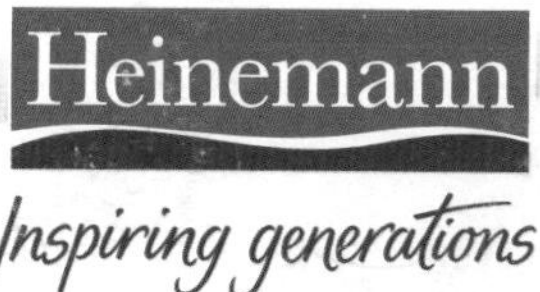

Heinemann Educational Publishers
Halley Court, Jordan Hill, Oxford OX2 8EJ
Part of Harcourt Education

Heinemann is a registered trademark of
Harcourt Education Limited

First published 2005

10 09 08 07 06 05
10 9 8 7 6 5 4 3 2 1

British Library Cataloguing in Publication Data is available
from the British Library on request.

ISBN 0-435-45947-3
ISBN 978-0-435459-475

Edited by Susan Ross, Ross Economics and Editorial Services Ltd
Typeset by Integra (India) Ltd

Illustrated by Integra (India) Ltd/Techtype

Cover design by Wooden Ark

Printed by Bath Colourbooks

Cover photo: © Getty

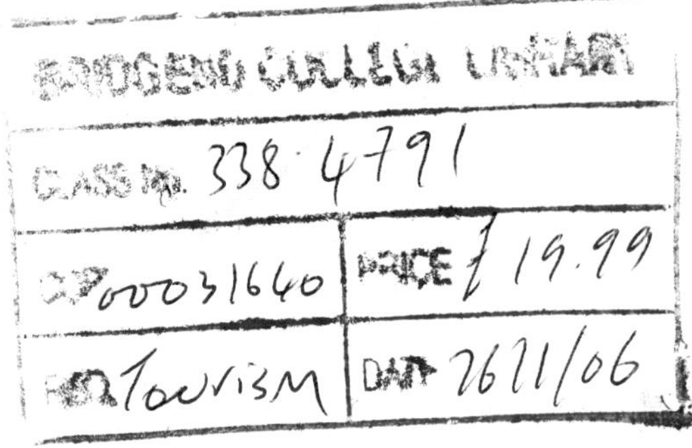

Contents

Acknowledgements

The authors and publisher are grateful to those who have given permission to reproduce material.

Pearson Education, p4 and p16; By kind permission of British Airways, p16 and p98; First Choice, p29; VisitBritain, p44; Jorvik Viking Centre, p47; Kuoni Travel Ltd, p62; Sunday Independent (Ireland), p85; Jan Carlzon, p86; Mandarin Oriental: The Hotel Group, p111; Holiday Inn Hotels, p115; easyJet, p113; Southwest Airlines, p113; Club 18–30, p139; Saga, p139; Avis Rent A Car System, Inc., p146; Mercury Direct, p154; Emirates News, p160; Guardian Newspapers Limited 2004, p172; Guildford College of Further and Higher Education, p202; BBC News website, p206.

Photos

AIGA, p105; Airtours Ltd, p5; Alton Towers, p271; Arnos Design Ltd, p129, p150, p155, p184, p185, p186, p249, p271; Brittany Ferries, p94; Richard Campbell/Visit Scotland, p271; Corbis, p11, p28, p52 (top and middle), p59, p64, p67, p68 (bottom), p69, p70 (bottom), p77, p78, p153, p164; Dartmoor National Park Authority, p51; Andy Dukes (BMF), p142; Eurostar, p171; First Choice, p5, p137; Getty, p30, p31 (top); Getty Images/Photodisc, p18, p21, p24, p27, p32, p44 (bottom), p49, p52 (bottom), p55, p63, p65, p68 (top), p148, p161; Getty Images Sport/Stuart Franklin, p211, p280; Harcourt Education Ltd/Debbie Rowe, p44 (top), p46, p102, p107, p120; Harcourt Education Ltd/Digital Vision, p13; Harcourt Education Ltd/Jane Hance, p149; Harcourt Education Ltd/Photodisc, p7; Inghams, p36, p57, p179; International Hotel Groups PLC, p81; International Olympic Committee, p210; Andre Jenny/AIAMY, p214; National Geographisical Data Centre, p31 (bottom); P&O Ferries, p9, p23; Photodisc, p44 (middle), p87, p91, p152, p157, p181, p182; Rex Features, p226; St Lucia Tourist Board, p61; Thomas Cook Ltd, p5; Thomson Holidays Ltd, p5, p33, p96, 104, p162; Virgin Atlantic, p8; VisitBighton.com, p271; Warwick Castle, p70; www.incameraphotography.com/Alamy, p281; YHA, p175.

Introduction

The travel and tourism industry is one of the fastest growing industries in the world. It employs thousands of people in the UK and millions worldwide. Tourism generates millions of pounds of income every year for the UK economy, and most of us participate in its activities, whether it is going for a day trip to a shopping mall or spending two weeks on a beach.

Working in the industry can be tiring, and dealing with a variety of customers can sometimes be frustrating, but you can also enjoy tremendous job satisfaction helping people to make the most of their trip. You may also get the opportunity to travel yourself and experience a variety of cultures and destinations.

What's in this textbook?

Your BTEC First Diploma in Travel and Tourism is certificated by Edexcel, one of the country's leading awarding bodies for vocational qualifications. This textbook covers all of the core and optional units:

Core units

Unit 1 Introduction to the Travel and Tourism Industry
Unit 2 Introduction to Tourist Destinations
Unit 3 Introduction to Customer Service in Travel and Tourism

Optional units

Unit 4 Introduction to Marketing in Travel and Tourism
Unit 5 Introduction to the Business of Travel and Tourism
Unit 6 Organising a Travel and Tourism Event
Unit 7 Work-based Project within the Travel and Tourism Industry
Unit 8 Travel and Tourism Study Visit

Assessment

You will be assessed by a series of assignments. You will need to demonstrate your understanding of a number of learning outcomes. Each unit may be assessed by one large or a series of small assignments. These will cover the grading criteria published by Edexcel and will be available for you to check your progress against. Each unit has a Pass, Merit and

Distinction grade. You will need to provide evidence for each of the criteria at Pass grade to obtain a Pass; all of the Pass grade and the Merit grade criteria to obtain a Merit Grade, and all of the Pass grade, Merit grade and Distinction grade to obtain a Distinction.

How will this book help you?

You will find throughout this book a number of features which will encourage you to pause and think about what you have just read. There are also a variety of exercises to reinforce what you have been learning. Features include:

- **Activities** – which will guide you towards further research.
- **Over to you** – questions which you should think about, or discuss.
- **Talking point** – questions for you to discuss in your group.
- **Key points** – a list summarising the key topics.
- **Case studies** – examples taken from the travel and tourism industry which will help you to understand the theories.
- **Practice assessment activities** – these will help you practise your skills for final assessment.
- **In summary** – this sums up the main points throughout each unit.

As well as reading this book and completing the exercises, you should try to be aware of all the information available to you in the media. There are many television programmes such as 'Wish You Were Here', 'Airport', etc. which are made for prime-time television but which also give you an insight into the industry. Look at the travel supplements of weekend newspapers, visit as many different kinds of attractions as you can with a 'professional' eye and look at brochures, posters and guides.

The more aware you are of all the many and varied ways of being a 'tourist', the easier you will find it to obtain the higher grades, and the more you will enjoy learning about this vibrant and exciting industry!

Unit 1 Introduction to the Travel and Tourism Industry

Introduction

Most of us have experienced tourism at some time or other, whether it's trekking in the Andes Mountains of South America, enjoying a week's package holiday in Spain or simply spending a day out at a visitor attraction in the UK. To get to any of these places, tourists need to travel!

In 2003, UK residents made 61.4 million leisure or business visits abroad and spent £28.6 billion on those visits. The figures do not include domestic visits, that is visits made by UK residents within the UK. In turn, the UK received 24.7 million visits from abroad. Overseas visitors spent £11.9 billion. By any measure, travel and tourism is a big industry!

So what is the travel and tourism industry all about? This unit will develop your knowledge and understanding of this fascinating and complex industry.

The unit first considers the structure of the travel and tourism industry including an introduction to its many components, its history and development since 1945 and the purpose and functions of different organisations. It then investigates the products and services provided by the travel and tourism industry. The next section examines recent developments in the industry and considers how these affect the products and services provided. Finally, the unit considers the many and varied jobs and career opportunities on offer in the industry.

How you will be assessed

This unit is assessed by an externally set BTEC assignment. By completing the Practice Assessment Activities in this unit you will gain knowledge and skills that will help you with the assessment. Ask your teacher what to expect from the external assignment.

In this unit you will learn about:

① the structure of the travel and tourism industry

② products and services

③ recent developments in travel and tourism

④ job roles and career opportunities.

1.1 The structure of the travel and tourism industry

The travel and tourism industry is made up of a number of different organisations which work together for the benefit of the tourist. It is a service-based industry and most companies sell the tourist a service – there are no real products for the tourist to take away with them, just souvenirs, photos and memories. It is sometimes said that what the travel and tourism industry provides, most of the time, is dreams and experiences.

Definitions, descriptions and roles

What is the difference between travel and tourism?

Travel involves getting from one place to another, and there are a variety of means – by air, rail, road or sea.

ACTIVITY

How many different methods of transport have you used? Write a list of as many different types of transport that you can think of – some you may have to pay for, others may be free.

Tourism is what we do when we are at a destination away from our home. There are two main types of tourist:

- A **leisure tourist** is someone who is away from their home during their own free time for a variety of reasons such as a holiday, a shopping trip, to visit friends and relatives (known as VFR), to attend sporting events like the Olympic games or a sports world cup.
- A **business tourist** is someone who is away from their home or work and undertaking work while they are away. They may be attending a business meeting, trade fair or conference or be on a sales trip. Of course, a business tourist may become a leisure tourist during their visit.

ACTIVITY

Make a list of the reasons why people travel. Identify those that are business reasons and those that are leisure reasons. Don't forget that some people may have to travel for reasons other than pleasurable ones; try to include some of these reasons in your list as well.

KEY POINTS

Remember these definitions:

Tourism: comprises the activities of persons travelling to and staying in places outside their usual environment for not more than one consecutive year for leisure, business and other purposes.

Visitors: All types of travellers engaged in tourism.

Tourists: Visitors who stay away from home for at least 24 hours, that is, overnight visitors.

Although the definition of a tourist is that they are away from home overnight, it is generally accepted that tourism includes those who also only go on day visits.

Tourism statistics need to be treated with care. Some countries may not make the same distinctions between visitors and tourists, and between leisure and business. Accurate statistics are sometimes difficult to obtain. This may be because of relaxations of border controls between certain countries, for example within the European Union.

The travel and tourism industry consists of a number of different organisations that need to work together to provide the tourist with the products and services which cater for their needs. The industry is divided into three sectors:

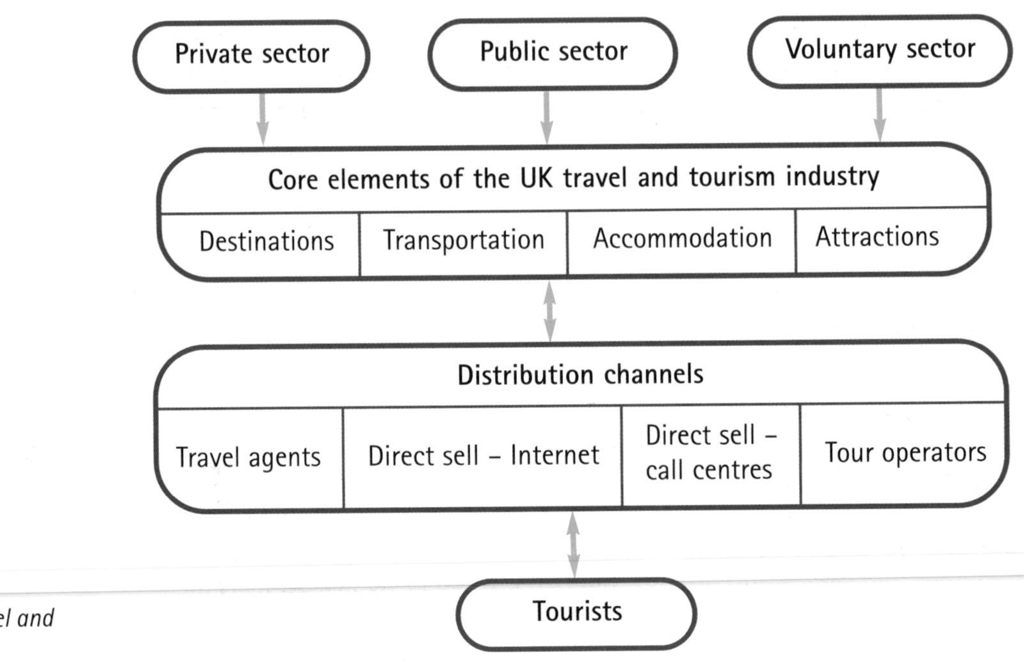

Sectors in the travel and tourism industry

KEY POINTS

The travel and tourism industry is divided into three sectors:

- Private
- Public
- Voluntary.

- The **private sector** is the commercial part of the industry that exists to make a profit for its owners or shareholders. This sector makes up the bulk of the travel and tourism industry and includes industries such as airlines, tour operators, travel agents, accommodation providers and some visitor attractions.
- The **public sector** is non-commercial. That means its aim is not to make a profit, but rather to provide a service or to educate. Central, regional or local government form the public sector and sometimes own (and run) attractions such as parks, gardens and museums. Tourist

boards, whether national or local, are public sector organisations. In some countries, governments own, or have a stake in, rail companies, airlines, etc.

- The **voluntary sector** is non-commercial and includes organisations such as the National Trust, English Heritage and the Youth Hostel Association. These organisations rely on members' subscriptions and sponsorship as well as, in some cases, admission charges as a means of funding in order to operate.

ACTIVITY

1 Contact the leisure and tourism department of your local council and find out what services it owns or runs. Look also at the council's website and see what information you can find.

2 Visit English Heritage's website (www.english-heritage.org.uk) to find out what properties they own in your area. You may wish to organise a visit, as English Heritage offers free entry to many of their sites for organised educational groups.

Let's look a little closer at some of the organisations involved in the travel and tourism industry.

Tour operators

Tour operators bring together different components of the travel and tourism industry, such as transportation and accommodation, and package them to sell at an inclusive price to tourists. That's where the terms 'package holiday' and 'inclusive holiday' come from. They either sell their products direct (personal callers, over the telephone, via the Internet) or through a travel agent to whom they pay commission.

Tour operators can be divided into three categories:

- **Outbound** tour operators such as Thomson, Airtours, Thomas Cook and First Choice are used by many people to book their holidays, typically a Mediterranean beach resort in the summer season. These companies generally offer a range of holidays, such as lakes and mountains, winter sun or winter sports. The four companies mentioned above are often referred to as the 'Big 4'. Between them they take more than 10 million people on holiday each year, which is nearly 50 per cent of the holiday market. There are specialist tour operators who specialise in holidays of a particular type or to

The 'Big 4'

a particular destination. Examples of European destination specialist operators include Mundi Color (Spain) and Citalia (Italy). There are also long-haul specialists including Kuoni Travel and Bales Worldwide. Specialist product tour operators include Sunsail (sailing) and Neilson (skiing). Club 18–30 and Saga (for those over 50) cater for specific age groups. Some specialist tour operators are owned by the 'Big 4'.

- **Inbound** tour operators deal with holidays in the UK for overseas visitors. They organise tours and accommodation to meet the needs of these tourists. Globus (Tourwise of London) and Miki Travel are two operators in this category (see www.BITOA.co.uk for further information on inbound tour operators).
- **Domestic** tour operators arrange holidays in the UK for British residents and include anything from holiday centres (Butlins, Haven, Center Parcs) and coach holidays (Shearings, Wallace Arnold – who also operate overseas holidays) to hotel breaks (Superbreak, Highlife).

KEY POINTS

There are three categories of tour operator:

- Outbound
- Inbound
- Domestic.

Travel agents

The purpose of the travel agent is to provide a link between the customer and the principal (airline, tour operator, hotel, etc.). Travel agents assess the needs of their customers and sell the right product to them. In return, they receive commission (payment) from the principal, although you will read on page 30 of changes in how travel agents get paid for their efforts.

In the UK there are leisure travel agents and business travel agents.

Leisure travel agents

Leisure travel agents are usually found in the shopping centres of your local town or city, and may be one of the following:

- Multiples are generally agents that have at least 50 branches and include companies such as Thomson, Going Places, Thomas Cook and First Choice. Some of these companies have more than 600 UK branches.
- Miniples are agents that have between five and about 50 branches. Often they are located in one region of the country such as Bath Travel which has branches in Dorset, Hampshire, West Sussex and Wiltshire.
- Independents are 'one-off' agents with up to about five branches in or around one particular area. Some independent agents may specialise in one particular part of the industry.

KEY POINTS

There are three types of travel agent:

- Multiple
- Miniple
- Independent.

Business travel agents

Business travel agents or business travel management companies cater for the travel needs of industry and the business community. They handle and manage the travel accounts of businesses both large and small, and specialise in making air bookings and hotel bookings for the business traveller.

Normally the company employing the traveller pays for the business travel arrangements rather than the traveller themselves. Many business clients travel frequently, so it is important for the travel consultant to build a rapport (a good relationship) with them.

Business travellers tend to make most of their bookings by telephone or email. Therefore, many business travel agencies are situated in office locations away from the high street. They do not need highly visible shops to attract customers in the same way as a leisure travel agency does. They may even be located within their clients' offices.

Business travel agencies include such companies as BTI UK and Portman Travel. Sometimes they are divisions or subsidiaries of larger travel organisations, for example American Express and Carlson Wagonlits. Some independent and miniple leisure agents also have thriving business travel departments.

ACTIVITY

Use the Internet or other resources to find at least one business travel agency. Identify what facilities they offer.

Compare your research with other members of your group who have researched other business travel agencies. What are the similarities and differences?

What services are offered by business travel specialists compared with high street leisure travel agencies?

Transport

Airlines

Airlines exist to transport their passengers safely from one place to another as quickly and efficiently as possible. There are three main types of airline:

- scheduled
- budget
- charter.

Scheduled airlines

Airlines such as British Airways, Virgin Atlantic and bmi all operate to a timetable and must fly regardless of how many passengers are booked on a flight. Seats are sold to the public, usually via the airlines' websites, or direct by telephone, or through a travel agent. The airline may have as many as four classes or levels of service and may include food and drinks in the fare.

Most provide interlining facilities for passengers who are connecting to further flights. This means passengers and baggage can also be checked in for their onward connecting flight at the first boarding point, which ensures they have an assigned seat on their connecting flight and saves them time at the connecting airport. If they are delayed by the first airline and miss their connecting flight, passengers are usually looked after by the airlines and alternative flights are arranged for them. Such airlines are often known as full-service airlines.

Budget airlines

Budget airlines are really also scheduled airlines. They also operate to a timetable and fly regardless of the number of passengers. However, they generally only sell seats to the public via their websites or direct by telephone.

Some budget airlines fly to airports that are further from the city centre. Passengers have to pay extra for food, drinks and any entertainment that may be available on board the aircraft. Some do not allocate specific seats when passengers check in for their flight, so they have to find a seat as if they were travelling by bus or train. They usually only offer 'point-to-point' facilities, that is, they will only accept passengers and their baggage to the destination of the first flight. Any passengers with onward flights have to check themselves and their baggage in again at the transfer airport, which can be a lengthy and tiring process. If the delivering airline is late and the passenger misses their onward flight, the airlines are unlikely to accept responsibility, and the passenger may have to buy a new ticket for an onward flight. For all these reasons, budget airlines are often called 'no-frills' airlines.

On the plus side, budget airlines provide a service to and from many regional airports in the UK, many of which have seen major growth as a result of the budget airlines. Ryanair and easyJet are the largest of the UK budget airlines.

Charter airlines

These airlines charter their aircraft to a person or organisation paying for the exclusive use of that aircraft. This might be as an *ad hoc* charter (a one-off arrangement), a series charter (several journeys between the same points) or a time charter (an aircraft which is chartered for a given period of time).

Because such flights have been chartered, seats on them are not directly available for sale to the general public. However, charter flights are normally for tour operators who sell the seats to the public as part of their package holiday programmes. Some tour operators charter a complete aircraft to operate a flight to a particular destination; others (generally smaller tour operators) buy seats on a charter flight to suit the needs of their holiday programme.

Tour operators own some of the charter airlines. Thomsonfly, Airtours, First Choice and Monarch are examples of charter airlines owned in this way.

Recently, the distinction between the three types of airline – scheduled, budget, charter – has become somewhat blurred, particularly on European routes. To compete with the budget airlines, some scheduled (full-service) airlines have been changing their products, introducing Internet fares which match or beat budget airline fares. Some no longer offer free food and drink on board, while retaining other aspects of full service like passenger and baggage interlining facilities, for example Aer Lingus. Many charter airlines now sell 'seats only' on their charter flights through travel companies. Some operate scheduled services as well as charter flights, for example Monarch. Passengers need to check carefully what their chosen airline will and will not provide.

Air travel is popular, but so are other forms of transport.

Cruise ships

Cruising is increasing in popularity. In 2004, over one million UK residents chose cruising holidays. Major companies like P&O and Cunard are building new ships and super ships to cope with the increasing demand for this market. Cruising can be a cost-effective way of taking a holiday as it offers an opportunity to visit a number of different destinations on one holiday and all food and activities on board ship are included in the price. In fact, it could be argued that cruising is the original all-inclusive holiday!

Car ferry and fast craft

Another popular method of travel is by car ferry and fast craft. Over 20 UK ports provide ferry services to other countries, such as Spain, France, Belgium, the Netherlands and Ireland, as well as to a number of destinations within the UK. Journey times can range from less than an hour to over 20 hours, depending upon the route and type of ship. On some of the longer sea crossings, for example between Portsmouth and Bilbao, the journeys are sometimes referred to as 'mini-cruises' and some people make the round trip for the pleasure of the voyage. This form of transport is particularly suitable for people who wish to take their own car and drive to their holiday destination. It is also an alternative for those who prefer not to fly.

ACTIVITY

Locate your nearest rail station. In pairs, work out which rail routes would take you via Eurostar to Paris.

Rail

Rail travel also provides a popular alternative form of transport. UK rail transport is experiencing major change and upgrading to enable it to compete with road and air travel and to compare favourably with other countries' rail systems.

Since the Channel Tunnel opened in 1994, the Eurotunnel service has been a serious competitor to the car ferry operators, particularly on the Dover to Calais route, as people are able to drive their car on to a train and arrive in France in little over half an hour. For passengers without a car, the Eurostar service operates from London Waterloo and Ashford to destinations such as Paris, Disneyland Paris, Lille and Brussels, and then high-speed rail connections are available to other towns and cities in Europe and beyond.

Coach

There are a number of scheduled coach services operated within the UK by companies such as National Express, which operates to approximately 1,000 UK destinations and carries around 16 million passengers a year. Services also operate between the UK and European destinations, which provide a cheap alternative to flying and an opportunity to see more of a country from ground level.

Several companies offer inclusive holidays by coach. These may be a tour, stopping off at a number of different points for a day or two, or drive and stay where you are taken directly to your destination and stay for a number of days. Many companies offer day excursions within the UK.

Car hire

There are many self-drive companies throughout the world, for example Avis and Hertz, providing self-drive cars for tourists, enabling them to have greater freedom and better access to their destinations. Chauffeur-driven cars are also available in many locations.

ACTIVITY

What are the advantages and disadvantages of travelling by each type of transport discussed in this section? How could each be improved?

Accommodation

There are several types of accommodation available. These are divided into two main categories:

- **Serviced** accommodation includes hotels, villas and apartments.
- **Non-serviced** accommodation includes campsites, caravan parks and holiday villages.

While most package holidays tend to include some form of accommodation, people are increasingly booking accommodation and flights or other transport separately on the Internet to create their own individual independent holiday.

Accommodation isn't just a bed. What else might it include?

Catering

Of course, tourists need food. This may be provided as part of the transport, accommodation or visitor attraction experience, but it may also be provided by independent or multiple caterers as stand-alone facilities.

ACTIVITY

Think about catering connected with:

- Transport
- Accommodation
- Visitor attractions

Guiding

Guiding is an invaluable feature of tourism. It can be, for example, the tour guide travelling on a two-week coach tour, the guide on a day excursion, the guide offering town or city guided walks, or guides at historic buildings and museums. In all cases, the guides are expected to be knowledgeable, friendly and good communicators.

ACTIVITY

In your group, look at a map covering a 20-mile radius from your home town. Identify three locations or attractions where guides may be used. What services would they be providing?

Visitor attractions

A visitor attraction can be natural or man-made. Natural attractions are part of the environment, like the Yorkshire Dales and Chesil Beach. Some areas of the UK have been designated as National Parks or Areas of Outstanding Natural Beauty (AONB). Man-made attractions range from those that have been built specifically to attract tourists like theme parks or museums, to those that were built for other purposes, such as cathedrals and castles.

Information services

Many cities, towns and visitor attractions have travel and tourism information offices which provide a range of information on local accommodation, attractions, public transport services, entertainment, etc.

Other services

Other organisations also serve the travel and tourism industry, for example travel insurance companies, taxis, the Post Office (passport application checks) and translation services.

Trade associations

A number of organisations support the travel and tourism industry and its customers. The largest in the UK is ABTA, the Association of British Travel Agents. Formed in 1950, the association now represents nearly 6,500 travel agency outlets and over 1,000 tour operators in the UK. Part of ABTA's responsibility is to ensure that all bookings through any of its members are financially secure. It also provides an arbitration service for customers who are in dispute with their travel agent or tour operator. (More information about ABTA can be found on their website www.abta.com. Check out the student zone in the careers and education section.)

AITO, the Association of Independent Tour Operators, represents about 160 specialist tour operators in the UK. The aim of AITO members is to provide the highest level of customer satisfaction and to promote responsible tourism.

ACTIVITY

Find out about the organisations below by visiting their websites. Which organisations in the travel and tourism industry do they represent? How many members do they have? What is their aim?

- Federation of Tour Operators (FTO): www.fto.co.uk
- Civil Aviation Authority (CAA): www.caa.co.uk
- Guild of Travel Management Companies (GTMC): www.gtmc.org
- International Air Transport Association (IATA): www.iata.org

VisitBritain markets Britain to the rest of the world, and England to the British. It is funded by the Department of Culture, Media and Sport and is the official tourist office for visiting Britain.

Government

Many government departments and similar public organisations perform travel and tourism related activities, including the Foreign and Commonwealth Office, Passport Office, Department for Culture, Media and Sport, HM Customs, HM Immigration and embassies.

ACTIVITY

Discover how the roles and purposes of the government departments below relate to the travel and tourism industry:

- Foreign and Commonwealth Office: www.fco.gov.uk
- Department for Culture, Media and Sport: www.culture.gov.uk

CASE STUDY

A business woman is travelling to Japan and South Africa. In what ways might she find the Foreign and Commonwealth Office useful?

History and development of the travel and tourism industry

The travel and tourism industry has grown rapidly since 1945. This is partly the result of technological improvements – faster and larger aircraft, better fuel efficiency, improved communications and transport networks, and the introduction of computer booking systems. People also tend to work fewer hours and are now entitled to a minimum of four weeks' annual leave from their employment, sometimes rising to five or six weeks depending upon the job or the length of time they have been working for a particular employer.

The table below lists the key events in the industry since 1945.

YEAR	EVENT
1945	Second World War ends
1946	London (Heathrow) Airport officially opened
1947	Fred Pontin enters the holiday business – opens Brean Sands holiday camp near Weston-super-Mare
1948	Holiday with Pay Act (1938) becomes effective
1950	First overseas package holiday organised by Vladimir Raitz of Horizon Holidays
1952	De Havilland Comet, the world's first passenger jet aircraft, goes into service
1958	Boeing 707, a long-range jet aircraft, makes its first non-stop commercial transatlantic flight
1960	UK residents take over 30 million domestic holidays and more than 3.5 million overseas holidays
1960s	First global distribution system (computer reservation system) developed
1965	Lord Thomson starts Thomson Travel Group
1968	World's first car-carrying hovercraft goes into service
1969	Development of Tourism Act
1970	Boeing 747 'jumbo jet' goes into service, giving a major boost to mass tourism
1974	Clarkson, the UK's number one tour operator, fails
1976	Concorde, supersonic aircraft, enters service
1977	Freddie Laker starts up Skytrain service from London to New York
1982	Laker Travel fails
1984	Richard Branson launches Virgin Atlantic with one leased Boeing 747
1988	UK residents take more than 20 million overseas holidays
1991	Intasum, UK's second largest tour operator, fails
1994	Channel Tunnel opened
1990s	Start of all-inclusive holidays and resorts

Continued

YEAR	EVENT
1996	UK residents take more than 30 million overseas holidays
1998	Approximately 1.4 million people buy travel tickets and services over the Internet
2001	September 11th terrorist attacks in the USA
2001	First tourist (Dennis Tito) goes into space
2003	Concorde makes last commercial flight and retires from service
2004	Queen Mary 2, world's largest cruise liner, enters service
2004	Richard Branson announces plans for tourist flights into space

Key events in the travel and tourism industry since 1945

Ever since the introduction of the jet aircraft in 1952, air travel has dominated the travel market. As air travel has grown in popularity so has the number of tour operators and travel agents in the UK, reaching a peak in the 1990s. The increase in leisure time and paid holidays from work has also contributed to this development. The chart below shows the number of UK residents who have travelled overseas for a holiday by any means of transport.

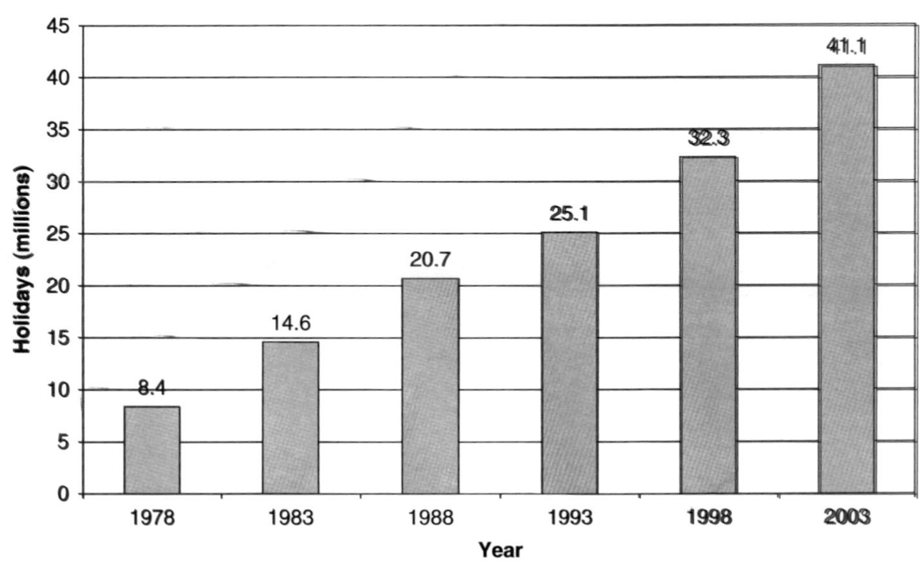

Since easyJet was formed in 1995, the number of UK residents travelling by air has increased by more than 68% whilst the number of residents taking a package holiday (inclusive tour) by air has increased by only 36% (source: www.statistics.gov.uk).

ACTIVITY

Look at table 3.07 of the International Passenger Survey available online at www.statistics.gov.uk or perhaps visit your local library to investigate the growth in holidays and travel. Draw a chart similar to the one shown to illustrate how travel by each mode of transport has grown. Draw another chart to compare the purpose of visits.

ACTIVITY

Using the Internet and other information sources, try to find the significance of some of the key travel and tourism events listed in the table. Why are they so important? What other developments did they lead to?

Horizontal and vertical integration

Horizontal integration exists when an organisation owns two or more companies on the same level of the buying chain. For example, the First Choice group of companies owns First Choice travel agencies and Holiday Hypermarkets, both of which are retail travel agents and on the same level of the buying chain. One advantage to the First Choice group of owning these two travel agent companies is that it can increase its market share by having two types of outlet in the same city. Another example of horizontal integration took place in 2002 when the airline easyJet purchased the airline Go from British Airways, although in this case the two companies now trade as one under the easyJet banner.

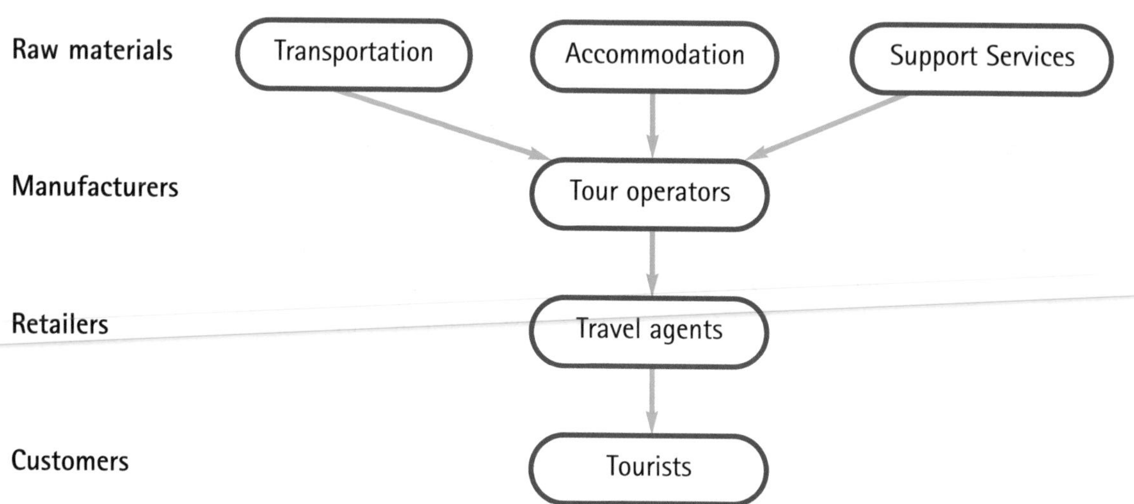

The travel and tourism industry buying chain

Vertical integration exists when an organisation owns companies on two or more levels of the buying chain. Each of the 'Big 4' travel companies are vertically integrated along with some others, including Cosmos and Bath Travel. The 'Big 4' all own an airline, a tour operator and travel agency. Until recently, some of these companies used different names for their airline and travel agency. However, they are now 'power branding' (using the same name throughout the organisation) so it is easier for the customer to see exactly who they are booking and travelling with. A good example of this is TUI UK, the UK's largest holiday company, which has re-branded its companies using the Thomson name:

	2004	2005
Airline	Britannia Airways	Thomsonfly
Tour operator	Thomson	Thomson
Travel agent	Lunn Poly	Thomson

Vertical integration allows an organisation to control the market and to retain more of the profits. For example, if a customer books a Thomson holiday that uses a Thomsonfly flight through a Thomson travel agency, the commission that Thomson pays to the travel agency stays within the organisation. The company might also be able to negotiate better rates with its own airline and, of course, the customer may also buy goods on board the aircraft and contribute to the overall profits of the company in that way.

The First Choice Group of companies is a good example of development through horizontal and vertical integration. First Choice was founded in 1973 as Owners Abroad. Through the 1980s it acquired other tour operators and set up its own airline, Air 2000. The company re-branded as First Choice in 1994 and formed its retail arm (Travel Choice) in 1998.

KEY POINTS

- Horizontal integration – when an organisation owns two or more companies on the same level of the buying chain.
- Vertical integration – when an organisation owns companies on two or more levels of the buying chain.

PRACTICE ASSESSMENT ACTIVITY

Level

M1.1 The full history of First Choice can be found by visiting their website (www.firstchoiceholidaysplc.com/firstchoice/corp_section/keyevents.jsp). Use this information to try to establish the impact of integration on the structure of the travel and tourism industry.

In summary

- The travel and tourism industry is very large and complex.
- Tourists stay away from home for at least one night and are either leisure tourists or business tourists.
- The private, public and voluntary sectors all play a part in the industry.
- Travel agents, tour operators, transport companies and accommodation providers are major sectors of the travel and tourism industry.
- The industry is supported by a number of trade, public and government organisations.
- The industry is fast moving, with many major events in the last 60 years having substantial impacts upon its development.

PRACTICE ASSESSMENT ACTIVITY

Level ✓

P1.1 Describe the structure of the travel and tourism industry.

P1.2 Describe the roles of different types of organisations in the travel and tourism industry.

1.2 Products and services

Tour operators

Tour operators offer a range of products and services to meet the needs of their customers and customer types. Most of the mass-market companies have a range of brochures to cater for these needs – city breaks, summer sun, winter sun, winter sports, lakes and mountains.

Our background, financial circumstances, age, interests and experiences are particular to ourselves. This sets a challenge for tour operators in meeting our needs. You will read about market segmentation in Unit 4 Introduction to Marketing in Travel and Tourism, but it is worth noting here that all sectors of the travel and tourism industry pay great attention to these differences and seek to provide products and services which will meet the wishes of potential clients. Some operators target particular segments of the market and specialise, perhaps in age groups or interests, or levels of luxury. They may offer four- or five-star hotel accommodation aimed at the luxury market, or one- or two-star hotels and self-catering apartments aimed at the budget or family markets. They may produce brochures specialising in holidays for the over 50s or 20–30-year-olds.

You read earlier that the main components of a package holiday are usually transport and accommodation. Tour operators may offer services to attract clients, like pre-booking of seats on the aircraft, in-flight meals, and transfers between the overseas airport and resort hotel, although there is an increasing trend to charge extra for such services. Most tour operators offer the option to buy travel insurance from them; in fact, many make having travel insurance compulsory. They will also arrange car hire, if required, at competitive rates. By pre-booking car hire in the UK, customers have greater control over their holiday budget.

At the holiday destination, tour operators usually provide an escorted transfer service between the airport and the hotel. A holiday representative will either be based at the accommodation or visit it, to ensure that their customers are happy and that any problems are solved. The holiday representative's role includes offering guidance and information, and organising and selling excursions.

Another major service provided by several tour operators is the holiday kids club. These are generally organised for different age ranges, for example Thomson has three Kidzone clubs: tots (3–5), team (6–8) and tribe (9–12). Specialist staff are employed to cater for the needs of these young clients and their parents, from organising games and activities to babysitting and early meal times. If the children are kept happy, it is quite likely that the parents will have a happy holiday too!

Travel agents

Travel agents offer a wide range of products and services. Whether a leisure agent or a business agent, the range is quite similar – it is just the product mix that will be different. Leisure agents rely on sales of package holidays to maintain their business which may account for about 70 per cent or more of their sales. Business agents rely on the sale of air tickets, accommodation and car hire, and will sell very few if any package holidays. The main products are:

Products offered by travel agents

In order to remain in business in a very competitive market some agents also offer coach tickets for scheduled services (National Express, Eurolines), excursion tickets and tickets for theme parks such as Disneyworld or Universal Studios in Florida. With many principals reducing the amount of commission they pay to the travel agent, some agents have started to diversify even further and now offer travel accessories such as suitcases for sale in their shops.

Travel agents provide other important services and information to their customers. The main ones offered are:

- passport, visa and health information
- country information and advice
- re-booking and reconfirmation of air tickets
- foreign currency exchange.

KEY POINTS

A passport allows travellers to leave and re-enter their own country. Visas may also be required by visitors to enter certain countries.

Some travel agents act as agents for the UK Passport Agency. For a fee they will check a customer's passport application form and ensure the correct documentation such as birth certificate, marriage certificate and photographs are present before submitting them on behalf of the customer. Some travel agents also obtain visas for which they are likely to charge a handling fee.

CASE STUDY

Planning a holiday

The Duffield family want to take a summer holiday together in August. Adele and James have two children, 11-year-old Victoria and 3-year-old Steve. They live in Cambridge and want to visit Adele's family in Zurich and then continue to a beach resort. They don't want a package holiday.

1. **What questions would you ask the Duffields?**
2. **What suggestions would you make to them about transport and accommodation?**
3. **What other services might you offer them?**

Transport

Airlines

Airlines need to cater for both the business traveller and the leisure traveller, so the larger scheduled airlines may offer as many as four classes of service: first class, business class, premium economy class and economy class. The price of the ticket and the level of service the passenger receives will vary depending upon which class they travel in. The main differences when travelling in a class other than economy is the amount of legroom, known as the seat pitch, and the width of the seat. Long-haul airlines are increasingly equipping their first-and business-class cabins with sleeper seats. These seats recline to form a 'bed' to enable the business passenger to sleep more comfortably than they otherwise would.

The style of service and type and variety of meals and drinks offered will also vary by class of travel. Passengers in first- and business-class cabins are likely to be offered superior quality toiletry kits and gifts, as well as newspapers. Passengers travelling at higher fares will generally have greater flexibility to change their flights. This is particularly valuable for the business traveller who may need to change arrangements at short notice.

DINNER

A selection of canapés

Starters

Tiger prawn cocktail

Provençale tart with a sour cream and garlic dressing

Chicken and mushroom soup

Fresh salad leaves with your choice
of balsamic vinaigrette or lemon and chive mayonnaise

A selection of warm breads

Main

Grilled veal medallions with sage and wild mushrooms

Pan-fried sea bass with XO sauce

Fresh pasta with your choice of carbonara sauce or tomato and basil sauce

Tandoori chicken on Greek salad

Snacks

Bacon roll served with tomato ketchup

Chicken and mushroom soup with a side salad

Char-grilled chicken sandwich with honey Dijon relish

A selection of finger sandwiches

A selection of cheese and fruit

Dessert and Cheese

Fresh fruit and Scottish shortbread served with whipped cream

Warm cherry and Mascarpone pancakes

A selection of cheese

A basket of fresh fruit

Your choice of
Espresso, cappuccino, coffee, decaffeinated coffee, tea or herbal tea

A British Airways menu for first-class passengers

On long-haul routes airlines offer in-flight entertainment. This may include the latest movie releases, electronic games and a comprehensive selection of audio channels. Some airlines offer the opportunity to view films and video programmes on individual seat-back screens so that every passenger is able to make their own choice of entertainment.

Airports

In 2003, there were 154 million international passenger movements (arrivals plus departures) through UK airports. Airports may have one-third or more of their arrival passengers transferring to onward flights. London Heathrow, Paris Charles de Gaulle, Frankfurt and Amsterdam are major transfer airports and they compete fiercely to keep that traffic, as well as the traffic starting or ending in their countries. Airports work closely with the airlines, concessionaires and regulatory bodies to provide smooth processes and excellent play areas like shops, play areas for children and babies, catering outlets, business lounges, showers, fast-track, etc.

Cruising

The main cruising areas for tourists from the UK are the Mediterranean, Scandinavia and the Caribbean. Nowadays, many customers take advantage of fly-cruises which include flying nearer to the cruising area, for example Miami for the Caribbean, and then transferring by coach or taxi to the cruise ship. One major advantage of the fly-cruise is that passengers arrive at their main destination or cruising area far quicker than if they had taken the cruise from a UK port. Even travelling to the Mediterranean from a port such as Southampton may involve a couple of days at sea before arriving at the first port of call.

Cruises can be considered as package holidays: the ship provides the transport, accommodation (the cabin), catering, and entertainment (often live entertainment, cinema, library, casino, games, swimming pool, beauty salon and guest speakers who are expert on the destinations or specific interests). Apart from the pleasure of visiting different ports, perhaps every day, the cruise company provides extensive ground arrangements in the form of excursions from those ports, at an extra cost.

Car ferry and fast craft

In 2004, there were 25.8 million international sea journeys to or from the UK, with a further 3.6 million domestic sea journeys within the UK (e.g. to/from the Channel Islands, and Northern Ireland) (Source: Office for National Statistics, 2005). There was a slight downward trend over the previous five years, possibly influenced by the Channel Tunnel and budget airlines. This has heightened the competitive aspect of the ferry sector. Companies are competing on price, speed and facilities.

Cruise ships offer passengers an all-inclusive holiday

ACTIVITY

Research the Internet for ferry companies operating international routes from the UK. Discover what types of ship(s) they operate, how frequent and fast the journeys are, and what on-board facilities there are. Compare your findings with other members of your group.

Rail

At the time of writing, there are 26 train operating companies in the UK. In addition, there are private ones operated as visitor attractions for tourists. Most of these companies operate regional and local routes, for example Merseyrail and Island Line, but others operate trunk routes or in major areas of the country, for example First Scotrail and Virgin Trains.

Train companies seek to win customers by providing regular and punctual services on routes which meet the customers' requirements, with a range of add-on facilities at stations and on the train, at fares which customers feel meet their needs. Virgin Trains has introduced its Pendolino 'tilting' trains, capable of travelling at 140 miles per hour. Pendolino routes include the west coast line from London to Scotland. These luxurious trains offer an

ACTIVITY

What is offered to first class passengers on the new Virgin Pendolino?

onboard audio system with a range of music and radio channels; power points to charge laptop computers and mobile phones; a shop which sells hot and cold food and drink, magazines, books, sweets and toiletries; a quiet zone; and special seats and tables for disabled passengers. First Scotrail operates sleeper trains between London and several Scottish destinations. These provide single- and double-berth cabins, a lounge cabin and lounges at some stations. Transpennine Express and others carry bicycles free. Heathrow Express has large baggage storage areas and onboard TV.

Train companies offer a range of fares to suit the needs of their passengers. These may include first-class fares; advance purchase fares; Rover tickets; group fares; off-peak fares; student, senior citizen and disabled persons' fares; and season tickets. It is also possible to arrange inclusive holidays by rail.

Coach

Scheduled coach companies offer a wide range of competitive fares, including young persons' fares (16–26 years), senior citizens' fares, overseas visitors' fares, family fares, advance purchase fares and special promotions. At the time of writing, National Express was offering 'Fun fares', enabling anyone to travel on designated routes and services for just £1. Day excursions and longer UK tours are either targeted at UK residents (and are particularly used by older age groups) or at overseas visitors to the UK. Overseas tours are targeted at UK residents.

Onboard services include TV with headsets, comfortable seats and toilet facilities. Some coach holiday companies offer their customers the convenience of a door-to-door service collecting them by taxi from their home and taking them to a central location for the coach journey.

Use the Internet to find out about products and services offered by car hire companies

Car hire

Self-drive car hire is very popular, particularly for business travellers and overseas visitors. Major companies like Budget and Alamo have offices in major cities and airports across much of the world.

The companies offer different sizes of cars at a range of rates. Incentive rates are offered to frequent hirers, those hiring for longer periods (e.g. one week) and those who have travelled on an airline with whom the car hire company has a partnership agreement.

To avoid waiting in long queues and having to give the same information every time they hire a car, regular hirers can join the company's frequent customer club. Quoting the number on their membership card enables the company to refer to existing information held about the customer, for example name, address, driving licence and credit card details, car preferences, etc. This means the documentation and car keys can be ready when the customer comes to the fast-track counter at the pick-up location.

Another form of car hire is chauffeur driven. This may be for business people or those who wish to treat themselves to some luxury (for example stretched limousines), or those who are travelling in small groups and require chauffeur-driven people-movers. Chauffeur-driven cars can be waiting for the customer at their point of arrival, for example an airport.

Accommodation

Accommodation can be selected on the basis of lots of different factors:

- Location
- Facilities
- Level of comfort
- Cost
- Interests

It can be booked as part of an inclusive package or independently. It may be:

- A four-star hotel
- A bed and breakfast home
- An apartment
- A villa
- An inn
- A holiday park or village
- A cruise ship or canal boat
- A caravan or a tent

It may be booked on a room (or pitch) basis, or a bed and breakfast, half board or full board basis. Some overseas destinations have all-inclusive resorts, where the price includes accommodation, meals, drinks and all other hotel facilities, including sports and entertainment.

The needs of guests will also differ widely. For example, a businessperson may want a comfortable hotel, with room service, a business centre and Internet connections in the room, whereas a family on holiday is more likely to be interested in interconnecting rooms, a baby-sitting service, family-focused restaurants and children's activities.

Accommodation is often given a rating or recommendation to assist potential customers to make their choices. In recent times, there have been attempts to rationalise rating systems into a single system, but several still apply in the UK and overseas. The rating is normally based upon the quality of accommodation, facilities and service. It is likely to include such issues as cleanliness, room service, porterage, facilities, catering, availability and quality of staff.

ACTIVITY

In a small group, collect a selection of travel brochures, some of which include UK accommodation and others which include overseas accommodation. Refer to the paragraph above to ensure you seek as wide a range as possible.

Compare the facilities offered by each provider of accommodation. What type of guest might be interested in staying in each type of accommodation? What forms of transport are offered?

Catering

The choice of catering is enormous as it forms an important part of most tourists' enjoyment. It can range from formal dining in a hotel or restaurant to independent eating in a café. Just as for accommodation, some countries have rating schemes for their catering establishments. Catering is not only important at the tourists' destinations but also during their travelling, so such places as airports, seaports, train and coach stations often have a range of catering outlets. Transport companies may provide refreshments or meals during the journey, for which they may charge.

Guiding

There are many types of guide, meeting a range of tourist needs. A knowledgeable guide, whether a town guide or a guide at an historic site or other visitor attraction, can add considerably to the good experience the tourist will have.

The national standard guiding qualification in the UK is the Blue Badge. Blue Badge guides have a wide range of specialities and interests and can guide on foot or in cars, coaches, trains or boats. They have detailed knowledge of their location and subject and are skilled in presenting.

Tourists on package holidays will often be encouraged to take day excursions and these will frequently have a guide. Coaching holidays may also have a guide travelling with the coach party for the entire holiday. It is important for guides to have knowledge both of the language(s) of their clients and of the country they are in.

Information services

Tourists can also obtain guidance and information in other ways. It may be from Internet websites which sometimes give virtual tours of the destination, etc., or it may be from audio/visual presentations at historic houses and museums. Maps and leaflets on attractions are available from tourist information offices and hotel lobby display stands.

Visitor attractions

Visitor attractions, whether they be natural, such as Snowdonia, or man-made, like the National Railway Museum in York, provide services to their visitors to enhance their experience. Natural attractions may have signs which tell the visitor something about the history of the attraction, or the views, or the wildlife in the area. Such attractions may have picnic areas or simple catering facilities. There may be rangers or guides who provide educational group tours. Man-made attractions often provide additional services. Perhaps a cathedral will have musical events, displays, guides, hand-held audio players available in several languages, leaflets and a shop. Apart from the rides, theme parks may have parades, cartoon characters, shops, catering, firework displays and facilities for disabled people and young children.

In summary

- Tour operators create and provide packages consisting of at least two of transport, accommodation and other significant services.
- Travel agents provide a wide range of services for the business and leisure tourist, ranging from package holidays to individual accommodation, transport and other arrangements. They also provide advice and secondary products, e.g. currency exchange, travel insurance.
- Transport includes airlines and airports, ferries and cruises, trains, coaches and car hire. There is competition between and within those sectors, and the transport companies provide many options to target specific market segments.
- The accommodation and catering sector gives potential clients a substantial choice, depending upon their needs, wishes, interests and personal circumstances.
- Guiding is a valuable addition which enhances tourists' experiences but needs professional knowledge and skills on the part of the guide.
- Visitor attractions may provide enjoyment, experiences, enlightenment, information, catering, shopping and facilities for those with specific needs.
- Information services use many forms of media, including the written word, visual and audio systems, Internet and virtual tours, and verbal information.

PRACTISE ASSESSMENT ACTIVIY

P1.3 Describe the range of products and services provided by travel and tourism organisations.

CASE STUDY

As a tour operator, you plan to offer inclusive holidays to Italy for those interested in art and history. Drawing upon what you have learned in this section, write a proposal which identifies:

- at what stages transport will be required, identifying at least two forms of transport
- what type of accommodation will be required
- what other services you will provide.

Justify your choices.

1.3 Recent developments in travel and tourism

The travel and tourism industry is constantly developing to keep up with the way in which our lifestyles are changing and the ever-increasing pace of technological change.

Distribution methods and technological advances

One of the greatest changes to affect the industry in recent times is the Internet. In 1998, it was estimated that 2.3 million UK households (9 per cent), had access to the Internet from home and 1.4 million people used it to purchase tickets. By 2005, 12.9 million UK households (52 per cent) had Internet access and the market research organisation Mintel reported that more people would be booking their holidays independently than by taking a pre-arranged package tour. The Internet is dramatically changing the way many people book holidays, and tour operators and travel agents are having to respond for survival. Nowadays, tour operators and travel agents have their own websites so that they can capture the increasing Internet market. An advantage to tour operators is that they will not have to pay commission to travel agents on holidays booked directly through their website, so they tend to offer customers online discounts. Travel agents may also offer incentives for customers to make bookings themselves.

Within the travel agency itself there is an increasing amount of technology to help the agent make bookings and handle administration. Software links an agent's in-house booking system with that of a tour operator so that transaction times can be speeded up. Agents also have back-office systems that automatically make diary entries to check that customers' holidays have been paid for and that tickets have been received.

ACTIVITY

Use the Internet, newspapers, trade journals etc to find out about mergers and takeovers within the travel and tourism industry.

Technological advances have also been responsible for the growth of a new type of travel agent specialising in e-commerce (electronic business). ebookers and Expedia, for example, offer customers the facility to book accommodation, travel, car hire, etc. online. These and some of the Big 4 agents also use call centres to handle the bookings of those customers who prefer not to visit a travel agent's shop or who have not the time to do so. Teletext and digital TV channels devoted entirely to holidays are all designed to make the buying process simpler for the customer and enable travel agents and tour operators to keep up with today's lifestyle.

In 2000, First Choice announced that it was investing £10 million in the following two years, developing new travel sites, cybercafes and digital TV services. Holiday hypermarket shops give potential clients the opportunity to surf the web in the shop for deals, before making a booking. Holiday cybermarkets would also be a key to e-commerce, with interactive screens in the shops showing video footage of hotels and resorts, making clients feel as though they are there. Interactive TV enables potential clients to 'chat' with a travel agent on the interactive TV while looking at maps, images and video clips of the destinations. Visitors to First Choice's website can 'leaf through' an e-brochure, make bookings, order foreign currency and read its magazine.

Technological advances have also enabled staff to become homeworkers, accepting calls and making bookings on their home computers, thus creating virtual travel agencies.

ACTIVITY

In pairs, try to find evidence of recent technological changes in your local travel agent's business or on the Internet. What are they? What other technological advances do you think they could make to benefit their clients?

Technology is also having a major effect upon how well airlines manage their yields – the amount of revenue per flight. Huge databases track the past booking pattern of flights, often as detailed as recording the pattern

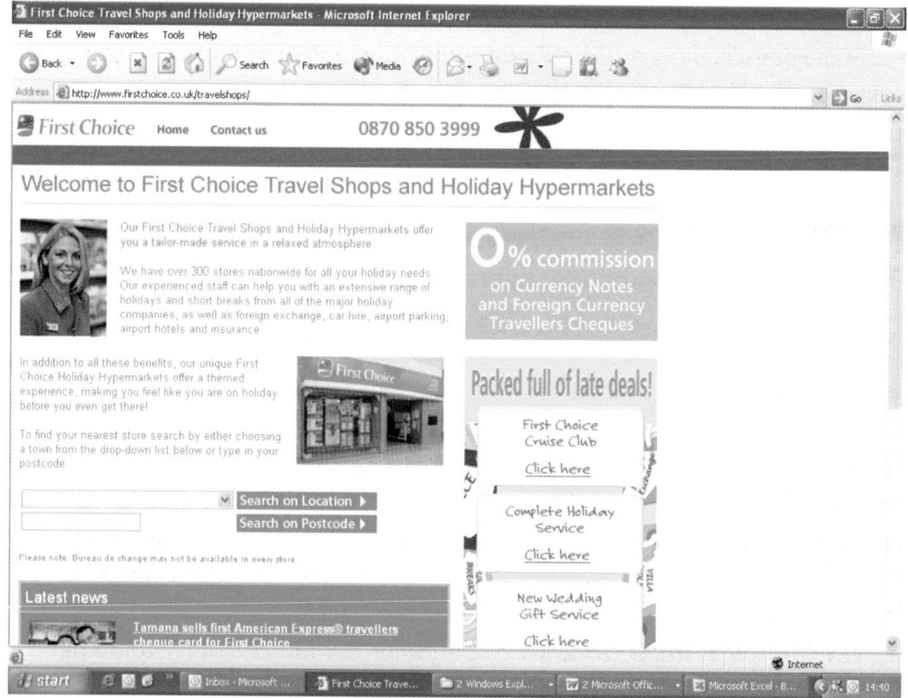

An Internet travel shop and holiday hypermarket

for a flight which has operated a particular route on a particular day at a particular time, for a given period. With that historic data, the airline is able to forecast how many more seats it will sell by the next time that flight operates, and can adjust the fares on it, to get the best revenue result.

Transport

The arrival of budget airlines has had a big impact on the industry, with many people prepared to give up added services such as flexible tickets and in-flight food and accept sometimes less convenient airports. Many full-service airlines are fighting back with fares which often compare favourably with those offered by the budget airlines.

These changes are having an impact on the type of holiday that people choose – more people are 'unpackaging' the traditional package holiday by booking their flights and accommodation separately. The disadvantage for customers is that, by doing so, they would not have the protection of the ABTA Bond if the airline couldn't provide the flight. There are also disadvantages for the travel agent, as airlines in particular are reducing the amount of commission they pay to the travel agent for booking flights, making it more difficult for the agent to make a profit. Instead, some travel agents are charging their clients fees for making their travel arrangements.

Over to you!

What are the effects on travel agents if more people decide to book their own holidays?

To cope with the increasing demand for air travel BAA is building a fifth terminal at Heathrow Airport. A government White Paper published in 2003 identified proposals for the development of air transport and airports over the next 20 years. It supported a number of development proposals around the UK including a further runway at Stansted by 2012 and a third runway at Heathrow to follow that.

ACTIVITY

Find out all you can about the fifth terminal at Heathrow Airport. How many passengers will it handle?

By 2006, some of the world's airlines will be operating the superjumbo Airbus A380. Virgin Atlantic and Emirates are just two airlines that have placed orders to purchase this new aircraft. The airliner will have two decks throughout the entire length of the plane and has been designed to carry up to 555 passengers in three classes. Its length is 73 metres and it has a wingspan of 79 metres. Because of its size, airports around the world will have to make adjustments to departure gates in order to make space for the plane. Heathrow is demolishing a pier at terminal 3 and building a new one that will allow passengers to offload and board on both levels. Being a wide-bodied, twin-deck aircraft it is possible that some airlines may have shops or boutiques and play areas on board. (For more on the Airbus A380, see the case study in Unit 4 Introduction to Marketing in Travel and Tourism, page 160.)

To reduce queues and waiting times at airports, airlines are introducing innovative ways to check in. Passengers may be able to check in remotely, perhaps at a town terminal, or by phone, fax or Internet. Those who check in at the airport can do so at self-service machines. Local innovations also improve service to customers; in Barbados, because passengers have to check out of their hotels several hours before their evening flight to the

UK, Virgin Atlantic have introduced a mobile check-in facility. A vehicle visits key hotels and passengers can check in there and dispose of their baggage, enabling them to enjoy more time on the beach.

Cruising is proving increasingly popular and cruise lines are introducing magnificent new ships. At 345 metres long, 45 metres wide, 72 metres high and at approximately 150,000 tonnes, Cunard's *Queen Mary 2* (*QM2*) is the world's largest, longest and tallest ocean liner. The supership can carry over 2,600 passengers and has a crew of approximately 1,250. The ship boasts 14 decks, sports facilities, five swimming pools and ten restaurants plus the only planetarium afloat. In a few years time, Cunard plans to introduce another new ship, the *Queen Victoria*.

Accommodation

Since the mid-1980s, all-inclusive resorts and hotels have developed. These generally offer all meals, locally produced drinks and sports facilities at an inclusive price. An advantage of this type of holiday is that you can budget your holiday spending much more easily before leaving the UK – you may only need to take money for some excursions and souvenirs. Within the UK there has been a dramatic increase in the number of budget hotels such as Travelodge, Travel Inn and Formula 1 either at airports or on main road routes. This type of accommodation has developed to cater for the needs of the ever-increasing travelling public.

Other developments

The general public are becoming more adventurous in terms of where they want to go and what types of holiday they want. People are also taking more holidays. Some tour operators are planning to withdraw their holiday representatives from some resorts, perhaps because the holidaymaker is becoming more confident and more individualistic, and because technology is assisting communication. Retired people are the fastest growing sector of the business and their needs must be catered for.

Areas affected by the tsunami in 2004 have been encouraging tourism

Tourism can damage local environments, so there is a focus upon sustainable tourism which considers and supports the needs of the local community and habitat. Following the devastating Indian Ocean tsunami in 2004, the tourism business in several affected countries had to embark upon a road to recovery which is likely to create change and take a long while.

In summary

- Technological advances are a major cause of change for the industry. Tour operators and travel agents are particularly experiencing changes in the way they must work.

- Changes such as new runways and airport terminals need to be planned many years in advance.
- The general public are becoming more confident in making their own travel arrangements, more independent and adventurous, and more comfortable with using technology.
- There is a trend towards more responsible tourism.
- Those in the travel and tourism industry must be alert to changing needs.

Level ✔

PRACTICE ASSESSMENT ACTIVITY

Select one of a tour operator, travel agent, transport provider or accommodation provider.

P1.4 Describe recent developments which have caused changes in the organisation you chose.

M1.2 Describe how these developments have affected the products and services being offered.

D1.1 Analyse how that sector responded to the situation, in terms of changes to the products and services offered.

1.4 Job roles and career opportunities

The travel and tourism industry offers a vast range of fascinating and exciting careers. Even once you are employed in your chosen sector, you will almost certainly have a wide choice of career specialisations to choose from, as you develop your interests in particular types of work.

Although job roles are described over the next few pages, it is important to remember that the skills you learn are going to be 'transferable', which means they are skills that can help you progress your career in travel and tourism.

Some jobs are generic. That means they are common to several sectors of the industry. Below are some examples.

Reservations call centre agent

Agents take telephone calls from the general public, or an intermediary like a travel agent, and use computer systems to check availability of their products, e.g. inclusive holidays, airline seats, self-drive cars. They answer

A reservations call centre agent

related queries and make reservations. In many ways, this role is similar to that of a travel agency consultant.

- This role is a popular route into the industry. Employers may seek GCSE grades A*–C or equivalent, particularly in English and Maths, and evidence of a vocational qualification would be useful, e.g. First Diploma/National Diploma or AVCE in Travel and Tourism, but they are particularly interested in what type of person you are. Do you like helping people and working in a team? Do you have a good telephone manner? Are you PC literate? Do you have customer service experience?
- In-house training is often given in telephone selling skills and sector-specific subjects.
- There are opportunities to progress to positions such as team leader and reservations manager.

Administration and/or finance assistant

Every organisation needs administration and finance support. This may mean issuing tickets and other travel documents and ensuring clients' special requests are dealt with efficiently and promptly, e.g. notifying airlines and hotels of dietary requirements. The work may also include issuing and receiving invoices and ensuring payments are received and made.

- Skills, attributes and qualifications will depend upon the job but may include GCSE grades A*–C or equivalent, being organised with an eye for detail, and being PC literate.
- In-house training is often given.
- Progression can be to team leader or manager, or into other specialisations within the industry as a whole.

Marketing and sales staff

These two functions are linked but undertake different roles.

Marketing staff

Marketing is responsible for promoting the company's products. This includes market research; using the best channels to sell through; advertising; creating promotional campaigns; brochure production and website management (making sure the product looks right and is designed correctly so as to attract customers).

- Employers are likely to look for people with GCSE grades A*–C or equivalent, who are organised, creative team players who can work to tight deadlines. A professional qualification would be an advantage, e.g. those related to the Chartered Institute of Marketing.
- Progression can be into senior marketing, sales or general management positions.

Sales staff

Sales staff are responsible for achieving sales targets by selling direct to the customer or an intermediary. The reservations call centre is usually part of the sales department. Some tour operators, accommodation and transport providers also employ field sales teams that visit travel agents and other businesses.

- Employers may seek those with GCSE grades A*–C or equivalent, particularly in English and Maths, and a vocational qualification, such as the one you are studying. They are particularly interested in what type of person you are. Do you like interacting with people, selling and negotiating? Do you have selling and customer service experience?
- Progression in sales can be into senior marketing, sales or general management positions.

Customer relations assistant

Customer relations staff respond to the concerns, complaints and compliments of their customers, in writing or by telephone. They may also ask customers to complete questionnaires, which are then analysed and distributed to relevant departments, providing feedback on their performance.

- While GCSE grades A*–C or equivalent, particularly in English, are likely to be needed, reinforced with a vocational qualification, employers will look for those who enjoy helping people, have high levels of tact and patience, and are good written and verbal communicators. Customer service experience is also valuable.
- In-house training is often given in complaint handling techniques and sector-specific subjects.
- There are opportunities to progress to positions in a range of customer service areas.

Let's have a look now at some sector-specific careers.

Tour operators

Each tour operator will have its own structure and, depending upon its size, its UK office will probably have reservations, administration, contracting, product development, sales and marketing, and customer relations departments which will require staff from junior or trainee positions to heads of department and managers. Non-generic departments which are particular to tour operators include product development and contracting.

Product development and contracting

Product development staff seek new destinations and activities for new holiday opportunities, and research options for accommodation, transport, excursions, etc. Larger tour operators have contracting staff who identify providers, e.g. hotels, airlines, and coach operators, of the right quality and negotiate with them to obtain the right number of rooms, seats, etc., at the right price, so that a holiday package can be created. Once a holiday programme is operating, supply and demand may change and staff have to ensure there are enough holidays to sell, or that the tour operator does not have over capacity (more holidays than their clients require). Smaller tour operators may combine the product development and contracting tasks.

- Business-related qualifications are valuable, e.g. ABTOC, HND in Business Studies. Staff must be able to use their own initiative but also work well in teams and relate to various nationalities, so travel experience and a foreign language are advantageous. Communication, negotiation, selling, numeracy and PC skills are essential.
- Progression is typically into more senior product, contracting and marketing roles.

Overseas positions

There are several roles available for those who wish to work overseas, including holiday representatives (reps), resort reps, children's reps, entertainers (or all of these jobs rolled into one). All represent the overseas face of the tour operator and are responsible for ensuring clients have a great holiday.

CASE STUDY

Rachael is a resort rep and meets clients at the airport and escorts them on coaches to their accommodation. During the journey, she welcomes clients to the resort and provides them with general information. She organises a 'Welcome' meeting to tell holidaymakers more about their accommodation and resort, places to visit and who to contact in an emergency, as well as answering any questions. She also sells excursions, on which she earns commission, so she needs to have selling skills! She must resolve problems such as overbookings, rooms in a poor state of repair, etc. She acts as liaison with hotels and coach companies, and reports any changes in accommodation, building works or other problems to head office. These positions are uniformed and involve shift work. Long hours may have to be worked, particularly when on airport duty.

- Most tour operators have a minimum recruitment age of 19–21 years and want four or more A*–C GCSEs, including English and Maths. A vocational qualification is also valuable (children's reps should have a qualification such as NNEB). An outgoing personality is required, as well as the ability to remain calm under pressure, use initiative, solve problems, act in an organised manner and handle administrative matters. Good communication skills are important and a second language is useful.
- Most holiday reps' positions are seasonal, so the first progression to aim for would be a permanent position. Progression is then available to team leader and resort area manager.

Travel agents

There are two main groups of travel agencies: leisure and business. Although there is similarity between jobs, there are also some important differences.

Leisure travel consultant

Positions in a leisure travel agency branch range from a modern apprentice or trainee travel consultant up to manager.

The consultant's role is to give guidance on holidays and travel-related issues and sell travel products to clients, using either telephone or online links to suppliers. Consultants may be required to carry out administrative tasks such as:

- making diary entries to keep track of bookings
- issuing tickets and other travel documents
- checking invoices and travel documents received from tour operators
- checking and paying in cash and cheques to the bank
- checking brochure stocks and arranging brochure displays
- ensuring window displays are current and relevant and all offers are up to date.

Many leisure travel agencies open six or seven days a week, so consultants need to be flexible and prepared to work at weekends. They usually wear uniform.

- Many people starting work in travel agencies begin their training on a modern apprenticeship scheme and study for an NVQ in Travel Services while training. Consultants need good oral and written communication skills; numeracy and cash handling skills and should be PC literate. They must be able to build a rapport with customers, be a team player and be comfortable working under pressure. As the products they sell are wide and varied, they must have good selling skills and product knowledge.
- Sometimes consultants are invited by tour operators or other providers, on educational visits to experience different countries, resorts, hotels and apartments, so that they are able to give customers first-hand knowledge of a destination or product.
- Consultants can progress to senior sales consultant, customer service manager and then branch manager level. In larger companies progression may be to regional sales manager or into head office management roles.

Business travel consultant

Business travel consultants handle the accounts of business customers. They spend much of their time dealing with business travellers or their companies, on the telephone or by email rather than face to face. If the value of the business account is large enough, the consultant may actually work on the customer's premises – this is called an 'implant'.

- Business travel companies prefer applicants to have some experience in the travel industry and be able to work quickly and accurately. Making a mistake for a business travel customer may not only be costly in losing that one sale, but could ultimately lose that company's account, which could be worth millions of pounds.
- HND/C in Business Studies and Travel and Tourism qualifications are valuable. Qualifications in global distribution systems (GDS), e.g. Galileo, Amadeus or Worldspan are desirable. A fares and ticketing qualification such as GTMC/Virgin Airfares and Ticketing at Levels 1 and 2 is important as it will provide the skills to deal with complicated and multi-sector itineraries that many business clients require. This training may be provided in-house.
- Progression can be to team leader, account manager and branch manager. Like leisure travel, there will also be a number of head office roles for career development, alongside field sales roles such as business development manager.

Foreign exchange consultant

Some travel agencies have a foreign exchange bureau which stocks a range of currencies and travellers cheques to sell to their customers. The role involves maintaining stocks of currencies to ensure there are enough to sell to customers who have placed an order and to those who may walk in off the street. It is important not to run out of a currency, but it is equally important not to be overstocked for security reasons and in case there is a sudden major change in exchange rates.

- Speed, efficiency, numeracy, accuracy and good communication skills are important.
- This role is sometimes combined with that of the leisure travel consultant, so qualifications, skills, experience, in-house training and progression is similar, although in-house financial and currency training may also be given.

Airlines

Whether on the ground or in the air, the service given by airline staff is expected to be of a very high standard.

Cabin crew

Ask anyone to name a 'glamorous' job in the travel and tourism industry and the chances are they will say 'Air cabin crew'. It may be glamorous at times, but it is a demanding job and can be tough on the personal lives of crew, because of shift patterns, being away from home, disruption and jet lag. Passengers want safe, comfortable and enjoyable flights, and it is the responsibility of cabin crew to provide this. Their role includes:

- welcoming passengers on board
- demonstrating emergency procedures
- ensuring passengers and cabin are in a safe condition
- providing information
- resolving problems
- assisting those with special needs such as unaccompanied young passengers, the elderly or people with disabilities
- serving meals and drinks
- selling from the in-flight shop and reconciling the accounts and payments
- dealing with any emergencies.

Cabin crew can progress to purser, responsible for a cabin, and cabin service director, responsible for all the crew on a flight and the service they give.

ACTIVITY

Investigate three airline websites. Find out the skills, attributes and qualifications required to become air cabin crew. Compare your findings with what the rest of the group has discovered.

Airline customer service agent

The customer service agent's role has four main functions:

- checking passengers and their bags in for their flight and checking that passports, visas or other travel documents are in order
- boarding passengers on to the aircraft
- meeting and escorting arriving passengers
- providing an airline information and assistance service.

However, the over-riding responsibility is to ensure a smooth, efficient and pleasant experience for passengers while at the airport.

- To be successful in this role, applicants must enjoy meeting people, have experience of providing customer service and be educated to a good standard. A second language is desirable. It can be a very demanding role, particularly at times of disruption, and shift work can be tiring, but there is much satisfaction in assisting passengers and resolving their problems.

- Typically, customer service agents can progress to team leaders, then duty managers.

ACTIVITY

Explore the websites of companies providing airport services to discover requirements and progression routes for staff working in such jobs.

Airports

Airports provide opportunities to experience a number of different careers. The airport operators, for example BAA, usually provide information desk and security staff and staff working behind the scenes ensuring safe operations on the runways, etc. There are many other airport employers such as shopping outlets, catering and bars, car hire companies, rail and coach operators, customs and immigration, police and hotels. All belong to the community of airport staff.

Other transport companies

Cruise lines, ferry companies, rail operators and car hire companies all recruit staff, often initially at junior level, in a wide range of jobs. Many are customer-contact, uniformed jobs involving shift work. The attributes, skills, qualifications and experience required vary depending upon the job. Good sources of career information will be found on their websites and in career centres and company brochures, etc.

Accommodation and catering

While there are many types of accommodation, for example hotels, guest houses, holiday camps, and caravan parks, the major employers are in the hotel sector. Jobs in areas such as reception, bar tending, housekeeping, coordinating conferences, reservations and catering are frequently advertised in newspapers and trade publications, and on employers' and agency websites. Some hotel groups offer their own structured in-house training programmes (see, for example, www.elitehotels.co.uk; www.accor.com). Staff at holiday centres such as Rank Leisure and Center Parcs are usually employed on a seasonal basis. Useful sources of career information in the hotel and leisure industry are:

- www.caterer.com
- www.hcareers.co.uk
- www.prospects.ac.uk.

Guiding and information services

Vacancies for professional guides are limited and mostly seasonal, and often on a self-employed basis. Tourist information centres operated by regional or local tourist boards or councils sometimes have vacancies for assistants.

Visitor attractions

Given the extensive range of visitor attractions from natural to man-made, from very small to very large, with few facilities or comprehensive facilities, jobs and careers are equally broad. Many are seasonal. Most have customer contact, so it is important to enjoy meeting and helping people.

In summary

- There are many sectors of the industry, which means career choice is wide.
- Many organisations require vocational qualifications.
- In-house training is frequently provided to develop staff.
- Many jobs are uniformed and require staff to work irregular hours.

Level

PRACTICE ASSESSMENT ACTIVITY

P1.5 Choose two jobs from different sectors of the industry. Describe the jobs and the qualifications, skills and attributes required. What role do these jobs perform?

M1.3 Compare the progression routes for the two jobs chosen.

D1.2 Analyse how recent developments in the travel and tourism industry affect career opportunities and job roles.

TEST YOUR KNOWLEDGE

1. There are three sectors in the travel and tourism industry. One is the private sector. What are the other two?
2. What is the difference between a tourist and a visitor?
3. Name the 'Big 4' tour operators.
4. What is a miniple?
5. Name six products a leisure travel agent might sell.
6. What is the difference between a charter airline and a scheduled airline?
7. What are the main cruising areas for UK holidaymakers?
8. What are the two recent main competitors to Channel ferries?
9. Name the English National Parks.
10. Name four trade organisations. What are their roles?
11. When did the Boeing 747 make its first commercial flight and why did that aircraft have such an effect on the industry?
12. Give an example of (a) horizontal integration, and (b) vertical integration.
13. Name six jobs in a hotel.
14. What are the two main components of a package holiday?
15. Why has Heathrow had to demolish a pier?
16. Who will Cunard name a future cruise ship after?
17. Describe the role of the product development department in a tour operator.
18. A business travel consultant is likely to progress to a leisure travel consultant. True or false?
19. What jobs might there be at a theme park?

Unit 2

Introduction to Tourist Destinations

Introduction

Imagine you were going on holiday tomorrow, where would you go? Somewhere hot with great nightlife? A trekking holiday? A bustling city? Now ask yourself why different destinations attract different kinds of visitors. This unit will help you to answer this by giving you a better understanding of key tourist destinations in the UK, Europe and the rest of world.

The unit looks at where a variety of these destinations are located and how this influences their appeal. Some destinations attract people because of their culture – you will learn why these cities and towns are so important to tourism. Other resorts are successful because of their climate; for example it could be either the sunshine or the snow which draws tourists.

You may want to travel yourself, and this unit will help you to decide where you would most like to go – there is a huge variety of destinations and it can be exciting to explore them!

How you will be assessed

This unit is assessed internally, so the centre delivering the qualification will assess you against the criteria.

In this unit you will learn about:

① the location and appeal of major tourist destinations

② the cultural aspects of tourist destinations

③ climatic conditions and their effect on travellers' choices.

2.1 Location and appeal of major tourist destinations

UK destinations

Destinations in the UK attract thousands of visitors every year. The table below shows the number of trips and nights spent away from home by UK residents in England alone. It also shows how much these tourists spent.

	TRIPS (MILLIONS)	NIGHTS (MILLIONS)	SPENDING (£ MILLIONS)
UK residents	121.3	371.9	20,560

Source: VisitBritain, United Kingdom Tourism Survey, 2003

Number of trips/nights and amount of spending by tourists in England, 2003

ACTIVITY

Find out tourism statistics for Scotland and Wales.

The most popular destinations vary from large cities to National Parks, museums to theme parks, beaches to lakes and mountains.

The UK is made up of England, Scotland, Wales and Northern Ireland. Scotland has mountain ranges where people can ski in winter and climb or hike in the summer. The coastline provides hundreds of beaches, from the dramatic cliffs and bays of Cornwall such as Penzance, to the broad sandy beaches of the east coast of England such as Great Yarmouth. Wales has many historic castles and three National Parks (Snowdonia, Brecon Beacons and Pembrokeshire Coast). Northern Ireland has many areas of unspoilt coastline and countryside. People go on holiday in the UK for sporting activities, shopping, sightseeing and swimming – and a lot more besides!

ACTIVITY

1 On an outline map of the UK, locate and name England, Scotland, Wales and Northern Ireland.
2 Using a map or atlas, locate and name each country's capital city.
3 Locate and name a mountain or range of hills in each country.
4 Locate and name a beach resort in each country.

Now you have introduced yourself to the UK, you need to look more closely at different *types* of destinations.

KEY POINTS

Tourism destinations in the UK include:

- towns and cities
- seaside resorts
- spa towns
- the countryside, including the National Parks.

Towns and cities

Many of the UK's towns and cities have been around for centuries. They have a wealth of history and heritage in their buildings and traditions.

Towns and cities generally have a range of entertainment such as theatres or cinemas, leisure complexes and museums. Shops may range from unusual individual shops to large shopping malls such as the Metro Centre in Gateshead. These destinations will have easy access via trains or coaches, motorways and even airports, and they will also have a range of accommodation available from guest houses to luxury hotels.

More tourists visit London, the UK's capital city, each year than any other destination in the UK. It is easily accessible by air, road and rail. Parts of London have been in existence for nearly 2,000 years, and visitors can see centuries of different buildings. London is also the commercial and political centre of the UK with thousands of shops and attractions. Unusually, the UK still has its monarchy, and the royal family is a great attraction for many foreign visitors. Palaces, processions and guardsmen hold a fascination for many tourists of any age!

ACTIVITY

Look at a town or city near you or one you have visited. Mark it on a map and research reasons why people come to this destination. Write an email to a student coming on an exchange visit from France telling them all about this place and what people can do there.

Big Ben and the London Eye, popular destinations for tourists to London

ACTIVITY

Using a range of sources (guide books, tourist information centre brochures, the Internet), draw a poster advertising London to a particular client group, for example children or young people. Include a map with London clearly marked on it and a variety of suitable attractions.

There are numerous cities and towns in the UK other than London which attract visitors. Many are known for their heritage and visitor attractions and tourist facilities. Examples of these 'honeypots' (destinations which attract large numbers of visitors) are York, Bath, Edinburgh and Oxford. Business visitors may also visit for conferences or meetings – they too will need easy access and good accommodation.

CASE STUDY

York

A visit to JORVIK is the perfect way to discover Viking-Age York, one of the most fascinating periods of the city's dramatic history.

Discover what life was really like over 1000 years ago in AD 975 and get face-to-face with the Vikings on the very site where archaeologists discovered the remains of the place they once called home.

Meet our Viking residents, see over 800 items uncovered here, and journey through a reconstruction of actual Viking-Age streets – complete with sounds and smells!

Source: www.jorvik-viking-centre.co.uk

York is the County Town of Yorkshire, in the Vale of York, at the confluence of two rivers, the Ouse and the Fosse.

There has been a city here for thousands of years – the Romans had their settlement of Eboracum and the Vikings built Jorvik on its ruins. The medieval city of York can still be seen in the 'snickleways' (alleys) and 'bars' (gateways) in the Roman-based walls.

Thousands of visitors come to York every year for its history and heritage. The Jorvik Museum takes you 'back in time' on a ride through the sights – and smells – of the excavated Viking town. This was where the famous Viking helmet was found.

There are many other heritage attractions such as Clifford's Tower and the Castle Museum, as well as the beautiful York Minster (cathedral). Families can enjoy a visit to the Railway Museum or a trip down the river.

There are many bars and restaurants as well as clubs – the university and colleges ensure that there is plenty for young people to do as well! There are also individual shops as well as the usual range of department stores. A visit to 'Betty's Tea Rooms' is a treat not to be missed!

1 **List four attractions in York and add who you think would be interested in visiting each of them, e.g. children, young people, couples, etc.**
2 **Locate York on a map and draw in the nearest airport (Leeds/Bradford), the main roads to York and the railway line to London and Edinburgh.**

CASE STUDY

Portsmouth

Portsmouth has been an important naval town on the south coast of England for many hundreds of years. It lies in a natural harbour and is home to the Naval Historic Dockyard. This huge open-air museum has many ships which visitors can tour, including Nelson's

CASE STUDY

Portsmouth (Contd)

Victory, the sailing ship from which he commanded the Battle of Trafalgar in 1805, and King Henry VIII's sixteenth-century flagship, the *Mary Rose*, which sank in the English Channel in 1545.

Portsmouth also has two partly ruined castles which guard the harbour at Southsea and Portsea. There is a Millennium Coastal Trail which takes visitors on a walk around the old port, which has two shopping areas at Port Solent and Gunwharf Quays. Gunwharf Quays also has leisure attractions with multiplex cinemas and bars and restaurants overlooking the sea.

1 **Why might people want to visit Portsmouth?**
2 **Locate Portsmouth on a map and draw in lines to mark the ferry routes to the Isle of Wight and France.**

Seaside resorts

As an island, Britain has thousands of miles of coastline. The National Trust protects over 600 miles of coast keeping it accessible to the public and in its natural state. Seaside resorts vary from small villages in coves, such as Porthcurno in Cornwall, to large towns with miles of flat sandy beaches such as Torquay on the English Riviera. There are traditional 'bucket and spade' resorts with piers and candyfloss, crazy golf and arcade games when it rains. Families visit seaside resorts year after year as children can spend hours making sandcastles and paddling in the waves. Visitors find the ever-changing sea relaxing and walks along the 'promenade' can be exhilarating, even in winter.

ACTIVITY

Find out how many beaches around the UK have the 'Blue Flag' award. (The award is made annually and lasts for one year.) Mark these on a map and add a key describing what a Blue Flag means.

However, resorts in England find it difficult to compete with the sun of the Mediterranean, so they have developed other ways to encourage tourists. For example, Blackpool has its casinos and illuminations as well as the Pleasure Beach theme park and Bognor has its 'Birdman' competition to see who can fly furthest from the (broken) pier!

European Blue Flag award

Beaches awarded the European Blue Flag have proved that they:

- have reached a certain standard of cleanliness, including water quality
- offer facilities such as toilets
- meet safety requirements – lifeguards must be on duty during the bathing season
- display environmental information
- are environmentally managed – the beach is cleaned regularly and litter bins are provided.

Spa towns

Spa towns such as Bath, Harrogate and Tonbridge Wells were very fashionable in the 18th century. Even the Romans went to Bath to use the hot springs for spa baths! The mainly Georgian buildings, where the rich and famous went to bathe in the baths and springs, are very popular with tourists.

CASE STUDY

Bath

The hot springs of Bath led to the Romans building 'Aquae Sulis' (a temple and baths dedicated to Minerva) around two thousand years ago. The Roman baths can still be seen today, where it was fashionable for people to 'take the waters' for their aches and pains. Bath has a wealth of elegant Georgian architecture, including the Royal Crescent and the Pump Room next to the baths.

The River Avon runs through the city, crossed by the beautiful Pulteney Bridge. It is also the home of the 'Bath Bun', which can still be eaten at Sally Lunn's café.

1. **Why did people want to go to these 'bathing pools'?**
2. **What is the equivalent today?**

Countryside areas

The UK is densely populated and guards its countryside areas against development! One of the most effective ways of ensuring that underdeveloped areas remain that way is the National Park. There are nine National Parks in England, three in Wales and two in Scotland. Much of the land is still privately owned, but it is protected by legislation against unsuitable building projects, use of insecticides, etc. The Parks are also required to encourage visitors so that everyone may enjoy the beautiful scenery.

Talking point

The National Parks are there to protect the environment and also to encourage visitors. Think about:

- the effects that thousands of cars and pairs of feet can have on fragile environments and animals and birds
- the way traffic and important areas are controlled in an area near you.

In groups, discuss ways the National Parks can minimise these effects.

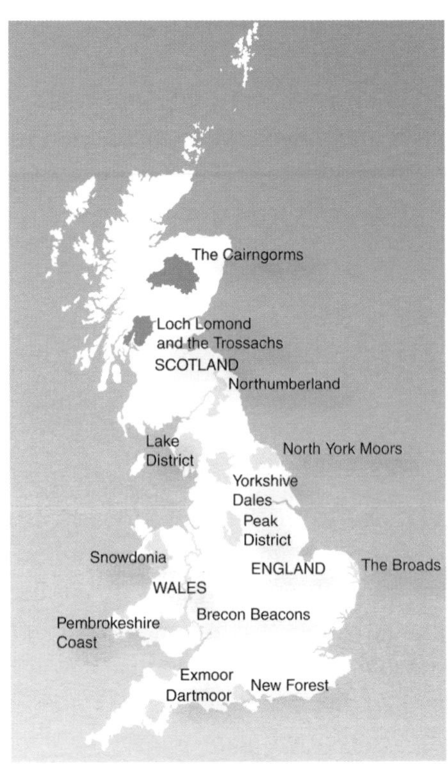

The National Parks of England, Wales and Scotland

CASE STUDY

Dartmoor

Dartmoor is an area of 368 square miles, in the south west of England. It receives around 10 million visits a year, and varies from undulating hill to open moorland with granite tors. The River Dart flows through it and at Dartmeet the East and West Dart flow together.

It is a beautiful area, and many people go simply to walk and ride through the region. There are many villages on Dartmoor – one of the most famous is Widecombe-on-the-Moor, home of 'Uncle Tom Cobbley and all' in the song about the fair. There are facilities for horse riding, sailing, biking, etc., and children are often entranced by the Dartmoor ponies which roam free. After all the activity, visitors can settle down to a real Devon cream tea! More information can be found at the Visitor Centre at Bovey Tracey, near Newton Abbot.

There are other areas of the countryside which are visited because of their natural beauty – some

CASE STUDY

Dartmoor (Contd.)

are protected by law as Areas of Outstanding Natural Beauty (AONBs), which restrict building and land use so that the general public can enjoy the area.

1 **Who do you think visits the National Parks? Write a list.**

2 **Choose one of the National Parks and list the activities which people can do there – now who do you think goes there? Look at your original list and compare them.**

3 **For the chosen park, draw a sketch map and add the facilities and amenities, e.g. visitor centre.**

Visitors to Dartmoor National Park enjoy a range of activities

In summary

- Tourism in the UK is very important – visitors come from all over the world, as well as different parts of Britain.
- People visit towns and cities for the facilities and shops, buildings and heritage. Spa towns are popular for their architecture and heritage.
- The seaside is popular for traditional 'bucket and spade' holidays as well as entertainment and leisure facilities, while people visit the countryside for leisure and sporting activities as well as to enjoy the beautiful scenery.

European destinations

Continental Europe is a popular tourist destination, but differs slightly from political and geographical Europe in that travel 'Europe' brochures often include Scandinavia (Sweden, Norway and Denmark) and North Africa (Tunisia and Morocco).

Most visitors travel either on 'city breaks' to capital and other major cities, or to resorts around the Mediterranean Sea or mountains. Some countryside areas, particularly in France, are popular for leisure activities such as hiking, boating, etc. The Alps and Pyrenees are centres for skiing in the winter.

ACTIVITY

On a blank map of Europe locate and name the following countries, and mark on their capital cities:

Austria	Germany	Portugal
Belgium	Greece	Spain
Czech Republic	Hungary	The Netherlands
Denmark	Italy	Tunisia
France		

Even more than the UK, Europe provides great contrasts. The ancient cities of Rome, Florence and Athens have been part of the cultural education of wealthy people for centuries, as they completed the 'Grand Tour' of Europe. The recent fall of the communist regime in the USSR has meant that access to the old eastern European countries has become easier. The rise of low-cost airlines has made transport much cheaper, and the Internet has made it simple to find information and make bookings in other countries.

Many people in industrialised countries are working long hours and are 'cash rich – time poor', and a short break to Europe which can be taken over a long weekend is increasingly popular.

KEY POINTS

Popular European tourism destinations:

- City break destinations
- Summer sun
- Winter sun
- Mountains and ski areas
- Rural destinations.

City break destinations

One of the nearest to the UK (and the most popular) is Paris. It is known as a most romantic city and is easily accessed by air, rail (Eurostar) or road. Everyone knows the Eiffel Tower and the boats on the River Seine, but there are lots of other reasons to visit Paris.

CASE STUDY

Paris

Paris – popular city break destination

Paris has long been the favourite destination of UK visitors. In the valley of the Seine, it is a city of boulevards and squares, parks and pavement cafés.

Many people go to visit its galleries and museums such as the Louvre (home of the famous painting of the Mona Lisa), where a huge glass pyramid dominates the entrance. Nineteenth- and twentieth-century art is found in the Musée d'Orsay, home of many Impressionist paintings.

For people who enjoy visiting beautiful churches, there are many, including Notre Dame (home of the 'hunchback') and the Sacré Coeur, high on the hill of Montmartre overlooking the city. For even better views, you can go to the top of the Eiffel Tower or the Arc de Triomphe.

It is a very romantic city, and lovers can cruise down the river on the *bateaux mouches*, or stroll through the Tuileries gardens.

CASE STUDY

Paris (Contd)

There are many designer shops such as Chanel and Gucci off the Champs Elysées and smaller individual shops, all with Parisian 'chic'.

You can stroll down the Left Bank of the Seine and see the artists' quarter and the flea markets selling pictures and bric-a-brac. This is truly a city for everyone, and can now be reached in less than three hours from central London by Eurostar.

1 **Why is Paris popular with young couples?**
2 **Where can people interested in art and culture go in Paris?**

CASE STUDY

Budapest

Budapest is the capital of Hungary, just over a two-hour flight from London. The city is one of those which has emerged from communist rule and is becoming a very popular destination.

The River Danube flows between the old centres of Buda and Pest, merged in 1873. Buda has a medieval city with palaces and churches on top of Castle Hill, a limestone crag overlooking the river. Pest is much flatter on the river plain, with boulevards, shops and grand buildings.

The city is full of bars and restaurants, art galleries and museums of local Magyar heritage. There are many natural hot water springs where people can swim in indoor or outdoor pools. In the winter, you can skate in the City Park, or in summer travel on the children's railway from Moskvater. For music lovers there is the Liszt Academy and the Autumn Festival in October.

The city has a definite eastern European feel but with modern comfort and facilities.

1 **Why is Budapest suitable to visit all year round?**
2 **What is the difference between the two halves of the city?**

ACTIVITY

In small groups, draw a spider diagram of the images of a European city. You may like to look at Paris, Amsterdam, Rome, Venice, etc. Just write down the first things which come into your head about the chosen city, for example Venice might be gondolas and singing gondoliers!

Summer sun destinations

Although short breaks are becoming more popular, more people still spend a one- or two-week holiday on the Mediterranean beaches. Many of the big resorts, such as Torremolinos in Spain, were once fishing villages, but now have all the leisure attractions to keep visitors occupied. As well as almost guaranteed sunshine and high temperatures from April to October, food and drink tend to be relatively cheap and there are many facilities such as water parks, golf courses and water sports. There are also bars, restaurants and clubs to ensure an interesting nightlife!

Some resorts, such as Puerto Pollensa in Majorca, still retain their original atmosphere, and are much more peaceful. These are suitable for older couples or families.

Mediterranean sea resorts are found in the Spanish Costas, Balearic Islands, the Algarve in Portugal and many Greek islands.

ACTIVITY

In groups, discuss any summer sun destinations you may have visited.

Draw up a list of attractions and facilities found at these resorts, and display them on a poster.

Why have these resorts been so successful?

Why do so many people prefer to holiday at these resorts rather than in the UK?

ACTIVITY

On a blank map of Europe, mark three destinations for each country around the Mediterranean Sea. Keep this map safe as you'll need it for other Activities in this unit.

Winter sun destinations

Much of the Mediterranean is too cool to be a year-round destination, except the Costa del Sol in southern Spain. The islands further south in the Atlantic, nearer to the coast of Africa, stay relatively warm and receive visitors all year. These include the Canary Islands of Tenerife and Gran Canaria, and Madeira. The coast of Africa is popular, too, particularly Tunisia and Morocco.

CASE STUDY

Tenerife

Tenerife is one of the Canary Islands, which although Spanish, with a real flavour of mainland Spain, are situated off the coast of Africa. This means that Tenerife has warm weather and sunshine all year round and is very popular as a winter sun destination. The beaches in the south are soft and sandy, but in a dramatic contrast, the north has dark, volcanic beaches. A major tourist attraction, the dormant volcano Mount Teide, is in the north of the island.

There are many resorts, such as Playa de Las Americas, which are lively and cosmopolitan and offer a wide choice of bars, discos and nightclubs. The resorts also have a range of shops and boutiques selling international as well as Spanish goods. There are restaurants and cafés which serve a variety of food. The atmosphere is lively and appeals to a wide range of people from young families and teenagers to older travellers. There are also many water sports facilities from water-skiing to scuba diving.

There are also smaller resorts such as La Caleta, which was a picturesque fishing village and still retains much of its character. Here there are small bars and restaurants, without the hustle and bustle of the larger resorts. This would be ideal for families with small children or those looking for a peaceful getaway. Resorts like Puerto de Santiago are in the steep hilly area, perfect for walkers and nature lovers.

Using a tour operator's brochure, find a resort on Tenerife which would be suitable for:

a a family with small children

b a middle-aged couple looking for peaceful walking and water sports.

ACTIVITY

Add the Canary Islands and Madeira (part of Portugal) in a different colour to the summer sun destinations map.

Mountains and ski areas

Of course, some people don't want to spend their winter holiday in sunshine, but in snow! Skiing can be an exhilarating experience in the sunshine and crystal clear air, and once people have experienced the freedom they are often 'hooked'. Snowboarding is becoming a popular winter sport, particularly among younger people, and the ski resorts also offer their own culture of clothing and music.

The Alps and the Pyrenees have ski resorts which operate between December and March. These can vary from traditional 'chocolate box' destinations such as Seefeld (Austria) to purpose-built skiing towns such as Flaine (France).

CASE STUDY

Valloire

Valloire is situated in the French Alps. It has been a winter ski and summer walking destination for many years, and grew out of a farming community in the lush river valley.

There are year-round ski-lifts to take people to the mountain top. In the winter, a number of lifts mean that the sides of the valley can be skied by people of all abilities, and in summer the walkers are accompanied by herds of cows with tinkling cowbells eating the lush grass and flowers!

The village has many bars and restaurants, where visitors can relax in the evening – in winter this is known as *après-ski* where *vin chaud* (warmed, mulled wine) soothes the aching muscles! There are also bars and restaurants on the mountains to refresh skiers as they ski down the pre-prepared runs, the pistes. There are many shops which cater for skiers, climbers and walkers, where boots, skis and snowboards can be hired in

CASE STUDY

Valloire (Contd)

winter and hiking and climbing equipment in summer. There is also a swimming and sports complex, and children's playground. In winter a ski-school operates, with a children's section.

1 **Why do you think Valloire is so successful as a ski resort? What facilities does it have for skiers?**
2 **Look at a ski brochure. Find out what the different colours on the pistes mean.**

ACTIVITY

On your map of Europe, add the Alps and the Pyrenées mountain ranges. Mark on five ski resorts in different countries.

Rural destinations

Just as in the UK, there are areas in Europe which are popular for their scenery and countryside. You have already looked at an Alpine resort, Valloire, which encourages summer visitors who come to walk and climb in the mountains. Lakes such as Lake Geneva in Switzerland offer visitors sailing, fishing and other water sports. Rivers such as the Dordogne in France are popular for boating and rafting.

ACTIVITY

On your map of Europe, mark three rural destinations.

In summary

Europe has been receiving visitors for hundreds of years. It offers mountains and valleys, coastlines and cities. There are contrasts between established cultural destinations and emerging eastern European cities and a range of sporting activities from skiing to rafting. Each country is unique, and offers different experiences to all types of visitors.

Long-haul or worldwide destinations

Long-haul destinations are normally those over four hours' flying time from the UK. This would include Africa, Asia, Australia and the Americas.

Now that European countries are becoming common destinations, visitors are looking for new experiences and cultures. Falling prices, due partly to an increase in charter flights, mean many more people can afford to travel to other continents. These are seen as excellent value for money. Indeed, Florida in the USA is treated almost as a European destination and is often featured in mainstream summer sun brochures!

USA

Both San Francisco and New York are also 'week-end break' destinations. People often travel here for shopping (some clothes and electrical goods are much cheaper in the USA) and the 'buzz' these exciting cities have. So much of the USA is familiar to visitors through American films and TV programmes that many of the sights are greeted like old friends.

The most popular US destination is Orlando, Florida, where giant theme parks like Disneyworld, Seaworld and Universal Studios ensure that there is always something to do for visitors of any age.

Australia

Australia has many destinations popular with visitors. The city of Sydney has a huge appeal with its opera house, beautiful bay and bridge and nearby beaches. There is a huge range of destinations across the vast continent from the arid interior and Uluru (formerly Ayers Rock), sacred to the Aboriginal people, to the sub-tropical North. Despite the fact it takes nearly a whole day to travel there, Australia is very popular with gap-year students and older people visiting relatives.

Over to you!

Many resort hotels are all-inclusive. Visitors seldom go beyond the hotel's grounds and everything a tourist needs, including activities, is included in the pre-paid price.

Do you think that the benefits of tourism to local people are as great on these kind of holidays? Why?

ACTIVITY

1 On a blank map of the world, name the continents.
2 In the USA, locate and name New York and Boston (short break destinations); Orlando (Florida) and Los Angeles (California), both Disney entertainment destinations.
3 In Australia, locate and name Sydney and Perth.

You will need this map for the next Activity.

The Caribbean Islands

The Caribbean Islands lie in the Caribbean Sea, close to the east coast of Central America. They are known for their beautiful sandy beaches and waving palm trees – the ideal of a 'paradise' destination. The islands have different cultural heritages – in the past they were colonies of Britain (Jamaica and the Bahamas), Spain (Dominican Republic) and France (St Lucia), among others.

CASE STUDY

The island of St Lucia

St Lucia enjoys a warm climate all year round. The island is covered in lush vegetation and tropical forests, cooled by Trade winds in summer. The beaches are all you would expect, with palm trees and golden sand. It is an unspoilt Caribbean paradise for all.

St Lucia is the perfect setting for a wedding, and the island offers a variety of wedding packages, with specialist brochures available to make the 'big day' easy to organise.

Many of the resort hotels offer a wide range of sports activities, from golf to sailing and windsurfing, as well as tennis and fitness areas. There are also children's clubs with sports for older children.

The many bars and restaurants serve international and French Caribbean cuisine.

This is an island for anyone who wants luxury and unspoilt beauty, as well as a variety of activities.

Look at a long-haul tour operator's brochure which features St Lucia.

Pick a hotel which would be suitable for families, and write a letter to a friend,

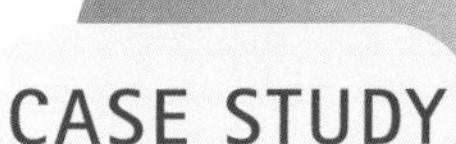

CASE STUDY

The island of St Lucia (Contd)

persuading them to go with you on your next family holiday there. Tell them why you want to go, what you can do there and why it would be a special experience.

The 'paradise' island of St Lucia

ACTIVITY

On your map of the world, locate and name three Caribbean Islands and the Caribbean Sea.

Safari holidays

Safari holidays give visitors the chance to drive (or even walk) into the bush of the African game reserves such as the Masai Mara. Usually in four-wheel drive vehicles with guides and animal experts, tourists are taken to see animals in the wild – from lions and elephants to flamingos and emus.

CASE STUDY

Cheetah safari, Kenya

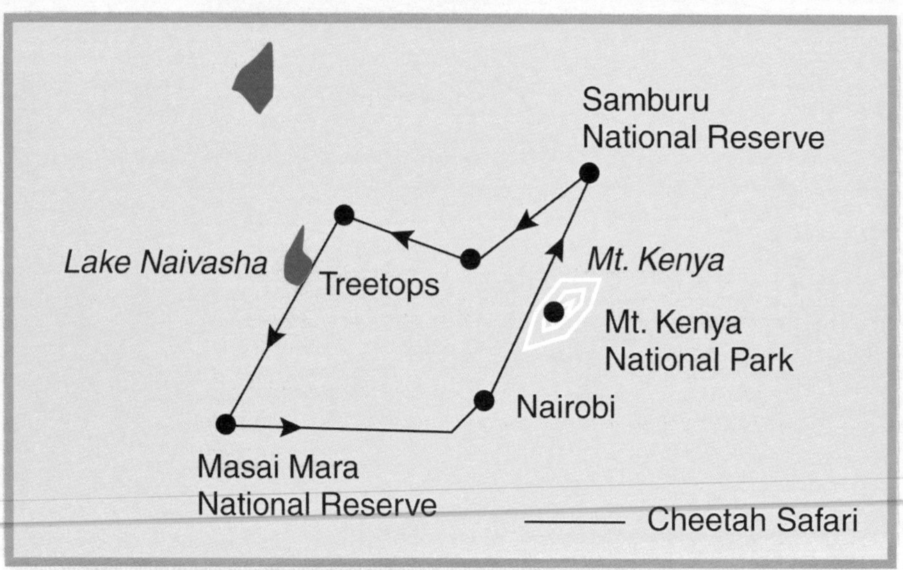

The Cheetah Safari is our most popular safari covering a wide area of Kenya and is designed to show you the very best in Kenya.
Our opinion
Stay at Block Lodges througout the safari which are in some of the best locations in the game parks. Mileages are quite long some days, but this is to ensure you see everything and the wildlife is quite unforgettable.

Source: Kuoni

1 **Where can the tourists stay?**
2 **What kind of tourist might be attracted to a safari?**

ACTIVITY

Add Kenya, its capital Nairobi, and Tanzania to your map of the world and add a key for safaris.

PRACTICE ASSESSMENT ACTIVITY

Level ✓

P2.1 Good news! If you have been keeping your maps all the way through this unit you should have produced evidence for:

Locate a range of UK, European and worldwide destinations.

In summary

Destinations are as individual as people: one visitor's ideal may be totally wrong for another. Each one is different – celebrate the differences!

Destination types

Some destinations, particularly southern Spain and the Balearic Islands (Majorca), have been popular since the beginning of the boom package holiday years in the 1960s. Once large aircraft arrive regularly, with thousands of holidaymakers every week, the destinations become mass market – that is, popular with high-volume, low-spending tourists. However, after a while, the 'been there, done that, bought the T-shirt' feeling kicks in, and people look for different places to go to.

Two different types of destination: Spain and Iceland

Some destinations are thought of as 'exclusive' – this could be because of the cost of getting there (Cambodia), the cost while you are there (Iceland) or because only a limited number of people are allowed there at any given time (Galapagos Islands, off Ecuador). These destinations are unlikely to become popular package holiday, mass-market resorts for any of the above reasons, or combinations of them.

Appeal

All the destinations you have looked at so far are important to tourists for one or more of the following reasons:

- climate
- topography (landscape)

Talking point

In groups, choose a tourist destination you are familiar with and discuss the following:

- Why do visitors go there?
- How does the destination encourage tourists to visit?
- What sort of tourists might go there?
- What is its main selling point?

Present your findings to the other groups.

- facilities
- access
- safety.

Each destination will encourage people to visit because of its own 'selling point'.

Climate

Some destinations are popular because of their weather. The Caribbean has warm sunshine and cooling breezes all year round; the Mediterranean area has hot summers and in the south, mild winters – these areas draw people who would like some 'warmth' after the chill of a northern winter.

However, not everyone wants sun! Parents with young children and particularly the elderly often prefer gentler climates in the summer, such as in Scandinavia or northern France where it may not get too hot.

Skiers need snow, so they will want to be in cold mountainous regions to get the best chance of good fresh snow fall.

If you are going to a cultural destination, the weather may not matter, but if you intend to sit on a beach or by a pool all day, then the sun might be a definite requirement. Remember, different areas will be less welcoming at certain times of the year, for example hurricanes in the Caribbean in September or the monsoon rains in India during the height of the summer.

Topography

This simply means a description of the physical features of a place. Some destinations are where they are because of their geographical features, for example cities were often built on rivers (London, Paris, Prague).

Some rivers are so important that visitors will go to look at the river valley itself – think of the castles of the Loire, rafting on the Dordogne and the vineyards of the Rhone in France. The Alps are important because of their height and steep mountain slopes; the Lake District (see the National Parks map on page 50) is important for – yes – its lakes! Some destinations are significant because of special natural features such as a volcano (the ruins of Pompeii, Italy), a forest (the New Forest in Hampshire) or a spectacular waterfall (Niagara Falls, North America).

Facilities

Tourists require the following services to help make their visit trouble-free and enjoyable:

- **Information**. Visitors will need to know about their destination. Tourist information centres in towns and cities or visitor centres in the National Parks will be able to provide leaflets and maps.

- **Shops and markets.** Shops are an important part of a holiday, whether it is for souvenirs or food and equipment. Many people enjoy shopping in local markets with their unfamiliar sights and smells – this is particularly so in countries with unfamiliar foods and goods.
- **Accommodation.** This may range from luxury hotels to a tent in the countryside or the African bush. Many families prefer self-catering accommodation for greater flexibility.

KEY POINTS

Reasons for choosing a destination include one or all of the following:

- Climate
- Topography (landscape)
- Facilities
- Access
- Safety.

Access

Visitors will need to be able to get to their destinations easily and to move around once they are there. The transport infrastructure (airports, ports, rail, roads) may be more important in a city than at a beach destination.

Safety

Safety has become a particularly important issue since the September 11th terrorist attacks on the USA (2001). While safety can never be guaranteed, tourists will want to avoid areas of conflict or war and areas of political unrest and terrorism.

PRACTICE ASSESSMENT ACTIVITY

Level ✓

P2.2 Now you have looked at a range of different destinations, choose *one* UK, *one* European and *one* worldwide destination and describe their appeal to visitors. Make sure that you cover all of the aspects above, and illustrate your answers well.

2.2 Cultural aspects of tourist destinations

'Culture' in this context means the way people live, their art, music, traditions, their beliefs – essentially what makes each area unique.

One of the main reasons why people go on holiday is to experience other cultures and traditions. Obviously, there are fewer variations within the UK, but there is quite a difference between spending a weekend in London and a week self-catering in the Yorkshire Dales National Park.

Over to you!

In pairs or small groups, think about and discuss the differences of the holidays in London and the Dales. You may need to do some research first, but list your answers under the following headings:

	London	Dales
Ease of transport		
Range of accommodation		
Environment		
Activities		
Suitable for?		
Information available		

Areas within the UK have different climates, different local dishes and different traditional crafts.

ACTIVITY

Match up the local food and drink with the home area.

Cider	Yorkshire
Cream teas	Bakewell, Derby
Batter pudding, served with beef	Somerset
Almond-flavoured dessert with pastry base	London estuary
Oatcakes and porridge	Devon
Jellied eels and whelks	Scotland

Customs, attitudes and values

Many destinations are now dependent on tourism and so make sure their welcome encourages visitors to return! However, some resorts, particularly in the former communist countries of eastern Europe, have expanded very quickly and some local people find the sudden appearance of plane-loads of (comparatively) wealthy tourists confusing and may resent the change.

Visitors must be careful not to cause offence and to be aware of local customs. In southern Europe, for example in Spain, Italy and Greece, it is usual for several generations of families to go out together. It is much less acceptable, even now, for young people to be alone together before marriage, and young women are expected to behave appropriately. 'Binge-drinking' is also much less common, as wine is usually drunk with food and children are often given a little with water. Some resorts are no longer willing to clear up after British 'lager-louts', and are making sure all visitors are aware they may be arrested for drunkenness.

In Islamic countries, such as Egypt or parts of Turkey, women are protected by their dress and may be expected to be escorted in public. Consequently, female western visitors may feel uncomfortable in some areas if unaccompanied, particularly if head and shoulders are uncovered and shorts or short skirts are worn. In some areas such as Egypt or South East Asia, you should always ask permission to take photographs of local people – otherwise you may cause offence. In the case of military sensitive areas, it could also cause arrest at worst and the film destroyed at best!

Local cuisine

Although hamburgers are everywhere, countries still retain their traditional dishes. Many people find buying food from markets and local restaurants a most enjoyable part of a holiday, and are eager to try unusual dishes and ways of eating.

ACTIVITY

See if you can match these worldwide dishes with their host country.

Houmus	Japan
Souvlaki	Spain
Sushi	Greece/Turkey
Tortilla	Greece
Fish chowder	USA

Unacceptable behavioural practices

You should always make sure you know what is acceptable locally – for example, showing the sole of the foot in South East Asia is considered very rude and the thumbs-up OK sign has a different meaning in parts of southern Europe.

Talking point

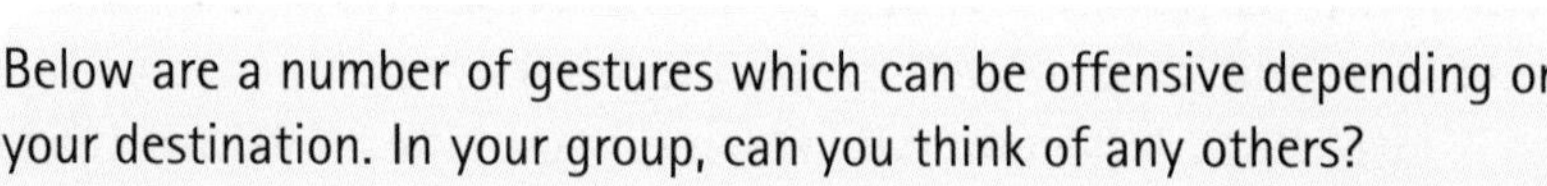

Below are a number of gestures which can be offensive depending on your destination. In your group, can you think of any others?

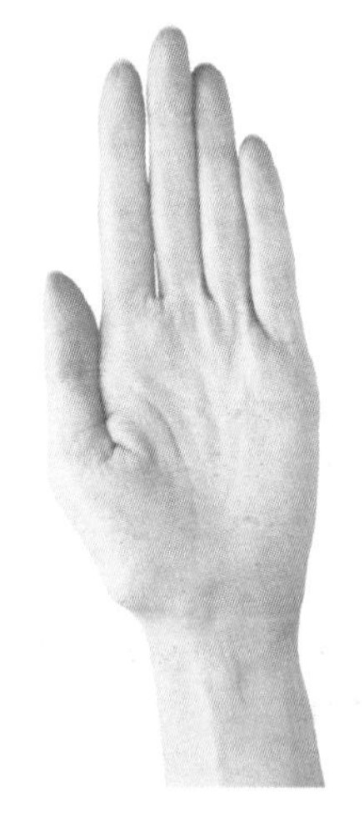

Gesture	Country	Meaning
Touching lower eyelid	Saudi Arabia	Stupid
	South America	Flirt
Palms thrust forward	Greece	Insult
	UK	Stop
Tugging at earlobe	Spain	Sponger
	Greece	Warning
	Malta	Sneaky
	Portugal	Wonderful
Thumbs up	UK	OK
	Sardinia	Obscene gesture
Ring/circle gesture	USA	A-OK
	France	Zero
	Japan	Money
	Tunisia	I'll kill you
	Columbia	Deadly obscenity!

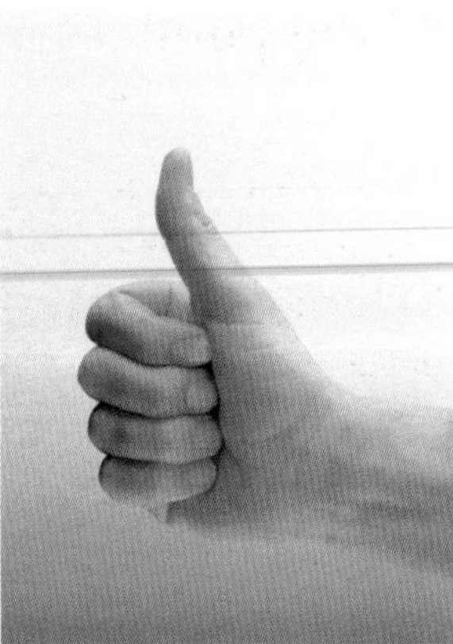

When in . . .
Islamic countries – the right hand is the 'clean' hand and should be used for eating
China – using a finger to point or beckon is rude
Indonesia – hands on hips is rude
Japan – smiling can mean happiness, anger, embarrassment or sadness
Korea – it is rude to blow your nose in public
Sri Lanka – moving head from side to side means yes, nodding up and down means no.

Religious practices

Some destinations such as Jerusalem are holy places for Jews, Muslims and Christians. Tourists may wish to visit holy sites but will need to be flexible because different religions will need to be able to worship in their holy places at various times of the day. Muslims, for example, pray regularly throughout the day. Most cities will have a cathedral, mosque, synagogue or other religious building.

Long-haul destinations are likely to have the most differences in culture and this is one of the main reasons why visitors go there! These destinations have become increasingly good value for money, and visitor numbers are rising. Local people may have different religious beliefs from visitors, and care should be taken not to offend by wearing shoes and shorts in a mosque or skimpy swimwear in a temple, for example. Women must be particularly careful in Islamic countries such as Egypt where the traditional burka, which covers much of the female body, is sometimes worn.

Muslims do not drink alcohol and some Arab countries may be 'dry' – alcohol may be difficult to obtain. There may be periods of the year, such as the Islamic Ramadan, where fasting between dawn and dusk is expected of most Muslims.

In Israel, you will need to remember that the Jewish Sabbath begins on Friday evening and lasts for 25 hours. In some countries, away from beach resorts, the Christian holy day of Sunday may well be observed, with all shops closed.

ACTIVITY

In small groups or pairs, research either Islam, Buddhism, Hinduism, Judaism or Christianity.

Buildings

Many tourists visit cultural attractions, such as castles, towers, historic houses and palaces. Think, for example, how the Tower of London spans hundreds of years of history.

The UK has many castles, which were built for the safety of the original inhabitants, such as Warwick Castle in England, Caernarfon Castle in Wales and Blair Castle in Scotland. In Europe, for example, dozens of castles or *chateaux* line the Loire Valley in France.

Further afield, the Taj Mahal in India and the ruined Inca city of Machu Picchu in Mexico attract thousands of visitors a year.

ACTIVITY

Ask ten people to name a favourite building in the UK or anywhere in the world. What do they like about it? Why is it their favourite?

Make a big chart and write all the details on it – see if you can find a picture of each building. Which is your favourite out of these and why?

Talking point

'Take only pictures, cast only shadows, leave only ripples of understanding as you travel the world.'

Discuss this view of the environmentalist David Bellamy who asks us to minimise the effect of tourism on sensitive areas. Why is it important that tourists are aware of local customs and make an effort not to cause offence?

Historic buildings such as Warwick Castle attract thousands of visitors each year

Arts and entertainment

Many destinations are important cultural centres with a range of art galleries and museums. These often display examples of local arts and crafts, as well as collections of international items. London, for instance, has the British Museum which actually houses items from all over the world, including Egyptian mummies and the Elgin Marbles from Athens.

Paris's Louvre Museum is home to the world-famous painting of the Mona Lisa by Leonardo da Vinci. Your local town may have a museum on a smaller scale, containing local archaeological finds, or local crafts.

Some cities are known for their theatre districts such as the West End in London and Broadway in New York. Most will have at least one theatre and/or opera house. There are many beautiful and well-preserved theatres throughout Europe, where international plays and operas are staged in different languages. At any performance in London's Shaftesbury Avenue, there will be many different nationalities present to experience the unique atmosphere and excitement!

You may also find that there is a local festival, which can range from the unusual (welly-throwing, lawnmower races) to the 'high arts' such as Glyndebourne Opera Festival. Mediterranean Europe has many festivals, often linked originally to religious celebrations. Some Hindu festivals in India can last for days.

ACTIVITY

Design a questionnaire to ask ten people where they have been to a festival or fair:

a in the UK

b in Europe

c worldwide.

Be prepared to share your findings with others and plot each festival on a map.

PRACTICE ASSESSMENT ACTIVITY

Level

P2.3 Describe the cultural aspects of *one* UK, *one* European and *one* worldwide destination. You may use the same three destinations you chose for the assessment activity on page 65, or you can choose three different destinations.

M2.1 Explain how *one* UK, *one* European and *one* worldwide destination appeals to different types of visitor including cultural aspects.

KEY POINTS

What makes a holiday destination unique?

- Its customs, attitudes and values
- Its local cuisine
- Its religious practices
- Its historic buildings
- The arts and entertainment facilities that it offers.

2.3 Climatic conditions and their effect on travellers' choices

As you read earlier in the unit, people travel to different places for a number of reasons. One of those is to experience different climatic conditions! Now, let's look at the influences of climate on different destinations and the kinds of tourists who will choose to visit them.

Global conditions

First, you will need to know the location of the world's major geographical features, so complete the activity below before reading on.

ACTIVITY

1 On an outline map of the world, locate and name: North Pole, South Pole, Equator, Tropic of Cancer, Tropic of Capricorn, Atlantic Ocean, Pacific Ocean, Indian Ocean, Arctic Ocean, Southern Ocean, Mediterranean Sea, Caribbean Sea.

2 Name the continents: Europe, Africa, North America, South America, Australasia.

3 Add the deserts of Gobi, Mojave, Sahara, and the Amazon Rainforest.

The northern and southern hemispheres

The Equator divides the globe into two halves – the northern half, or hemisphere, has its summer during June to August, and in the southern hemisphere summer falls from December to February. This means Christmas in Australia can be celebrated with a barbeque on the beach! Because of the tilt of the Earth as it orbits the Sun, countries on the Equator have a steady climate with temperatures ranging between 19°C and 27°C throughout the year. Rainfall here occurs throughout the year.

Either side of the tropics, the temperatures are also fairly steady at around 25°C and rainfall tends to peak in late summer and autumn.

The world can be divided into climate zones, which depend on a country's distance from the Equator – its latitude. Height above sea level will also affect a destination's climate.

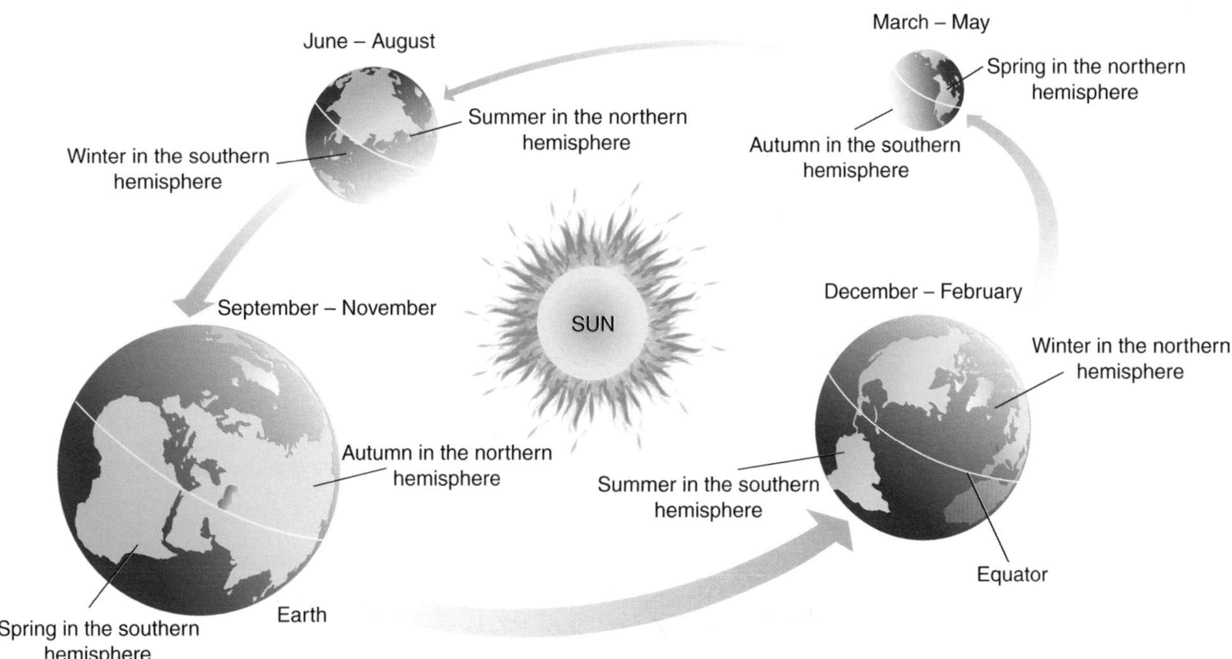

Seasons in the northern and southern hemispheres

Daylight

The tilt of the earth also means that daylight and darkness at the Equator are roughly equal all year round – further away from the Equator the proportion of day/night varies, so that the north of Norway, for example, may have only a few hours of light in the winter but in the summer it can be light for about 21 hours! This will make a difference to some visitors, who may want to see the Aurora Borealis (Northern Lights), a natural cosmic light show in the dark skies!

Visitors from the northern hemisphere may fly south during the winter (like birds!) to get more daylight and sunshine.

Deserts and rainforests

Deserts are found where the lack of rain (perhaps only a few centimetres may fall every few years) means that little natural vegetation can survive, and the soil and sand is constantly shifting. Often rain falls over mountain ranges or land mass before it can reach the desert. While the world's deserts do attract some visitors who want to have a unique experience, the extreme temperatures do not encourage mass tourism.

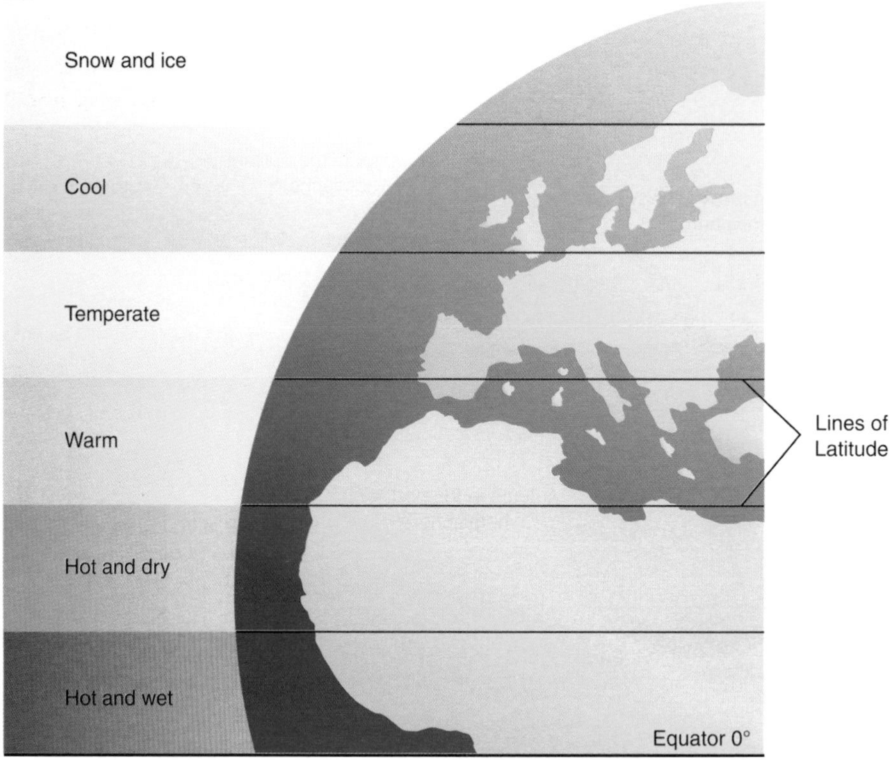

The world's climatic zones

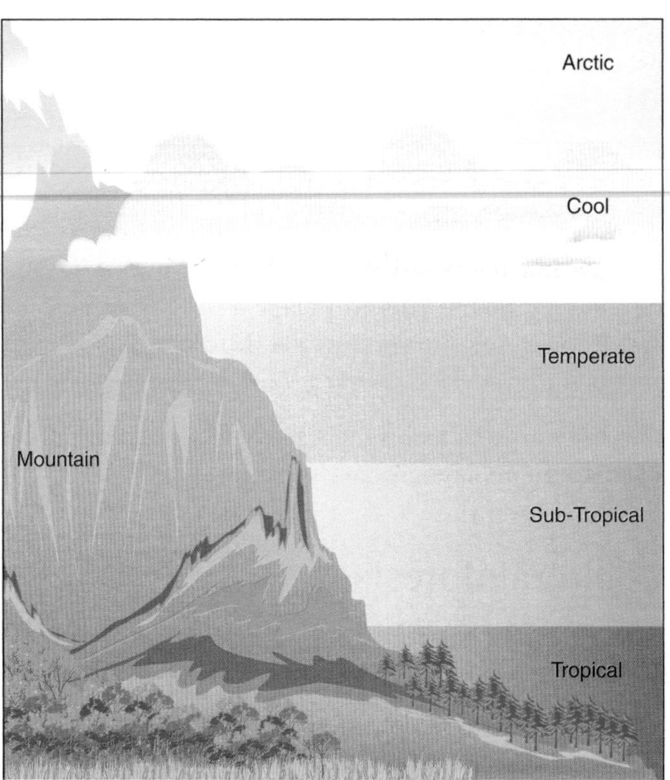

Height above sea level will affect a region's climate

An exception to this is Las Vegas, USA, which receives millions of visitors to the city (which is surrounded by desert) in order to gamble and see the bizarre hotels on 'The Strip'.

Rainforests occur where there is heavy and frequent rainfall, together with high temperatures. These can be found particularly in south America, and tourists visit them for the variety of plants and birds which live in the area. Again, the high humidity is not always comfortable, so it is not a market for mass tourism.

Seasonal conditions and effects on travellers

Winds

Winds are very important to climate. Winds that pass over oceans pick up moisture, which will fall as rain when a land mass is reached.

Look at the map of the world's prevailing (predominant) winds (see page 76). You can see that the eastern seaboard of the USA, the southern California coast and the Caribbean Islands have winds which cool the coasts and make them pleasant destinations even in the summer. The Canary Islands also benefit from this type of wind.

Winds are not always beneficial – some such as the Sirocco, which blows from the deserts of north Africa to Italy and the Mediterranean, are hot, dry and dust-laden, and can make you choke!

ACTIVITY

Many of the prevailing winds have names which suit their character! See if you can find out what they are.

Canary Islands and Hawaii

These popular islands are known for constant high winds and the resulting surf waves – although Hawaii is on a much bigger scale! Water sports are popular and high summer temperatures are tempered by the winds to a pleasant level.

Over to you!

Watch the weather forecast on television for a few days. Look at how the winds affect the rainfall and the temperatures in the UK. Consider the effects of this on exposed areas.

Rainfall, hurricanes and monsoons

You read earlier about summer and winter destinations. Somewhere like the Alps can be both, because visitors are able to ski in the snow in

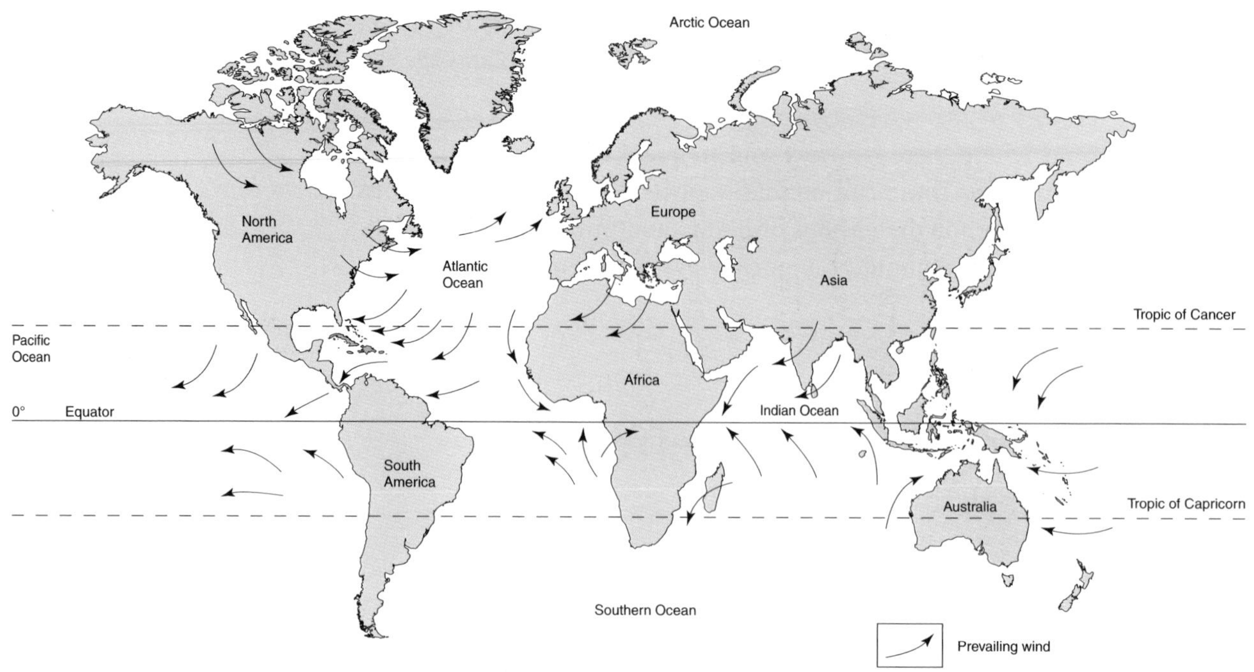

The world's prevailing winds

winter, and walk and climb in the mountains in the summer, using the same lifts and facilities. Other areas such as the Caribbean are also year-round destinations, since their temperatures do not vary a great deal. However, their rainfall may vary considerably! Look at the chart opposite.

The Caribbean and South East Asia

The temperatures in these regions are pleasant in winter and hot in summer, but the coasts and islands often have cooling breezes, which make their resorts popular with UK tourists all year round. However, in late summer there is a risk of rain and thunderstorms. The air gets so hot, and absorbs so much moisture that when the hot air rises in the early afternoon, it can no longer support all the moisture, and daily afternoon showers are common! Sometimes storms beginning in the Pacific and Atlantic oceans near the Equator develop into hurricanes (known as cyclones or typhoons depending on the part of the world in which they occur). The peak hurricane season in Florida and the Caribbean occurs in late summer/early autumn; in South East Asia the main typhoon season takes place during the summer months, with a lesser typhoon season during the winter.

South East Asia also experiences monsoons where there is heavy and prolonged rainfall after drought. Although prices are cheaper, tourists need to be careful to choose the right time of year to avoid these seasonal rains. Monsoons occur because of the relative difference between the temperature of the land mass and the sea, and an imbalance of high and low pressures, and the wet winds resulting from this.

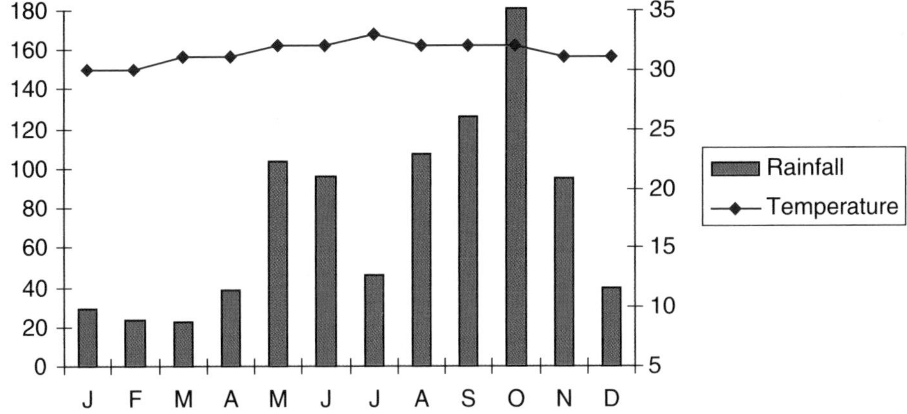

Jamaica's daytime temperatures are fairly constant but its rainfall varies considerably

Snow and avalanche risk

The amount of snow is governed by the height of the mountains and the aspect – whether facing the sun or not. Popular destinations for UK visitors are the Rocky Mountains in the USA and the European Alps and Pyrenees. The Rockies are much higher and the snow is much deeper and can be guaranteed, whereas in Europe there is often concern that there may not be enough at lower levels.

Where there has been an unstable base of snow, followed by a large dump of snow, there may be a risk of avalanche when the snow begins to melt. It is always important to take safety advice and a local guide when skiing off-piste. Some alpine resorts are prone to this and there has been considerable loss of life in the past.

KEY POINTS

It is important for you to know something about the seasonal climatic conditions of popular tourist destinations when advising customers on their holiday choice.

In summary

A destination's climate depends on many factors:

- Its distance from the Equator (the further north or south you go from the Equator, the greater the temperature variation).
- Its distance from the oceans (the further away, the more extreme the temperature and the less rainfall).
- Its height (the higher the destination, above sea level, the cooler it will be).
- Whether the destination is in a prevailing wind area (temperatures will be moderated).
- Beware hurricane and monsoon seasons.

Remember:

- Not every visitor wants hot sunshine!
- While seasons can be predicted, there may always be natural disasters such as earthquakes, tsumanis (giant waves caused by an undersea earthquake), droughts, floods, which can happen at any time. There is always a risk to any travel, and visitors will need to be aware of the forces of nature.

Level ✓ PRACTICE ASSESSMENT ACTIVITY

P2.4 Describe climatic conditions and how they can affect the traveller's choice of destination.

M2.2 Explain how climatic conditions affect the appeal of *one* UK, *one* European and *one* worldwide destination (again this could be the same choices as in earlier assessment activities,

Level ✓

PRACTICE ASSESSMENT ACTIVITY (CONTD)

or you could choose three different destinations to illustrate your knowledge).

D2.1/D2.2 Evaluate the significance of the key factors that influence the appeal of a destination. Choose any *one* destination that you think you can evaluate in detail. Work independently, using a range of sources of information that are clearly referenced in work that is presented clearly, logically and coherently.

Choose destinations that you have either visited, or know someone who has visited, or destinations you are really interested in! It will make a real difference to your work if you have a 'connection' with your destination.

Travel destinations try to sell themselves to visitors, so there is a huge quantity of information and images available. Use tourist boards and tour operators' brochures, newspaper articles as well as the Internet. It will make it even more interesting if you can use your own holiday photos!

ACTIVITY

1 Look at the following destinations and put together a chart describing the climate. Lines of latitude describe the distance from the Equator (0°).

Destination	Latitude	Average temperature: January	Average temperature: July	Height above sea level	Average annual rainfall
Paris, France					
Jamaica, Caribbean					
Denver, Colorado, USA					
Colombo, Sri Lanka					
Perth, Australia					

2 What differences do you notice between the destinations?

3 Explain the variations (look at the summary above to help you).

TEST YOUR KNOWLEDGE

1. a What are the countries which make up the UK?
   b Name the capital cities of these countries.
   c What is a 'honeypot' destination?
2. Destinations can be divided into different categories. Name them and give two examples for (a) UK, (b) Europe, (c) worldwide destinations.
3. What is the difference between short-haul and long-haul destinations?
4. a What is a safari holiday?
   b Name two countries which offer safaris.
   c Name a game reserve.
5. Explain how the climate and topography (physical features) might attract visitors to Lanzarote, Canary Islands.
6. a How many countries do the Alps go through?
   b Name four activities visitors can do in the Alps.
7. a Name three worldwide religions.
   b How might a religious culture affect how visitors dress and behave?
8. Explain how climate may affect the appeal of the following areas:

   a Nice, France
   b St Lucia, Caribbean
   c St Moritz, Switzerland.

Unit 3 Introduction to Customer Service in Travel and Tourism

Introduction

Travel and tourism is about people, all of whom have customer service needs. When these needs are met or better still, exceeded, customers will want to return to you again and again. Customers also tell others how good (or bad!) you are.

Whether you work directly with customers, or behind the scenes, you will be involved in the challenging, exciting and satisfying world of providing excellent customer service.

This unit examines what customer service is; what your customers need and like; and how customer service can be provided. Completing the unit will help you to understand and provide excellent service.

Providing excellent customer service is both challenging and rewarding

How you will be assessed

This unit is assessed internally, so the centre delivering the qualification will assess you against the criteria.

In this unit you will learn about:

① skills and techniques to provide good customer service

② the needs of different types of customers

③ how different organisations approach customer service

④ applying customer service and selling skills in travel and tourism situations.

3.1 Skills and techniques to provide good customer service

What is customer service?

Every day of our lives, we experience customer service. It may be when we buy something in a shop, or when we travel on a bus, or go to a swimming pool, or even when we go to the dentist. Most of the time, we don't even notice it. Sometimes we will, either because it is particularly bad or because it has been especially good.

Talking point

In a small group, brainstorm as many words and phrases as you can to describe good customer service.

Now, brainstorm as many words and phrases as you can to describe bad customer service.

Review the words and phrases you have chosen and, in one sentence, write a definition of customer service.

Did your group suggest any of these words (see top of next page) when you brainstormed good customer service?

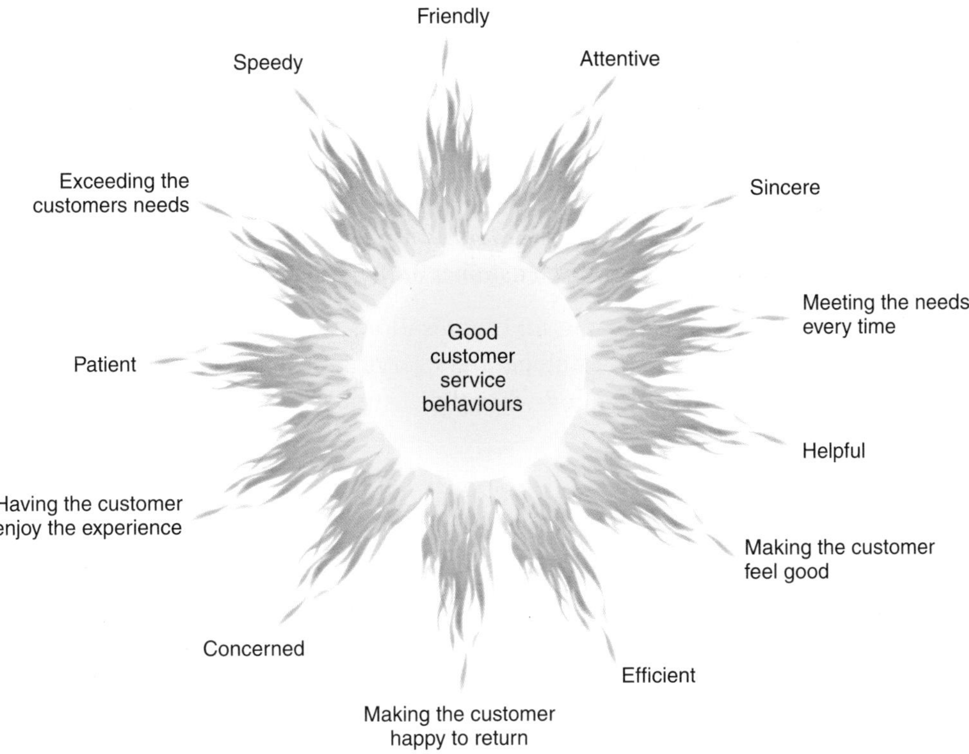

Examples of good customer service behaviours

These are some of the words and phrases your group might have suggested for bad customer service.

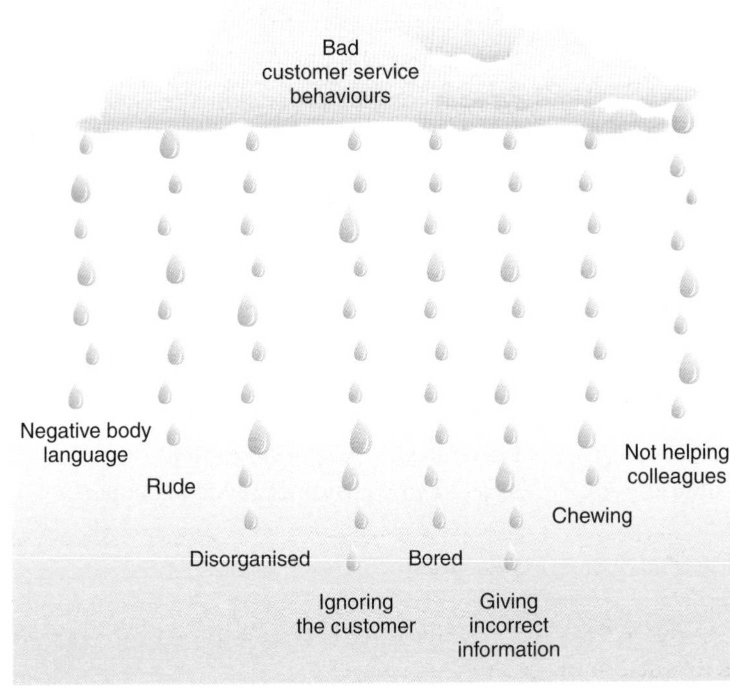

Examples of bad customer service behaviours

Customer service is difficult to define, but it is important to remember that it is the customer who will decide what customer service is. Customers can be very different from each other, so will measure customer service in different ways.

The Institute of Customer Service defines customer service as:

> *'The sum total of what an organisation does to meet customer expectations and produce customer satisfaction.'*

This means that everyone in an organisation, whether or not they have direct contact with the customer, and everything that an organisation does, should be aimed at providing what the customer wants, so that the customer is satisfied.

Delighting the customer

However, it is not enough simply to 'meet customer expectations and produce customer satisfaction'. If that is all you do, the customer may feel that the customer service is all right, but nothing special. What you and your organisation have to do is *delight* every one of your customers, so that they will remember you, enjoy dealing with you, come back to you again, and tell other people about you.

CASE STUDY

Going the extra mile!

Passenger Agent Maria had a tricky situation at Toronto airport. An elderly couple who had been visiting their son and his family were checking in to return to the UK. Their son drove them 100 miles from his home, left them at Toronto airport, and set off home again. When the couple checked in, they discovered they had left their passports in his car!

Maria could have taken the easy way out by telling them they could not travel until they had their passports. However, she wanted to help the distraught couple. Their son did not have a mobile phone, so she asked if he had had the car radio on. He had, and they remembered the programme he was listening to. Maria called the radio station and asked them to put a message out to the son, to return to the airport. The son heard it and drove back to the airport just in time for his very relieved parents to catch their flight!

Maria had gone the extra mile and had delighted the couple and their son.

Write down as many reasons you can think of as to why customer service is important. Discuss your reasons with someone else in your group.

Customer service is important because you must ensure the customer is so pleased with doing business with you, that they will keep returning to you.

There are other reasons why customer service is important:

- You have to keep your customers away from your competitors.
- It costs five times as much to win a new customer as it does to keep an existing one.
- Dissatisfied customers tell others of their bad experience, and those people will avoid using your organisation.
- You need the customer to feel that your organisation is great to deal with.
- Your organisation needs to be able to compete on value rather than just price, that is, customers are prepared to pay more for your product or service.
- Your organisation needs to be secure and develop, and so do you.
- You want the buzz you get out of providing excellent customer service!

Over to you!

A customer bought a £1 loaf of bread from her supermarket. How much is that customer worth to the supermarket? Just £1?

Ryanair will send staff to charm school

Ryanair's famously outspoken boss Michael O'Leary has performed the biggest U-turn of his career – by ordering his staff to be nice to airline's frazzled passengers. . . .

At two meetings in London, Ryanair executives revealed plans to focus on providing a kinder, softer approach to its customers. . .

James Freemantle of the Air Transport Users Council said: 'The slide show and presentation was strongly focused on punctuality, behaviour by staff towards customers and a greater emphasis on understanding air travellers' needs. It's not just about cost anymore.'

Source: Based on Jerome Reilly, *Sunday Independent* (Ireland), 8 August 2004

In summary

- Customer service can be defined as: 'The sum total of what an organisation does to meet customer expectations and produce customer satisfaction.'
- The customer decides what is good customer service.
- Customer service is important for many reasons; the most important of which is that you must ensure the customer is so pleased doing business with you that they keep returning to you!

Level

PRACTICE ASSESSMENT ACTIVITY

P3.1 Choose an organisation you know well. Perhaps it is an organisation you work for, or a club you belong to, or a college where you are a student.

How do you rate the customer service of this organisation? What skills and techniques are used by the organisation to provide customer service? Are any of the skills and techniques used by your chosen organisation also used in the travel and tourism industry?

If you were head of your chosen organisation, what two proposals would you make that might improve customer service so that you delight your customers?

Communication methods and skills

Effective communication is a major factor in customer service. This section considers types of communication and the skills and techniques useful in communicating well.

CASE STUDY

Moments of truth

Jan Carlzon was the Chief Executive Officer of Scandinavian Airlines System (SAS). He realised that the reputation and success of SAS depended upon how highly the passengers judged their communication with SAS staff. That communication could be at any time in their dealings with the airline. It could be for any reason and by any method, lasting for several minutes or just a few seconds. He called these contacts, 'Moments of truth'.

He realised the airline had to do everything to ensure those 'moments' were highly successful. He said: 'These "Moments of truth" are the moments that ultimately determine whether SAS will succeed or fail as a company.'

What did Jan Carlzon mean by a passenger's 'Moment of truth'?

Why do we communicate?

We communicate with others to:

- inform
- instruct
- seek information
- motivate.

Inform

You may be a holiday representative and want to tell your customers verbally about the resort. You may need to leave a written message for a colleague.

ACTIVITY

You have just taken a phone call from Brian. He wants Caroline to discuss the complaint from Mrs Harrison, in his office at 11.30 am. She is to bring all the paperwork about the complaint. She must call him by 11 am on extension 2403 if she cannot make the meeting. Write a suitable message for Caroline.

How did you do? Your message to Caroline should say who it is from, who it is to, when the message was taken, the accurate detail of the message, and what Brian's extension number is.

Instruct

This may be a verbal safety instruction given by cabin crew. It may be a notice to passengers telling them what they cannot carry in their hand-baggage.

ACTIVITY

You work in a three-storey tour operator's office. Your manager has left you a note:

'I've had the Fire Service here this morning. They've told us to get signs up about fire evacuation, pronto. Something about what to do if a fire is found, how to get out, where to go, what to do, what not to do. Apparently it's got to be clearly phrased and understood. Sort it out by this afternoon!'

So, the task is yours, to create a written instruction which meets the needs. Your instruction must be eye catching, clear and logical.

Seek information

Some of your verbal communication will be to seek information from a customer, so that you can respond to them. You may need to write a letter asking for information. A common type of written communication seeking information, is a customer service questionnaire (see page 115).

Motivate

You may want to verbally encourage your customers to go on an excursion. You may want to compliment an employee on their good work, in writing.

ACTIVITY

Some words and phrases are motivational – they can make people feel good when used about them. Here are some examples:

Caring	Friendly	Knowledgeable
Committed	Good humoured	Patient
Concerned	Helpful	Polite
Confident	Kind	Went the extra mile

Choose some of these words and phrases to complete the following letter to an employee:

Dear Lorna

I had a phone call from Mrs Simpson this morning, telling me how ________ and ________ you had been to her when she made a booking with you.

She told me she was travelling to visit a sick relative and was very uncertain about the flight arrangements she needed to make. She said you were ________ and ________ and helped her in a very ________ manner. You were very ________________ about Switzerland and ________ about what you were doing. Once you had helped her decide which city to fly to, and had booked her flight, you ____________________ and found details of the train connection she needed to make.

Clearly, you were very ____________ and ____________ to help Mrs Simpson. I am very pleased to add my thanks to hers. Keep up the good work!

The style of communication

You use different styles of language depending upon whether you are talking or writing to a friend, a tutor or a grandparent. Different customers and situations also require different styles. How would you talk to a client during a happy holiday experience, or during a complaint situation, or if the hotel was on fire?

How do we communicate?

We communicate with each other

- face to face
- electronically, e.g. by telephone
- in writing.

Whichever way we communicate, the same process occurs:
Stage 1: The sender wants the receiver to understand a message.
Stage 2: The sender puts the message into a logical language and style.
Stage 3: The message is transmitted.
Stage 4: The message is received.
Stage 5: The receiver 'decodes' (interprets) the message.
Stage 6: The receiver understands the message and may respond.

Over to you!

Communicating isn't just about sending *messages. It is also about* receiving *messages. We waste a lot of time, and create bad impressions, by talking when we should be listening. If we listened more, we would gain more information more quickly and demonstrate greater respect for our customers.*

We were all given 'two ears and one mouth. We should use them in that proportion!'

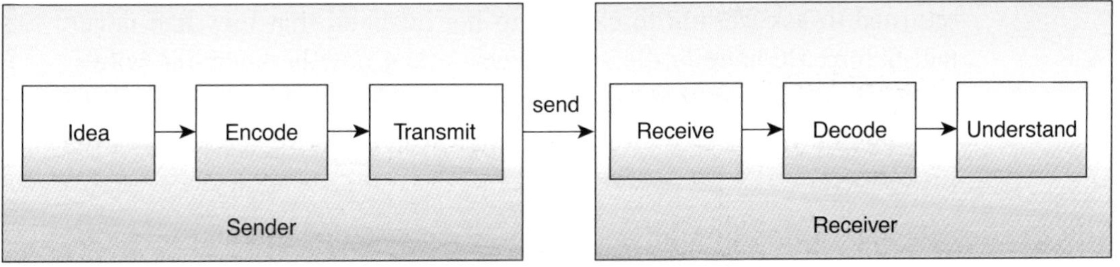

The communications process

Communicating face to face

We tend to think that the important thing to do when communicating is to *say* the right things. In truth, the 'words' we use are only one part of communicating, and it is the part which has the least impact!

The **words** we use account for around 10 per cent of the impact of our communication. Thirty per cent of the impact comes from the **pitch** and **tone of our voice**, what we can call the 'music'. The part which has the most impact – 60 per cent – is the **body language**, what we can call the 'dance'.

Words

The first few seconds of communication will have particular power, because it is then that the customer will receive their first impression of you! These are powerful 'Moments of truth'.

'Hello', 'Good morning', 'Can I help you?' are common opening statements you will use when dealing with customers, but how might that first communication be strengthened?

Personalise it! Use the customer's name as soon as you know it. Look for clues. The customer might give you a ticket showing their name, or have baggage with their name prominently showing on the label. However you discover the customer's name, make sure you use it.

Dermot King is the Chief Executive of a supermarket chain. He believes in spending time with the customers. Once, he was assisting staff when a family came to the till. He bagged their goods and said, 'Thank you Mrs Connolly for shopping at King Supermarkets.' Minutes later, the customer returned to ask Dermot to explain to her husband that they had never met before. He happily did so, and was asked how he knew the wife's name. He explained that, when paying, she had put her shopping list on the counter. It was written on an envelope addressed to her. How's that for observation!

People of different ages and cultures might have different views on how they should be addressed. An older person may prefer formality and like to be addressed by courtesy title and surname, for example Mrs Green. A young person may prefer to be addressed by their first name.

ACTIVITY

Write down opening remarks you might make to personalise your communication in the following situations:

a You are a coach escort. Among the passengers joining the coach is a woman with a young child eating an ice cream.

ACTIVITY

b You are a hotel receptionist and a woman wearing a wet raincoat and shaking water off her umbrella approaches you to check in.

c A man checks in at your desk with a lot of baggage. You notice the name Maurice Connor on a label on one of the bags.

What opening remarks did you suggest? Here are a few you might use:

a 'Hello, are you enjoying your ice cream?'

b 'It looks as though it's raining pretty heavily. Let's get you checked in to your room quickly, so that you can change into some dry clothes.'

c 'You've got a lot of bags with you, Mr Connor. Are you going away for a long time?'

The travel industry uses lots of jargon, for example hotac, no-show, ETA. Don't use it when communicating with customers. They may not understand it and it is discourteous.

Remember also, the language you use may not be the first language of some of your customers. Be careful to use clear diction and not to speak too quickly.

Throughout your communication, think about what you want to say and how you will say it. Structure helps you manage the communication and demonstrates knowledge and confidence.

Pitch and tone

This is the 'music' of communication. The effectiveness of your verbal communication is powerfully altered by the pitch and tone of your voice. Varied pitch and tone can demonstrate interest and enthusiasm. Flat pitch and tone can demonstrate disinterest and boredom. You can vary the volume of your voice to create an effect. You might use a loud voice to communicate an instruction in an emergency, or a quiet voice to encourage a calm atmosphere. Avoid the temptation to speak more loudly just because someone does not understand you!

Body language

This is the important 'dance' of communication. Look around you. What does the body language – the non-verbal communication – of others in the room tell you? Do you see enthusiasm, boredom, anger, puzzlement, happiness?

How would you feel if the escort on your excursion leans against the coach door, legs crossed and arms folded? He is presenting a 'closed' style. You might assume he is bored, not interested in you and not about to give you a fun journey.

Is this person interested or bored?

What if the cabin crew member greets you on board with good eye contact, a smile and is standing upright? She is presenting an 'open' style. You will probably feel she is demonstrating interest, warmth and confidence, and that this should be a good flight.

Mannerisms

Be careful to avoid mannerisms. Think about how *you* speak and what your body is doing. Ask a friend if you have any mannerisms. You may be surprised. Do you 'um' and 'er', or use slang phrases like 'Gottcha!' or 'Y'know'? Do you put your hand in front of your mouth or stand on one leg? Do you have other mannerisms?

Over to you!

Is it possible to know if the person at the other end of the phone is smiling?

Electronic communication

Using a telephone poses a particular challenge. You cannot use body language, so you must learn to be skilled in using the remaining 40 per cent which comes from the words used and the pitch and tone of your voice. Remember that standing or sitting comfortably, upright and alert will affect the way you speak, as will smiling.

Written communication

The same principles apply to written communication as they do for verbal communication. Think about what you want to communicate, and about who you are communicating with. Choose a style you feel is most appropriate to your customer and the situation. Structure your communication to ensure it logically addresses the issue.

There has been a revolution in written communication in the last decade, through the use of email. It is a useful, speedy method. However, emails are not confidential and they can be misinterpreted, with the reader assuming a much tougher, less polite message than the sender intended. Beware of this and learn email etiquette.

Confidentiality and accuracy

Customers trust organisations to treat information about them confidentially. That means not discussing them or any details about them, or their arrangements, with others unless for valid business reasons. This would include discussions about bookings they make, their contact details, and credit card information.

Do not make casual remarks about customers or release information to people asking about them. Airline staff are sometimes asked if someone is on a flight, but they will not release that information. That might seem unfair. However, the caller might say he is the passenger's husband and she has asked him to meet her at the airport, but how do you know the caller is really her husband or that she wants her husband to know where she is?

This confidentiality is protected in law. The Data Protection Act is designed to protect individuals from misuse of computer data held about them. They have the right of access to that data, rights of compensation for inaccuracies or wrongful disclosure, and the right to have inaccuracies corrected.

Accuracy is very important. If you need to record or say anything which is supposed to be factual, make sure it *is* correct.

In summary

- We communicate to inform, instruct, motivate and seek information.
- We must listen!
- We communicate verbally (either face to face or electronically), or by writing.
- The impact of communication comes from the words, the pitch and tone of our voice and by our body language – the words, music and dance. Body language is by far the most powerful.
- There are techniques we should use when communicating.
- We must be accurate and confidential when recording or using information.

Selling skills

Selling is not just about having a customer buy and pay for a product – an inclusive holiday, a guided tour, a train journey. It is a key part of customer service and is a part of promoting your organisation, which will encourage the customer to buy from you.

Selling objectives

There are five selling objectives:

- **To achieve customer satisfaction.** If you meet the customers' needs, they will feel good about you and your organisation, and be more likely to return.
- **To increase profitability.** Your organisation has to make a profit to stay in business, and to continue to employ you.
- **To increase sales.** Effective selling and customer service means customers will want to buy more from you, and will recommend you to others.

- **To secure repeat business.** Repeat business, or company loyalty, is vital. You need the customers to keep returning to you. They are more likely to do so if your company meets their needs, is trustworthy, makes them feel valued, does not pressure them to buy, and gives them good advice and help tailored to their needs.
- **To secure a competitive advantage.** Other organisations want your customers! You can prevent this if you highlight the advantages of buying your product rather than that of your competitors and by giving customer service which delights them.

Shopping on board a ferry

The Eight Stages of Selling

The Eight Stages of Selling is a useful framework of selling techniques.

1. **Create an image.** Make sure you and your environment are creating the right image to attract the customer. Is your appearance smart? Are your office, shop, desk, equipment clean, tidy, attractive? Are the goods you want to sell, or the brochures you want to offer, in good condition and easily available?
2. **Establish a rapport.** Create a favourable first impression. Be warm and sincere. Personalise the experience for the customer. Pay attention to how you communicate, including your body language. Don't get distracted.
3. **Investigate needs.** Find out what a customer wants by asking appropriate questions. Start with **open questions** (questions which

start with who?, what?, where?, why?, which?, how?). These will give you a lot of information, e.g. 'What interests does your daughter have?'. Continue with **leading questions**. These will narrow down the subject to give you more information, e.g. 'If she uses perfume, what types does she like?'. Move on to **closed questions**. These will give you specific information or confirm something, e.g. 'Has she tried Stella McCartney's new Stella perfume?'.

4 **Actively listen.** We aren't good at listening – we need to work at it! Demonstrate that you are listening and have understood what has been said. Use your body language, e.g. by nodding. Say encouraging things, e.g. 'As you have already taken a cruise on the QE2, you know how enjoyable cruises can be'. Repeat key words and statements, e.g. 'You said you like cruises, but only if they call at a different port every day'.

5 **Present the product/service.** By now, you should know your customer's needs and preferences. Make sure you know your products/services. This will help you to select one or more suitable ones to offer them. Choose three or four features which you feel will particularly appeal to the customer. Sell the benefits, e.g. 'You said you like calling at a different port each day. This ship is a bit smaller, so it can get in to many ports which the larger ships can't visit'.

6 **Handle the objections**: Don't tell the customer they are wrong, but overcome the objection by finding something positive to say which addresses the objection, e.g. 'I understand why you feel you would be more likely to be seasick in a smaller ship, but don't worry, because this is a modern ship fitted with the latest design of stabilisers'.

7 **Close the sale.** Watch for clues that the customer is ready to buy, e.g. the customer might say 'I understand' or 'That seems like the holiday I'm looking for' or 'Do you need a deposit?'. When that happens, re-emphasise the benefits to reinforce the customer's comfort about buying, and ask them how they want to pay.

8 **After the sale.** Ask the customer if there is anything else they would like to purchase. Remind them about when the balance is due, or tell them about guarantees, etc. Package the purchase well, even if it is only a ticket. Present it with a flourish! Follow up after they have used the product, to enquire if all was as the customer wished, and encourage them to think about their next purchase.

In summary

- There are five selling objectives.
- There are eight stages of selling.
- Good questioning techniques are important to selling – open, leading and closed questions all play their part.
- Customer service skills and techniques are vital aids to successful selling.

Level 

PRACTICE ASSESSMENT ACTIVITY

In groups of three:

- Prepare three copies of a proforma with the eight stages of selling listed down the page.
- Take turns in a selling situation. The first person is the customer, the second is the employee, the third is the observer.

P3.4/M3.3 Agree a selling situation and have the employee sell a product or service to the customer, using each of the eight stages of selling.

The observer will complete the proforma, noting evidence of when and how each stage was used.

D3.2 Complete the sale and then discuss what the employee did well. Evaluate your own performance and what you could do to make it even better.
Rotate roles, think of another selling scenario, and start again until you have performed three different situations.

KEY POINTS

Presentations may be formal and on a particular subject or informal announcements. Quite frequently they will be made using a microphone and you should seek opportunities on this course and elsewhere to gain experience of using microphones.

Presentation skills

Many employees in the travel and tourism industry speak in public, for example guides, cabin crew and holiday representatives. Presentations may be to small or large groups. There are some useful techniques to help you on the next page.

Talking to customers

Preparation

However brief the notice you get to speak, there is always time to think about what you are going to say, and how you are going to say it.

- Plan a logical structure to your presentation.
- Prompt cards are useful, but avoid standing in front of the audience reading them. They want to see your face, not the top of your head!
- Practise your presentation. Ask a friend to give you feedback.
- Check the location is suitable. Are any changes needed to it?
- Make sure you know how to use the equipment and that it works.
- Decide on what you will wear. Make sure it is clean and smart.

Nerves

- Calm your nerves by rehearsing.
- Have a Plan B in case anything goes wrong, e.g. the projector fails.
- Take deep breaths.
- Check your personal appearance.
- Tell yourself you look good and that your presentation will go well.
- Think of the audience as your friends.
- Go out there and enjoy it!

Presentation

- The first few seconds of your presentation will be the most powerful. Make sure how you appear and what you say in your opening sentences create a positive image. Even if you have decided to use prompt cards or a script, learn what you are initially going to say off by heart.
- Speak confidently! Make sure you are clear in both *what* you say and *how* you say it.
- Keep your face towards the audience and speak clearly to them.
- Avoid speech mannerisms.
- Use the pitch and tone – the music – of your voice to keep the audience interested.
- If you are using a microphone, don't put it in front of your face. The audience wants to see you, not a metal stick! Hold it about a couple of centimetres below your chin.
- Use your body language to create a confident image. That will impress your audience and have a positive effect on you.
- Stand erect, legs slightly apart, to demonstrate that you are at ease with yourself.
- Scan the audience and make eye contact briefly with various members.

Over to you!

When giving a presentation, make sure everyone can hear you. You can do this by asking your audience directly or you can look for body language signs. What might these signs be?

Pace what you have to say. Don't rush it. It can be easy to speed through an announcement especially if you have made it lots of times. What might happen if you rush a presentation or announcement?

ACTIVITY

Work in pairs. One will make an announcement using a microphone and speaker and the other will observe. At the end of the exercise, discuss what the speaker did well and what they might do to make their presentation better, using the guidelines in this unit. Swap roles and start again.

You are a holiday representative in Barbados. It is 6 pm and your clients have just landed after a long flight from Manchester, which arrived two hours late. You are to escort them on the coach to their hotel. You need to make some mention of the flight, the delay, and how they might be feeling. You need also to tell them where the coach is going, and how long it will take to get there. You might like to give them other information, perhaps what the meal arrangements are tonight, what they are seeing en route to the hotel, etc.

Personal presentation

Customers will judge you and your organisation on the image you present, so you need to get it right!

Personal appearance

Many organisations require staff to wear a uniform. This promotes the organisation and presents a powerful image. The organisation should give a demonstration and written briefing on how the uniform is to be worn.

Jacket (male uniform)

- *May be worn fully buttoned or fully unbuttoned with uniform.*
- *Must be fully buttoned when wearing knitwear underneath as a warmth layer.*
- *Cabin Crew in flight gilet must never be worn underneath the jacket.*
- *Must not be worn draped around shoulders.*
- *Must always display relevant name badge and brevet.*
- *Must always be available whilst on duty.*
- *Collar must not be worn turned up.*
- *The 'senior' cabin crew member will make a diplomatic decision on whether it is 'jackets on' or 'jackets off' when boarding and when staff are visible in public places such as airport terminals, hotel lobbies etc. Once that decision has been made all Cabin Crew members must present a uniform appearance. It is not acceptable for some crew to be wearing/not wearing the jacket in isolation.*
- *It is recommended that staff ask their dry cleaner to place metal foil or plastic button protectors over the buttons on their jackets to maintain their appearance.*

Source: British Airways, *Uniform Wearer Standards*

British Airways provides staff with a uniform guide

Grooming

You may be given rules and guidance about grooming, including information on acceptable hairstyles, make-up, tattoos, jewellery, etc. Look your best, by ensuring you and your clothes are clean and smart.

Personal hygiene

Good personal hygiene is essential. Take regular showers or baths and use deodorants and perfumes appropriately. Make sure your teeth are clean and your breath smells fresh. You may be working in difficult environments, for example in dusty streets, in high temperatures and in crowded aircraft cabins, so it is a good idea to take hygiene products with you to use throughout the day.

Body language

Always make sure your body language gives a positive and confident message.

✔ DO	✘ DON'T
Lean forward slightly when listening to someone	Stand with your arms folded
Have a ready smile to use at appropriate moments	Have your hands in your pockets
Incline your head to the side to show you are interested	Chew gum
Use appropriate hand gestures	Fiddle with articles like pens, loose change or clothing

Body language dos and don'ts

Attitude

You owe it to your customers, the colleagues in your group, your organisation, and yourself to have a positive attitude. You want people to value and like you. A negative attitude will affect the way that you communicate. Have a positive attitude – it feels so much better!

Effective customer service

How can organisations ensure their customer service is effective?

Identifying customers' needs and obtaining feedback

It is the customer who decides what customer service is. Organisations must encourage feedback from their customers to find out what they want and what they think of their performance. If they do not, they will not learn of what has gone wrong and will not get the chance to put it right, so it will keep going wrong. Organisations must keep close to their customers. Dermot King found out what his customers wanted by spending time among them (see page 90.)

Quality and quantity of information

Customers value accurate and interesting information. There are numerous ways to provide this. Many hotels train key staff in local knowledge and provide information on local tourist attractions and events.

Timing of service and information provision

Customers want good quality information and service at the right time. For instance, BAA plc needs passengers to know what items are forbidden in cabin baggage, for example knives, needles. Posters in the airport help, but to ensure passengers are aware of forbidden items before they pack, BAA also communicates such information through its website and newspaper advertisements.

Appearance of the environment

If you arrived at a hotel where the reception area had flaking paint, an 'Out of Order' sign on the lift, dirty glasses on a table and last week's newspapers on a shelf, wouldn't you want to leave as quickly as possible? It is the responsibility of the organisation and everyone who works in it to ensure the environment, both in customer areas and behind the scenes, is kept clean, replenished and in good condition.

Training

Unless staff are given induction and refresher training, including product knowledge, technical training and customer service training, an organisation cannot expect its employees to give superb, effective customer service.

Being proactive and responsive

Excellent customer service depends upon being proactive – taking action before the customer asks for it. Watch good shop assistants, cabin crew, and waiters, for example. They constantly scan their area, looking for clues that a customer needs attention, and checking with them that their needs are met.

Good organisations will respond to customer and staff comments and ideas, and implement changes as a result. They will be alert to potential changes in the business environment and will seek ways to overcome, and take advantage of them. Customer service is always changing. As the public becomes more sophisticated, has higher disposable incomes and receives 'better' customer service, so it will change its interpretation of what excellent customer service is.

In summary

Good organisations:

- know customers' needs
- provide timely and quality information
- ensure the working environment looks good
- gain and act upon performance feedback
- train staff
- are responsive and proactive.

Level ✔

PRACTICE ASSESSMENT ACTIVITY

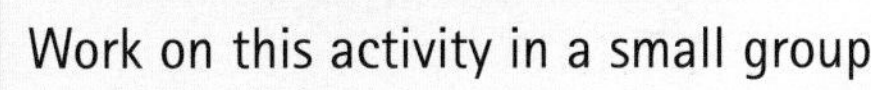

Work on this activity in a small group.

Choose an organisation in the travel and tourism industry. Imagine that the organisation has asked you to make a group presentation to them outlining:

1 What excellent customer service is.
2 How the organisation currently approaches customer service (**P3.3**).
3 How skills and techniques enhance customer service (**M3.1**).
4 The customer service challenges facing the organisation.
5 A training programme for staff detailing the skills and techniques that will be developed.

Choose another organisation in the travel and tourism industry. Repeat tasks 2, 4 and 5 for this organisation.

3.2 Needs of different types of customers

To work in travel and tourism you must be willing and able to meet the needs of a wide range of customers in a wide range of situations.

Types of customers

Segmentation

Whether we call our customers, clients, visitors, guests or passengers, their needs must be understood. To do so, we need to segment them. Segmentation is the grouping of people who have common characteristics (see Unit 4 Introduction to Marketing in Travel and Tourism, page 131). The spider diagram shows some of the customer categories which could be segmented.

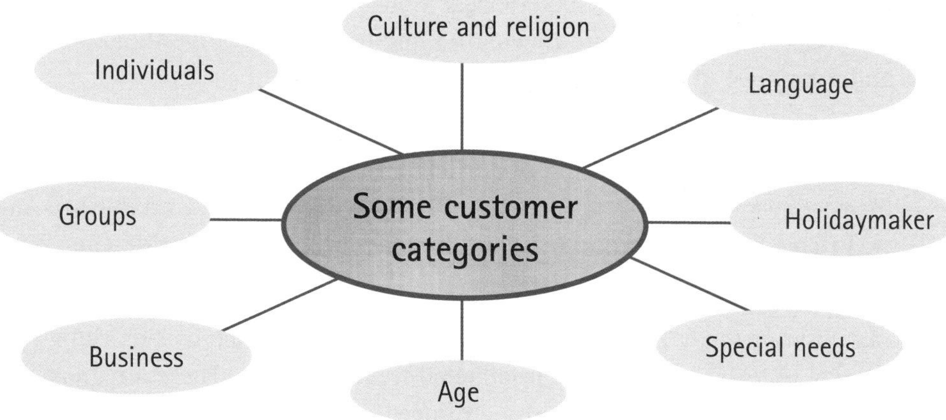

Travel and tourism customer categories which could be segmented

Individuals

Individuals may be people on their own, which means they can have your undivided attention. However, they may be in a small informal group, for example a family or business colleagues. Then you must share your attention between them, and give each the appropriate service. Women may have different needs to men. Children may have different needs to adults. Sometimes, you may be dealing with a VIP (very important person) like a film star or the chairperson of a major international company. These are very influential people and you may need to look after them in a particular way.

Groups

Organised groups usually have not just been formed for a specific occasion. Members will normally know each other. Examples include an orchestra or a youth club. They usually have a group leader who may share with you the responsibility for communicating with the group. However, although there will be common needs, each member still has his or her own concerns and it is important to relate to them.

The other type of group is formed by circumstance, for example they all happen to be on the same inclusive holiday, or are all taking a guided tour of a visitor attraction. They probably will not know each other and will not have a group leader. Such groups may have a wider range of members and a wider range of needs. This can be challenging, as you need to be alert to their individual needs and ensure they are met. Gather them around you, so that they can all hear you and feel included. You will probably be asked more questions by such a group, as there is a wider range of needs and no group leader to help you.

Age

You will meet people from every age group, from the days-old baby to the centenarian. Many customers are children. They want to enjoy themselves, but they might find their experiences a bit daunting, so they will be delighted to have someone they can relate to, who can give them help and assurance at the appropriate times.

A useful technique with young children is to crouch down to their level and talk to them about something of particular interest to them, for example their teddy's name. This has a 'halo effect' – while you have established an exclusive zone for you and the child to talk within, those outside your zone will see you are relating to the child, and recognise your caring approach.

Organisations may have special facilities for children, such as kids clubs at holiday hotels, play areas at airports and travel agencies. These are great for the children, but they also meet a customer service need for adults who can be relieved from looking after them. Some adults without children may also appreciate 'child-free' zones.

Kids clubs meet both children's and adults' needs

The fastest growing segment of the UK population travelling overseas is the over-54 age group. In 2000, compared with 1993, the number of overseas visits made by them increased by 98 per cent, compared with 63 per cent for the 0–54 age group.

With such growth, we must learn how to give the older age groups customer service they value. Older people generally tend to like a more formal approach and are likely to welcome recognition that they have had experiences which the rest of us have not had. Don't assume that they are losing their mental faculties or physical abilities. Saga Holidays caters for those in the 50+ age group. Its 'Go for it' range includes learning to scuba dive among the coral reefs of Borneo, wine tasting in South Africa and horse riding on a ranch in Arizona!

Cultures and religions

We all belong to a culture. We have beliefs, practices, traditions and preferences which influence our way of life. They become the 'norm' for us, but they may not be the norm for those with different cultures. Religion is often a strong feature of culture and can be a particularly sensitive issue. We should respect, learn about and respond to others' cultures and religions, so that we do not cause offence. By doing so, we can give excellent customer service.

KEY POINTS

- Muslims and Jews do not eat pork.
- In much of Asia, it is offensive to pat the head, as this is seen as the most sacred part of the body. Cabin crew should therefore be careful not to pass anything over heads.
- In northern Europe, greetings are quite formal, e.g. a handshake. In southern Europe, a greeting is more likely to include hugging and cheek kissing.

Language

Often we assume others can (and should!) speak our language. This shows disrespect to our customers and makes communication, and giving excellent customer service, difficult. Be patient, listen and look for clues as to what the customer is saying. Use your body language, or even quick drawings, to communicate. A useful aid to language is the use of symbols. These are often universal, so will be understood in any country.

International symbols. Do you know what each one means?

Holidaymakers

Holidaymakers, tourists and day trippers have a wide range of needs. Some will look for organised activities and entertainment. Some will want excitement, others will want a relaxing time. Some will want to learn new things, while others will simply want to be with their family and friends.

Each sector of the holiday business seeks ways to meet the needs of their customers in their segment of the business, so the types of customer service will be different, depending upon the market segment.

ACTIVITY

In small groups, brainstorm what facilities and style of customer service would be appropriate for:

- young travellers on an activities holiday in Australia
- families on a beach holiday in Spain
- retired couples on a Christmas cultural weekend in Vienna
- women on a health spa break.

Business people

Business people generally want speedy, efficient treatment. They are working away from home, so they need to be able to use their time effectively and have the facilities and support normally available at home.

A calm airport lounge with newspapers, computers and communication facilities is a need recognised by airlines. Hotels cater for business-people, by providing communication and Internet facilities, same-day laundry facilities, 24-hour room service, express check-in and check-out.

However, even business people need to relax, so they may become leisure tourists as well, and want customer service appropriate to leisure tourists.

Customers with special needs

All customers have needs which are individual to them, but some have additional needs beyond the general needs of most customers. These needs might arise because the customer:

- has a physical limitation such as being unable to walk or having a limb in plaster
- has a hearing or sight impairment
- has a learning disability
- has a severe language limitation
- is a child on their own
- is a woman travelling with a baby and/or young child.

All staff can help such customers, with care, empathy and a clear understanding of their specific needs. Some staff may be given special training to help them better meet the customer's needs, for example learning sign language, how to treat wheelchair passengers, escorting sight-impaired passengers. It is important when caring for a customer with special needs to ensure you introduce them to the next person who will look after them, and explain what is needed.

KEY POINTS

Here are some examples of caring for customers with special needs:

- A ferry has a special car parking space for people with physical disabilities. It is next to a ramp to the cabin deck, rather than stairs or a lift. A wheelchair is kept by the parking space. A trained staff member meets the passenger to assist them to cabin level.
- Several airlines have escorts who look after 'unaccompanied minors' at airports and sometimes fly with them. Some have special airport lounge areas with videos, soft drinks, nibbles and games. In flight, they are given comics, games and tuck boxes.
- Some holiday hotels have staff to look after and entertain children in exclusive 'Kids zones' and baby-sit, so that parents can enjoy their evenings.

External and internal customers

External customers are those who purchase and/or use your organisation's products and services. The distinction between those who buy your product or services – the purchasers – and those who use it – the consumers – is important. Think of the parent with a child in a shop. The child pleads with their parent to buy some sweets. The parent is the purchaser and the child is the consumer. Both are important customers and can influence buying decisions.

Internal customers are those who work for the same organisation as you and who may need your services. That includes departments that need timely and accurate information from you, so that they can meet the needs of the customer and the organisation. Everybody in an organisation, whether they are in finance, operations, catering, etc., is serving the customer, either directly or indirectly. Without them, the organisation will fail the customer. So, they are deserving of excellent customer service from you. They need you to be approachable, friendly, understanding, supportive, effective and efficient. Unless the whole organisation is working as one, with the customer at the heart of all it does, the customer will lose, and you will lose the customer.

Customers' needs

The common need

All customers share one set of needs. They want you to:

- make them feel important, that means valuing them and treating them as an individual
- know your products or services
- listen and show empathy (understand how they feel).

Over to you!

The customer's lament

Hey, I'm ME!

I'm not the last customer you had.

I'm not the next customer you will have.

Please treat me as an individual with my own needs.

I'm ME!

Types of need

Information, advice, instructions

As the travel and tourism industry is a people business, you will spend much of your time giving information, advice and instructions to customers.

ACTIVITY

For each of the following jobs, list three pieces of information that are likely to be asked for frequently:

a theme park ride assistant

b train guard

c historic house guide

d hotel receptionist.

Discuss your list with someone else in your group.

How did you do? You probably thought of questions specific to the job, for example an historic house guide might frequently be asked 'Who painted that picture?' but might also frequently be asked non-job specific questions such as 'Where is the cafeteria?'.

There is increasing dependence upon technology to provide information to staff and customers. Tour operators' computers provide information and booking facilities for their inclusive holidays; transport organisations use computers to make reservations and to provide 'real time' information on arrival times and destination weather. Heritage locations use visual and audio aids to provide information to visitors.

Assistance

Different customers need different levels of assistance. This may range from giving directions or carrying someone's bag, through to helping customers with special needs who need greater assistance than normally required.

Health, safety and security

Customers and colleagues expect you and your organisation to ensure their health, safety and security. The Health and Safety at Work Act 1974 requires employers and employees to ensure a healthy, safe and secure environment for the public and employees. You should always be observant to your environment and report anything which could be a risk, for example a loose carpet in a hotel or trailing cables in an office.

Customers will seek advice on health arrangements when travelling overseas. The SARS outbreaks in 2002–3 caused travellers concern, and staff needed to be up to date regarding the situation and preventative measures. They were assisted in this by information from various government and medical organisations, communicated particularly by the Internet and leaflets.

Weather can have an effect upon health, security and safety, for example hurricanes can result in flights being delayed or cancelled, hotels being changed and holiday arrangements being altered. Tour operators and airlines have emergency procedures, trained staff and support systems which they put into action when such emergencies happen. They must assist those who are at the destination, those who are concerned about relatives at the destination and those planning to visit the destination. Staff must be well trained, calm and able to use their initiative to assist their customers.

World concern regarding international security and terrorism has been heightened in recent years. Everyone in the travel and tourism industry has to be alert to security risks and customers need to be briefed and reassured.

In summary

- All customers want you to make them feel important, know your products and services, listen and show empathy.
- Different customers need different types and levels of help.
- Employers and staff have legal responsibilities to customers and colleagues for their health, safety and security.
- Each customer segment will have its own set of customer service needs.
- Each person within a segment also has their own needs.
- External customers are those who buy and/or use your products and services.

- Internal customers are those people and departments you work with within your organisation.
- It is as important to give good customer service to the internal customer as it is to provide it to the external customer.

Level ✓

PRACTICE ASSESSMENT ACTIVITY

Work on this activity in groups of three or four.

It's a foggy day at the airport. The flight to Milan is delayed overnight. It has 150 passengers. Hotel accommodation has to be arranged, as well as transport to and from the hotels. Some passengers want messages sent to people meeting them. Some passengers should have been making connections to other flights at Milan to continue to their destination. There are some families with young children and babies. There are 35 members of a Welsh male-voice choir due to sing in Milan tomorrow night.

You are the passenger agents dealing with the situation and are face to face with the customers, but you have the support of a control centre to make some arrangements for you.

In your group, decide:

P3.2 What different types of passenger you may encounter and their needs.

What support you will need from the control centre.

What your group of passenger agents has to do.

P3.5 What you will say to the passengers and how you will respond if any of them complain.

3.3 How different organisations approach customer service

The travel and tourism industry ranges from giants with integrated businesses to small independent companies, and from those which supply the main goods and services to those which supply the support services, for example:

- transport operators – air, sea, rail, road
- accommodation – hotels, villas, campsites, holiday centres, etc.

- attractions – theme parks, heritage sites, activity centres, etc.
- secondary services – insurance, airport representatives, tourist offices, passport offices.

As you will have read in Unit 1 Introduction to the Travel and Tourism Industry, some organisations, for example tour operators, integrate services vertically and horizontally. This gives them control over each level of the packages they market, with a consistency of style and objectives.

This section considers objectives, policies, procedures, resources and customer service for a range of organisations.

Approaches

Visions, missions, guiding principles, values, objectives

Many organisations have **vision statements** which set the scene for the kind of organisation they want to be. **Mission statements** are then created which describe the way the organisation will conduct its activities, covering its purpose, its strategy, its standards of behaviour and its values. Some organisations have **guiding principles** or **values** statements instead. Others may include in their mission statements the areas they intend to address and what they hope to achieve in a given time frame, for example five years. **Objectives** state what the organisation, or departments within it, specifically aim to achieve, how success will be measured and the time scale for achievement. Specific targets may then be quoted, for example '5 per cent improvement in punctuality compared with the previous year'.

Mission statements have a major influence upon the levels and styles of customer service of an organisation. An airline with the vision of being a computer-led business, with minimal staff contact with passengers, may decide to only accept Internet bookings and have self-service check-in at airports. This would require a different customer service approach to an airline with the vision of being the most friendly airline with staff available at every point of the passengers' travels. The first airline would invest in technology and procedures which enable the passengers to do things without human help. The latter airline would invest in selecting and training customer-caring staff, with procedures to support them. This does not mean one is better than the other. It merely identifies that there is more than one way to cater for passengers.

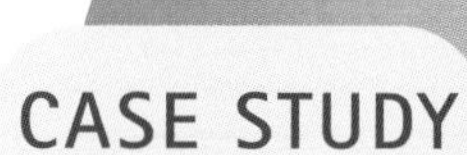

CASE STUDY

Mandarin Oriental hotel group

Mandarin Oriental hotel group vision, mission and guiding principles

Vision: To be recognised as one of the top global luxury hotel groups, providing exceptional customer satisfaction in each of our hotels. The growth strategy of our Group is to progress towards operating 10,000 rooms in major business centres and key leisure destinations around the world.

Mission: To completely delight and satisfy our guests. We are committed to making a difference every day; continually getting better to keep us the best.

Guiding principles:

Delighting our guests: We will strive to understand our client and guest needs by listening to their requirements and responding in a competent, accurate and timely fashion. We will design and deliver our services and products to address their needs. In fact, we are committed to exceeding their expectations by surprising them with our ability to anticipate and fulfil their wishes.

Source: Mandarin Oriental hotel group

The Mandarin Oriental's document also gives details of their other guiding principles:

- Working together as colleagues.
- Promoting a climate of enthusiasm.
- Being the best.
- Delivering shareholder value.
- Playing by the rules.
- Acting with responsibility.

The hotel group's statements clearly identify giving outstanding customer service as a major driving force for the company.

ACTIVITY

Read the following mission statements of two, low-cost airlines: easyJet, which is based in the UK, and Southwest Airlines, which is based in the USA.

> *'To provide our customers with safe, good value, point to point air services. To effect and to offer consistent and reliable product and fares appealing to leisure and business markets on a range of European routes. To achieve this, we will develop our people and establish lasting relationships with our suppliers.'* (easyJet)

> *'Dedication to the highest quality of customer service delivered with a sense of warmth, friendliness, individual pride and Company Spirit.'* (Southwest Airlines)

ACTIVITY

Discuss in your group the similarities and differences between the two, and the impact that they may have upon their levels and styles of customer service. Think about what each company chose to include in its mission statements, and what they did not include.

Responsive and proactive approaches

You will have already read that being proactive and responsive is essential if you want to provide good customer service (see page 101). Organisations must also be proactive and responsive, anticipating changes and developments in their business and their customers. They must be alert to external changes (sometimes known as P.E.S.T. – Political, Economic, Social and Technological) and take advantage of them. Organisations also need to be aware of changes *within* the organisation. Many companies, Boeing and British Airways for example, carry out staff surveys which add to the organisation's understanding of staff satisfaction. A survey might cover:

- What staff are happy with
- What staff would like more/less of
- What staff concerns are.

Simply having all this external and internal information is not enough however. Organisations must respond to the information so that customers and staff know the organisation is taking action to improve its customer service.

Customer charters

Many organisations tell their customers what they will do for them in customer charters. These might include:

- the information the organisation will provide, how and when
- their payment and refund policies
- what they will do in the event of a disruption to arrangements (e.g. delays, cancellations)
- the performance levels they will aim for (e.g. punctuality)
- the compensation they will provide.

Over to you!

Explore the websites of some travel and tourism organisations. Discover if they have published customer service charters (often found in their menus under 'Customer service' or 'About us'). Example organisations include Ryanair, GNER, United Airlines, South West Trains, but there are many others. Compare and evaluate them. Are they specific enough and measurable, so that there can be no doubt what will be done for their customers? Is there anything which you feel is missing from any of them? Why do you think this might be?

Processes

How an organisation expects its customers to buy and use its products and services also affects the style of customer service it gives them, and the amount of human interaction it has with its customers. For example, customers are increasingly using the Internet to research, establish what is available and then book their arrangements. Organisations must design dependable, user friendly websites. Customers make choices between organisations, depending upon how useful they find their websites. Increasingly, passengers make their bookings on the Internet and take a reference number to the airport, rather than obtain a paper ticket, to enable them to board the aircraft. Advances are also being seen in other forms of travel and for accommodation bookings.

Computer databases build information on customers' needs, preferences and interests, so that they can be taken into account each time a customer buys from the organisation. This personalises the experience, for example car hire companies will try to provide the preferred model of car and have the agreement and car keys ready when the customer arrives. The computer has stored the customer's credit card, billing address and driving licence details, so only a brief stop is needed at the car hire desk. If car keys become replaced by code numbers, even this brief stop may become unnecessary.

Passengers have a much wider choice between organisations and processes than they used to have. Some budget airlines may offer a limited choice of methods to check in, no extra facilities at the airport and possibly no seat assignments. Other airlines may offer a choice of check-in methods, for example with a passenger agent at a check-in desk or using a self check-in machine, or by telephone, or at a town terminal. They may offer a choice of assigned seat, and exclusive airport lounges to those travelling in premium cabins. On board, passengers may expect entertainment via seatback video screens and a choice of meal, particularly if they are travelling on a long haul flight. Budget airlines may not offer such facilities, or may charge for them.

Such differences between budget and full-service airlines do not mean that passengers should not receive customer service. Passengers make a value judgement when they decide whether to travel on a budget ('no frills') airline or a full-service airline, but the human element should exist on both. Southwest Airlines has shown that it is possible to offer a 'no frills' service, yet inject humour and friendly service through the performance of their staff.

Hotels offer different styles and levels of service. Businesspeople want fast check in and check out. The room might be pre-allocated, with the key ready to hand over at a special desk, in exchange for a booking reference and presentation of a credit card. They can check their bill on their in-room TV prior to check out, and just drop their key at the desk as they depart.

Organisations' processes require documentation. This may include booking forms, booking systems, customers' records, tickets, invoices, receipts, health and safety records, and communications with customers and contractors. While many of these are computer-based, many continue to be paper-based. Documentation and record keeping requires great care and accuracy. Much of it is required or affected by legislation, for example the Health and Safety Act and the Data Protection Act.

Follow-up

It is important to follow up after the event, both to discover the customers' views on what the organisation provided to them (and possibly to put things right) and also to have them start to think about their next purchase from that organisation. Excellent customer service will ensure that customers are gained and retained, which will improve image and profit, but how can we assess the quality and effectiveness of the service being given?

There are informal ways, like having conversations with customers while they are with you, or phoning them when they return home, as some travel agents and hotels do. There are also more formal market research methods. The most common is the customer service questionnaire, perhaps given to you during the flight, or placed at the exit to the tourist attraction, or left in your hotel room. These give feedback on how the organisation is doing

HOLIDAY INN HOTELS & RESORTS
GUEST SATISFACTION SURVEY

Correct Mark: ☒

		Very Satisfied ←				→ Not At All Satisfied
1. Please rate your overall satisfaction with this hotel.		5 ☐	4 ☐	3 ☐	2 ☐	1 ☐
2. How likely would you be to:		Very Likely ←				→ Not At All Likely
Return to this hotel if in the same area for a similar purpose?		5 ☐	4 ☐	3 ☐	2 ☐	1 ☐
Recommend this hotel to others?		5 ☐	4 ☐	3 ☐	2 ☐	1 ☐
3. How has your stay at this hotel influenced your decision to stay at other HOLIDAY INN hotels in the future?		5 ☐	4 ☐	3 ☐	2 ☐	1 ☐
4. Please rate this hotel on:		Outstanding ←				→ Unacceptable
Arrival	Speed and efficiency of check-in	5 ☐	4 ☐	3 ☐	2 ☐	1 ☐
Room	Maintenance of guest room	5 ☐	4 ☐	3 ☐	2 ☐	1 ☐
	Cleanliness of guest room	5 ☐	4 ☐	3 ☐	2 ☐	1 ☐
	Comfort of bed and pillow	5 ☐	4 ☐	3 ☐	2 ☐	1 ☐
	Quietness of guest room	5 ☐	4 ☐	3 ☐	2 ☐	1 ☐
	Room lighting	5 ☐	4 ☐	3 ☐	2 ☐	1 ☐
	In-room working space and environment	5 ☐	4 ☐	3 ☐	2 ☐	1 ☐
	Attractiveness of guest room	5 ☐	4 ☐	3 ☐	2 ☐	1 ☐
	Condition of furniture, carpet, etc.	5 ☐	4 ☐	3 ☐	2 ☐	1 ☐
	TV channels and movie options	5 ☐	4 ☐	3 ☐	2 ☐	1 ☐
Staff	Ability of staff to anticipate your needs	5 ☐	4 ☐	3 ☐	2 ☐	1 ☐
	Attentiveness of staff	5 ☐	4 ☐	3 ☐	2 ☐	1 ☐
	Promptness of staff in fulfilling your requests	5 ☐	4 ☐	3 ☐	2 ☐	1 ☐
	Accuracy of staff in fulfilling your requests	5 ☐	4 ☐	3 ☐	2 ☐	1 ☐
	Knowledge of staff	5 ☐	4 ☐	3 ☐	2 ☐	1 ☐
	Attitude of staff	5 ☐	4 ☐	3 ☐	2 ☐	1 ☐
Hotel	Cleanliness of common areas of hotel	5 ☐	4 ☐	3 ☐	2 ☐	1 ☐
	Attractiveness of the lobby	5 ☐	4 ☐	3 ☐	2 ☐	1 ☐
	Safety and security inside hotel	5 ☐	4 ☐	3 ☐	2 ☐	1 ☐
Restaurants/ Bars	Breakfast - food quality and service	5 ☐	4 ☐	3 ☐	2 ☐	1 ☐
	Room service - food quality and speed	5 ☐	4 ☐	3 ☐	2 ☐	1 ☐
	Other food and drink experience	5 ☐	4 ☐	3 ☐	2 ☐	1 ☐
Value	Value for the money paid	5 ☐	4 ☐	3 ☐	2 ☐	1 ☐

Source: Intercontinental Hotels Group

Holiday Inn Hotels & Resorts guest satisfaction survey

and also show customers that the organisation cares about them. Some organisations include questionnaires on their websites, for example Kuoni Travel and Caledonian Macbrayne Hebridean and Clyde Ferries. Others use market researchers to interview customers at the end of their journey. For example, some airlines interview customers in the airport arrivals area, while their views are still fresh in their minds.

An organisation must discover what its customers consider important when they are assessing customer service, so that they know what to measure. An example of criteria which customers might rate as important is shown below.

Typical criteria for assessing customer service

The outline criteria need to be broken down into specific detail to enable decisions to be made on *what* is to be measured and *how*, for example cleanliness might include cleanliness of hotel bedrooms. Measures might include waste bins empty; clean carpet; mark-free windows and mirrors; facilities replenished. These could be measured by observation.

There is no value in creating customer service criteria if they cannot be measured objectively. In the example questionnaire on page 115, the questions are graded 1 – 5. This is a way to statistically measure quality issues.

In summary

- Organisations need a vision of what kind of organisation they want to be, a mission declaring the areas they wish to address and what they wish to achieve, guiding principles/values to identify what is important to them and how they will behave, and measurable objectives to aim for.

- Such statements have a direct impact on the level and styles of customer service each organisation wishes to deliver.
- Some organisations publish customer charters, stating what they will do for their customers.
- Processes, procedures and styles will result from the organisations' statements of intent.
- It is vital to gain feedback from customers and staff on what is important to them and how an organisation is performing against stated criteria.

Level

PRACTICE ASSESSMENT ACTIVITY

Working in pairs, make a presentation to your group on *two* local travel and tourism organisations. Obtain copies of their missions, values, guiding principles and objectives.

Design a questionnaire or questionnaires to assess service quality at those organisations. Part of the questionnaire should address procedures, processes and training.

Visit them and complete the questionnaires.

D3.1 Evaluate your findings.

M3.2/D3.1 Identify the customer service strengths and weaknesses of the two organisations.

D3.1 Relate your findings to their mission and values and comment upon whether you feel they are reflected in what you have observed.

M3.2 Identify the similarities and differences between the two organisations.

3.4 Customer service and selling skills in travel and tourism situations

A wide variety of customer service situations require skills, techniques and initiative, often in unplanned, fast moving conditions.

Customers

Customers will have a range of experiences which affect their moods and attitudes.

Happy

By reflecting their mood and working with them, it is easy to gain their cooperation and have them enjoy their experience.

Aggressive

Customers may become angry because something has gone wrong or because they are in a situation they find frightening or worrying. Anger can turn to aggression, which needs a calm but firm response. Comments like 'I want to help you sir, but I can't do so while you are being abusive' may have a calming effect. Having the customer sit down may help. Diverting their attention to something else might assist. Alcohol, etc., may have affected their rationality. It is important to ensure the customer's safety and the safety of others around them. Stay calm and in control, and get assistance if necessary. If other customers see that staff are in control and looking after the interests of all the customers, they will be more likely to support the staff.

Exceptionally, a customer may behave very aggressively, in an environment which makes the situation very distressing for others and potentially unsafe. Some organisations give advance warning to customers of the potential consequences of such behaviour. British Airways has developed a policy and statement entitled 'Zero tolerance on disruptive behaviour' which is contained in its inflight magazine, *High Life*. It specifies what action BA will take in the event of a passenger disrupting a flight.

Distressed or concerned

Dealing with distressed or concerned customers requires a calm approach, patience, empathy, and gentle questioning to establish what is causing the distress or concern, so that the problem can be resolved.

Section 3.2 'Needs of different types of customers' identified techniques to handle various customers, for example those with special needs, those who did not speak English and those in groups or travelling as individuals.

Locations and environments

Locations and environments need to be considered when deciding which customer service methods are appropriate.

Indoors or outdoors?

Different types of customer service may be required, depending upon whether it is being given indoors or outdoors. A tour guide in a historic house can talk quietly, and conversation between the guide and the visitors is easy. Video displays often supplement the guide, as do hand-held audio guides in the user's language. Outdoors, acoustics are generally not so good, so the guide must draw the customers close and speak very clearly. If possible, some information can be given in the hotel or on the coach before arriving.

Crowds and noise

Tour guides may have fewer than 20 customers at a time, but there will be far more customers per staff member at airports and railway stations, which can be crowded and noisy. This is a problem for transportation organisations. When there is airport or train disruption, passengers sometimes complain that 'it was chaotic, and no information was given to us'. That is usually because face-to-face communication is very limited, given the numbers of customers involved, so there has to be heavy reliance upon display screens and public address announcements. These may give all or much of the required information.

However, in such situations where crowds and noise levels add to the stress, customers tend to want personal assurance from a staff member that all their concerns have been addressed. Patience wears thin and staff must draw upon their communication skills and initiative to minimise difficulties for the customers. It is important to identify and assist those who are finding the situation particularly difficult, for example the parent with a baby or other special needs passengers. They

ACTIVITY

Visit your local airport, ferry terminal, railway station or coach station. Look for customer service methods:

- face to face by staff
- using public address systems
- customer self-help equipment
- display screens
- leaflets
- notice boards
- signs and symbols
- other methods.

List each method and note what purpose it is serving. On your return, discuss your findings with your group.

can be helped, perhaps by bringing them to the head of a queue or getting them a wheelchair or some water. Other customers will think well of staff who do this.

Such locations rely heavily upon leaflets, display screens, signs, symbols, etc., to provide customer service. There may also be self-help equipment such as ticket machines and trolleys.

Situations

Customers expect help in many situations. Some situations may be very familiar and the customers' queries are easily resolved. Sometimes they can be more unusual or difficult, and initiative will be needed.

Information, advice and queries

Customers may ask a train operator employee the time of the next train; a holiday representative for advice on what excursion to take; an airline passenger agent to clarify which boarding gate they should go to. In each case, the customer expects the employee to recognise their need and provide an accurate, honest and knowledgeable response. Staff should be prepared for the most frequent questions and know where to find the answers to the more unusual. They can be aided by manuals and computer systems. If you are asked a question and do not know the answer, don't guess – ask a colleague or your manager.

Problems

Some people give excuses for not helping customers, either because they do not want to bother, or because they are not using their initiative. Statements like 'We're closing in five minutes', 'I can't leave my desk' or 'My computer won't let me' are negative and unhelpful. *Don't be part of the problem, be part of the solution!* It is your job to solve problems. The customer must feel yours is a good organisation to deal with. You will feel good by helping resolve customers' problems. You may have been asked the same question countless times before, and it may seem stupid to you. To the customer, it is the first time they have asked that question and it is not stupid. Respond in a positive, interested and helpful manner.

Complaints

However hard you and your organisation try, things will occasionally not be to the liking of the customer and they will complain to you. Few people like dealing with complaints, but by having the right attitude and using the right skills and techniques, the customer can be satisfied, which will make you feel great.

There is a bonus for getting it right. Surveys show that if you turn a customer from being unhappy with your organisation to being very pleased with how you handled their complaint, they are likely to be more loyal than customers who have not had cause to complain. That does not mean customers should be given cause to complain so that you can recover the situation, but it does emphasise the value of excellent customer recovery!

Customers may complain in writing, by phone or face to face. Face-to-face complaints can be the hardest, particularly when others are watching. However, there are some techniques which will help you succeed.

Do not take complaints personally. Hopefully, the customer is complaining about a situation, rather than about you. However, you represent the organisation with which the customer is dissatisfied. You have to take ownership of resolving it. Your objective must be to get to a 'win–win' situation, where both the customer and you are happy with the outcome.

Adopt a friendly, helpful but assertive manner. Being assertive means explaining your position while respecting the other person's feelings and situation. It enables you both to feel OK and valued.

If you are in a face-to-face situation, try to establish physical contact, perhaps by shaking the customer's hand. Try to take the customer to a quieter area where you do not have a crowd as an audience, then both sit down, as it is harder to be angry from a seated position.

Initially, the customer will be climbing the 'anger mountain', pouring out to you what went wrong and how appalling your organisation is. It is important to stay quiet at this stage. You have to let the customer vent their anger. If you try to interrupt, or give reasons or excuses why something happened, the anger mountain is going to keep growing, and the customer will continue to complain angrily, and perhaps heighten their demands.

The anger mountain

Indicate you are listening, by your body language, for example nodding and the occasional 'Ah ha' or 'I see'. Wait until the customer reaches the top of the anger mountain. By doing so, you will have allowed them the opportunity to tell you want went wrong, and to calm down.

Once the top of the anger mountain has been reached, it is time to speak. Apologise and make it clear that you are taking ownership to find a solution. Ask questions. This demonstrates that you have been listening and also gives you the opportunity to get the detail you need, for example 'You told me you gave your passport to the passenger agent. Can you tell me at which desk they were sitting?'. Put yourself in the customer's shoes. That will help you to understand how they feel and to understand how the situation may have arisen.

Now, you will have gained most of the information you need, so that you can investigate and resolve the situation. Make sure you know what the customer would consider to be a satisfactory conclusion. Sometimes it may be the provision of what they believe they should have been given in the first place, or it may be that they want additional recompense. Perhaps they just wanted to complain to someone and be assured that action will be taken to prevent it happening to others.

Once satisfied that you have the best solution, offer it in a positive fashion to the customer. It can help if you give them a choice, for example: 'I can either book you on the next flight to Berlin, which leaves at 16:00 and gets you there at 18:30, or I can offer you a flight to Frankfurt leaving at 13:00, with a connection which will get you to Berlin at 17:00'. By offering a choice, it shows that you are trying to meet the customer's needs. It also moves them away from thinking about what went wrong, to thinking about what choice to make.

Sometimes customers will make unreasonable or impracticable demands of you, and you may have to say no. If that is the case, do so clearly, explain why and move on to what you can offer them.

Even when you have resolved the immediate problem and satisfied the customer, you have not come to the end of your task. The matter may need further investigation, so make sure that you have a contact for the customer, so that your organisation can respond to them more fully when the investigation is complete. Make sure that whatever went wrong does not happen again, either to this customer or any other. You may need to let others know. For example, if a rail passenger complains that a wheelchair is not available at the departure station, tell the station manager and the staff at the destination, so that the customer does not have any further problems. You may also realise that the fault could happen to other passengers, so tell your manager to ensure it does not happen again.

In summary

- The method and style of customer service will depend upon many factors, including the type of customer, the location and environment, and the situation.
- Customers expect *you* to meet their needs, whether it is giving them information or advice, or resolving a problem or complaint.
- Your motto should be *'Don't be part of the problem, be part of the solution'.*
- Don't take complaints personally, but do take responsibility for resolving them.
- Aim for a 'win–win'.
- Remember the anger mountain and take steps to ensure the problem does not happen to this, or any other customer again.

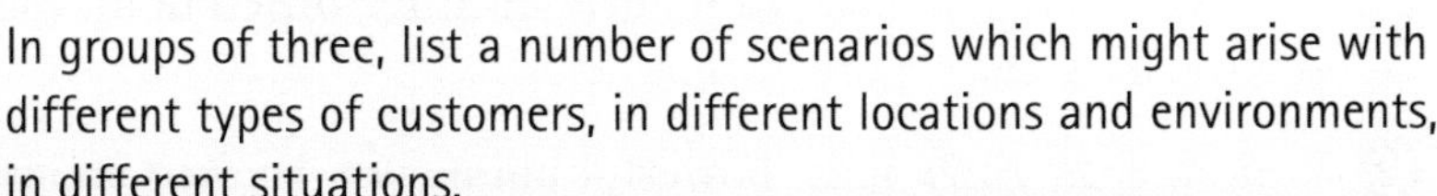

In groups of three, list a number of scenarios which might arise with different types of customers, in different locations and environments, in different situations.

Select three scenarios. Take it in turns to be the customer, the employee and the observer.

P3.4/P3.5/M3.3 Role play the scenarios, using the skills and techniques learned in this unit. The objective is to provide realistic and excellent customer service.

D3.2 After 5–10 minutes, discuss how the scenario was addressed and what skills and techniques worked well, and what could be done to improve the performance.

Change roles and undertake the next scenario.

TEST YOUR KNOWLEDGE

1. Define 'customer service'.
2. Give five reasons why customer service is important.
3. Explain four reasons why we communicate.
4. Think of five motivational words, other than those on page 88.
5. Think of three occasions from the time a holidaymaker checks in for their flight, to the time they arrive at their hotel, when staff may wish to communicate with them. What would they want to communicate and how would they do so?
6. Describe the eight stages of selling.
7. Consider three types of hotel clients with different needs. What are those needs? How can the hotel satisfy them?
8. Create a five-item customer charter for your local train company.
9. Discover what methods passengers on three different airlines can use to check in.
10. What are the three most powerful points you learned about customer service by studying this unit?

Unit 4

Introduction to Marketing in Travel and Tourism

Introduction

What are the principles of marketing and how are they used in the travel and tourism industry? In answering these questions, this unit will enable you to look at two different travel and tourism organisations and consider how they meet the needs of different types of customer. The unit also looks at how market research is used in the industry and will give you the opportunity to explore and develop promotional materials.

How you will be assessed

This unit is assessed internally, so the centre delivering the qualification will assess you against the criteria.

In this unit you will learn about:

① the principles of marketing in the travel and tourism industry

② travel and tourism products

③ market research

④ promotional methods.

4.1 Principles of marketing

Definition of marketing

Marketing is a complex management tool, which the Concise Oxford Dictionary defines as:

'The action or business of promoting and selling products and services'.

Marketing is totally focused on the customers' needs and could be easily described as providing:

- the right product
- at the right price
- at the right place
- with the right promotion
- at the right time.

As you can see, these are all directed at the customers' needs and wants. You will investigate each of these points in further depth later in this unit.

The marketing mix

The marketing mix is sometime known as the **4Ps**:

The marketing mix

The marketing mix makes up the full package that you are selling to the customer. If any one of these parts is not well developed, this can lead to a product being unsuccessful. After all, there is no point having the most suitable holiday in the world to offer a customer at the lowest price which the customer only needs to pop around the corner to buy if the customer does not know about it!

Product

This is the product or service that you are providing for the customer. This includes all services. The product in travel can change from customer to customer depending on their requirements. A different hotel or grading of airline seats will give the customer a different experience and, in turn, a different product.

It is very important for an organisation to understand its product, not only its features and details but also how the product is different from competitors' products. This is the product's **unique selling point** (USP) – what makes your product different from everyone else's. For example, does your theme park have a roller coaster with more loops than anyone else's? Does your holiday resort have a reputation for luxury and excellent customer service? Your USP could be something as simple as offering the warmest of welcomes or easier booking facilities.

KEY POINTS

The marketing mix, also known as the 4Ps, consists of:

- product
- place
- price
- promotion.

KEY POINTS

USP is the unique selling point that makes your product or service different.

It is important to remember that a product that is currently satisfying the customers' needs will need to be altered, adapted or even replaced. There may be several reasons for this:

- Technology can make a product obsolete. This is what happened to the horse and cart when the motorcar became an economical viable alternative.
- Tastes move on. In Unit 3 Introduction to Customer Service in Travel and Tourism, you learnt that to keep customers happy you need to satisfy their needs. However, every time you satisfy a customer's needs, the customer changes what their needs and expectations are, so you have to develop your product to meet those changing needs.
- Education through television programmes and through experience has led customers to become more demanding in their travel and tourism needs. This will affect how and where they travel and also the types of experiences they have when they reach their destination. These developing needs have led to ever-more diverse holiday destinations and even more choice, and have sparked the spectacular growth in special interest holidays.

Companies spend a great deal of time and money developing an image and reputation for a particular product. This is known as the **brand.**

Benefits of branding

- Customers can recognise a particular product.
- Customers become loyal to brands and trust the brands' products, leading to increased sales.
- It is easier for the organisation to develop an individual image for its products. This fits in with different types of products for different types of customers (you will learn more about this later in the unit).

ACTIVITY

Do a quick survey among 20 people in your class to find out the following answers:

1 What is your favourite soft drink?
2 What did you have for breakfast today?
3 What type of car do you or your household have?

Put your results on a tally chart.

From your results, work out how many answers are brands and how many are types of products, for example Ford is a brand but a 4 × 4 or estate car is the product.

This will give you an opportunity to practise Key skills Application of Number N2.1.

Place

Place is about the distribution point of your product. This is easy to confuse with the holiday destination. Try to think of 'place' as the location where the customer goes to buy the product or service. For example, you would not pop over to the Caribbean to buy your summer holiday; you would be likely to book it either through a local travel agent or the Internet. So, the place with regards to the marketing mix is where the product is sold.

In particular, 'place' will have a major effect on a travel and tourism organisation should it decide to look for or change premises or open up a new location. There is always a trade-off between location and cost. In general, the better locations cost more in rent and business rates. However, in a travel and tourism organisation a prime town centre location is not always needed. A tour operator, for example, does not benefit from being in the centre of the town as most or all of its business is carried out via computers or on the telephone. However, for a travel agency, location could be all-important.

The location of natural visitor attractions or even ancient monuments cannot be changed. You cannot move Stonehenge closer to London just so that you can increase its tourism numbers! In this situation, you need to consider how you can make your location more attractive to visitors. This might be by expanding your provision so that customers spend longer at the attraction. For a big attraction, it could involve improving signage to the destination so customers can find it easily.

The 'place' where you buy your product could be the travel agency in your local high street

Price

This refers to the price that is charged for the product, and includes discounts. Travel is a very price sensitive market place, with budget airlines competing on price of flights and some package holidays being sold almost solely on the price. Price is particularly relevant to last-minute deals and bucket shops.

Most organisations do not just have one fixed price for their products. With the use of computer systems **variable pricing** has become the norm.

Variable pricing

This is where an organisation offers different prices for the same product. There are a number of reasons for this:

- To encourage a particular group of people to use a product such as older people or students. Variable pricing is used at quiet times to encourage people to use a product or service. Museums and visitor attractions regularly offer variable pricing.
- When the product is going to be lost if not sold. A seat on a flight cannot be sold after the plane has taken off. This may sound silly, but if you own an airline, every empty seat is lost money. Several airlines have brought in computer systems to manage their sales so that they fill every seat in the aircraft with each customer paying as much money as possible.
- Changes in demand for the product can also change the price. There is a big debate at the moment about parents taking their children out of school early to go on summer holidays. This is because when the school holidays start and demand for holidays increases, travel agents and tour operators increase their prices (this could be because the tour operators' costs have increased).

Talking point

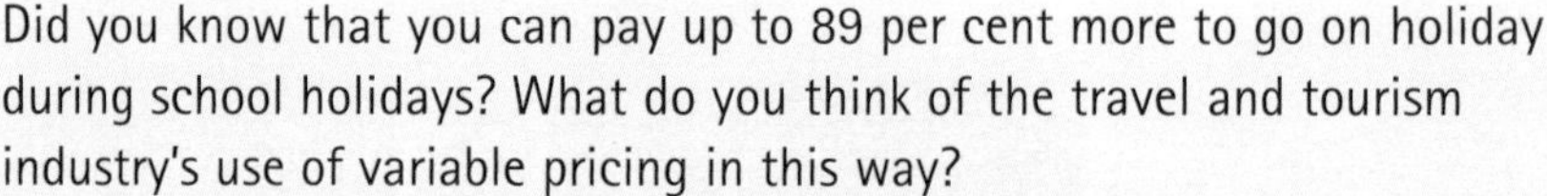

Did you know that you can pay up to 89 per cent more to go on holiday during school holidays? What do you think of the travel and tourism industry's use of variable pricing in this way?

ACTIVITY

Find out about the other types of pricing:

- Market skimming strategy
- Discount pricing
- Cost plus pricing
- Competitive pricing
- Market penetration pricing.

Promotion

Promotion is any activity that is designed to put across a positive image of the organisation or individual. In other words, any interaction with the public or media could be counted as a form of promotion. In fact, word of mouth (where people recommend a company) is one of the most influential forms of promotion (there is more information on promotional methods and techniques later in this unit).

Target marketing

Not every product is going to appeal to everyone. If there were just one summer holiday that suited everyone, then travel agents would only have to stock one summer holiday to sell! However, every customer is slightly different with different needs and expectations. For example, the holiday requirements of a group of four 18-year-old lads wanting their first holiday away from home without their parents will be different from a couple who have just retired and want a once-in-a-lifetime experience.

Target marketing is about creating products that are aimed (or targeted) at different groups of people. These groups are called **market segments.**

Market segmentation

Although it is possible to produce a different package for each individual customer, the cost involved in terms of time tends to make this either too expensive or not practical. In order to provide products that appeal to different groups of travellers, the travel industry divides the whole travel market into different segments.

A market segment is a group of customers with similar needs. Imagine the travel market is like an orange and that the different groups are its segments. The more specific you make each segment, then the smaller the segment becomes. For example, if the market segment was package family holidays, this is a large segment, but if you break it down further into package family holidays *to Spain*, the segment becomes smaller although it is still a large segment of the current market.

KEY POINTS

By grouping together a set of customers with similar needs – a market segment – you can develop product(s) for the group's needs.

The travel industry segments the market in many ways. The first segmentation is the split between business and leisure travel. Many travel agents and tour operators tend to specialise in one area or the other, for example Going Places concentrates on leisure travel and American Express and Hogg Robinson concentrate on business travel.

Imagine the travel market like an orange – each segment represents a different group of customers

This is quite a logical split as the two different markets have substantially different requirements with regards to level of service and needs (see Units 1 and 5). These two main market segments are further segmented to group different types of customer needs. Different methods of segmentation are covered in the next section.

CASE STUDY

A trip across the Pond to you!

You have just received the letter below.

Texas Tourism School
4011 93rd Street
Texas
USA

Hi

My name is Sue-Ellen and I am student at the Texas Tourism School. My class and I are planning to travel to the United Kingdom this summer for our European study visit.

We were planning to come to your area and I was hoping that you could help us by describing what there is to do round your way.

I would like to know at whom each place is aimed so that I can make sure that the right people go to the right place.

Thanking you all for your help.

Sue-Ellen Jackdoor

Can you help Sue-Ellen and her classmates? Make a list of visitor attractions in your local area and try to work out the target market for each one.

Marketing objectives

Marketing objectives are developed from an organisation's mission statement (see Units 3 and 5). The mission statement is the specific area that an organisation wishes to address and what it wants to achieve in those areas. For example:

> *'We are committed to provide unrivalled professional travel services with integrity, to travellers around the world'* (www.abletravel.com).

To achieve this mission the organisation develops a number of **aims**. These are the organisation's major goals to achieve the overall mission (the mission statement). These are some of the types of marketing aims that an organisation could have:

- Create awareness of the product or organisation.
- Increase market share.
- Challenge the opposition.
- Modify or develop new products.
- Improve image of product or organisation.
- Target new customers.
- Increase profit.

These aims are fine, but they are still general and do not highlight the steps to achieve the organisation's goals. The steps to achieve an aim are called **objectives**.

ACTIVITY

Choose an organisation in the travel and tourism industry. Come up with a specific objective for each of the marketing aims in the bullet list (left).

KEY POINTS

Without objectives no one will understand what the goal is.

SMART objectives

All objectives have to be SMART:

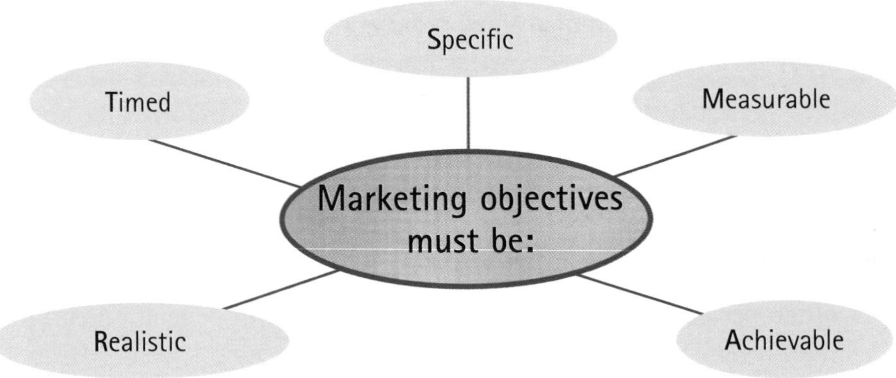

SMART objectives

KEY POINTS

SMART objectives are:

- Specific
- Measurable
- Achievable
- Realistic
- Timed.

Specific

The objective has to be stated in such a way that everyone who is involved in the objective understands what they are trying to achieve. The objective 'To make the airline better' is not specific and does not tell people how to improve the airline.

Measurable

You have to be able to measure your level of success against the objective. The objective 'To have more happy customers' is not particularly measurable and it is very difficult to measure how well you achieve the objective. However, the objective 'To reduce customer complaints by 10 per cent' is easy to measure your performance against.

Achievable

There is no point in setting an objective that is not achievable, as you will always fail to achieve it. The effects of this are that the staff can become demotivated and uninterested in trying to achieve other objectives.

Realistic

Although it is possible to sell every seat on an airplane or to have a fully occupied hotel, in most cases it is not realistic to expect to achieve this on every occasion. Goals have to be realistic for very much the same reasons, as they have to be achievable.

Timed

All objectives must have a time frame. Without a time frame there is no point at which you can stop and evaluate whether you have achieved an objective. The time frame is also important if an organisation is using objectives to help drive it forward. It is sometimes better to have many small, short-term objectives to help you achieve what could be a long-term aim. Your tutor does this by breaking a subject down into parts and teaching you one bit at a time in a lesson.

Here's an example of a SMART objective:

'Within/by the end of the next three months we will increase the amount of holiday insurance cover that we sell by 10 per cent.'

- It is specific in that everyone in the organisation knows what the aim is.
- It is measurable as the organisation can look at the financial records and see what percentage increase has been achieved.
- The current situation within the organisation has to be understood to ensure the objective is achievable or realistic. However, an increase of ten per cent is not an unusual amount, but will depend on current sales levels.

- The timeframe has been set so that at the end of the three-month period, it will be possible to compare the organisation's achieved results with the objective to see if it has been achieved and how and why it has been achieved, or not.
- It is very important to evaluate all objectives after they have been completed to see what problems and successes there have been. This will also help the setting of more realistic aims and objectives in the future.

ACTIVITY

Look again at the objectives you came up with from the activity on page 133. Make your objectives SMART.

ACTIVITY

1 Which of the following objectives are SMART objectives, and which are not?

a Increase sales over the next three months.

b Reduce customer complaints by 10 per cent.

c Increase average spend by 10 per cent by the end of the year.

d Have more happy customers.

e Increase the amount of customer feedback by 1000 questionnaires this year.

2 Rewrite the objectives that were not SMART as SMART objectives.

In summary

- Marketing involves promoting or selling a product or service.
- Each product or service has a unique marketing mix: Product, Place, Price, Promotion.
- Products are usually developed for a group of customers with similar needs. This is called a market segment.
- Objectives are targets for organisation to work towards. Objectives must be SMART (Specific, Measurable, Achievable, Realistic and Timed).

PRACTICE ASSESSMENT ACTIVITY

Level ✓

P4.1 Describe how the principles of marketing are adopted by travel and tourism organisations.

4.2 Travel and tourism products

Travel and tourism is a huge industry with a wide range of different products. Unlike in some industries, travel and tourism products tend to be services and experiences rather than tangible (physical) goods. For example, if you were going to buy a car, you could look at the car, give it a test drive and make a decision whether you were going to buy it – the car is a tangible product. However, if you were going to buy a holiday or a plane ticket, you could not try it first before making the purchasing decision.

Identification of different products

Package holidays

A package holiday is a holiday that has at least three different services put together. Two of these will be transport to and from the destination and accommodation while on holiday. The third part is usually made up of either transfer from the airport to the hotel or excursions.

A package holiday could be as simple as a weekend coach trip around the Cotswolds or as complicated as a two-week, fly-drive holiday across the USA.

Package holidays are created by tour operators. This is done in advance and then information about the package holiday is sent to travel agencies. When the customer goes into a travel agency the agent has a number of different packages that they can sell to the customer. It is similar to buying a computer package with everything you need, rather than buying each part and assembling your own computer.

The advantage to the customer is that they only need to buy one product for their holiday rather than having to organise each component, or part, separately.

Attractions

Attractions draw people to a particular area. There is a huge range of different attractions from natural attractions such as the seaside or beautiful scenery to man-made attractions like a theme park or a heritage site. Britain's main attraction to foreign visitors is the country's history and heritage.

Accommodation

This is where you stay on holiday. The range of different types of accommodation is wide, depending on your needs and how much you wish to spend. A tourist could stay in a suite in a five-star London hotel and spend

Spain is a popular package holiday destination for British tourists

hundreds of pounds a night; alternatively, a youth hostel or bed and breakfast accommodation would cost under £20 a night. The type of accommodation is dictated by where you are travelling to, your budget and your needs.

Transport

There are three main ways to get to your destination:

- by air
- by land
- by sea.

The type of transport used to go on holiday depends on the needs of the individual. Some people want to get to the destination as quickly as possible; others view the travelling as a part of the holiday. This is particularly so with walking and cycling tours where the travelling is the holiday.

ACTIVITY

In a small group, make a list of all the different types of transport you can think of for air, land and sea. Then compare your list with the rest of the class and see how many different forms of transport you have found.

Tourist destinations

A tourist destination is a place where tourists go on holiday. This might be a historical town or city like Chester or Rome, or it could be a resort like Blackpool or an island such as Ibiza or Corfu.

PRACTICE ASSESSMENT ACTIVITY

Level ✔

P4.2 For this activity, you will research *two* travel and tourism organisations. First, agree with your tutor the organisations you plan to look at. Describe the travel and tourism products that each organisation provides and identify who the products are aimed at.

Types of customers

Customers are individuals, with their own individual needs and wants. However, to produce a travel and tourism product for each individual would make holidays too expensive for the average person. To make the cost of a holiday affordable, travel and tourism organisations produce products that will appeal to large groups of people.

Grouping customers is done in many different ways; however, the main aim is to group customers with similar needs and wants so that the organisation produces a product that addresses the group's needs. This group would be called a market segment. Below are the different ways that are used to segment a market.

Segmentation involves some generalisation and you will always find exceptions to the segments. However, segmentation helps organisations to develop individual products for each group.

KEY POINTS

Socio-economic relates to social and economic factors.

Socio-economic groups

This method involves segmenting society on grounds of employment status and income. Below are the current Office for National Statistics' classifications.

1 Higher managerial and professional occupations
  1.1 Large employers and higher managerial occupations
  1.2 Higher professional occupations

2 Lower managerial and professional occupations

3 Intermediate occupations

4 Small employers and own account workers

5 Lower supervisory and technical occupations

6 Semi-routine occupations

7 Routine occupations

8 Never worked and long-term unemployed

Note: For complete coverage, the three categories (i) Students, (ii) Occupations not stated or inadequately described, and (iii) Not classifiable for other reasons are added as 'Not classified'.

Source: Office for National Statistics

Office for National Statistics socio-economic classifications

Although the groups are graded 1–8, it does not mean group 1 is better than group 8, just that they have a different employment. However, it is reasonable to say that groups 1 and 2 could have similar needs and wants.

Specific age groups

Another way of segmenting the market is by age. This is used in package holidays, with companies producing packages for different age groups. Saga Holidays, for example, specialises in holidays for the over-50s, whereas Club 18–30 produces a completely different type of holiday targeted at 18–30-year-olds. This segmentation works well for these products, but age is a very broad way of segmenting a market. After all, not all 18–30-year-olds are the same or have similar needs.

These brochures will appeal to different market segments

Lifestyle and family circumstances

Segmenting by lifestyle and family circumstances looks into how you live your life. Your needs will change as you go through the stages of the family life cycle.

At each stage of the life cycle a person's income and responsibilities change, and each change is significant because it will affect the individual's needs when they buy a product.

STAGE	COMMENTS
Bachelor	Young and single with limited or no family responsibility
Newly married	Young and married with no children
Full nest 1	Family with youngest child under school age
Full nest 2	Family with youngest child of school age
Full nest 3	Children are still at home but are now working
Empty nest 1	One partner working and children have left home
Empty nest 2	Both partners are now retired
Solitary survivor 1	One partner left who is still working
Solitary survivor 2	One partner left who is retired

The family life cycle

Talking point

In a small group, discuss what you think will be the changes in income and responsibility at each stage of the life cycle. Draw up a chart like the one below and complete it. The first stage has been done for you.

Stage in family life cycle	Change in income	Change in responsibilities
Bachelor	Single income	No family responsibilities

Lifestyle segmentation is slightly more complicated than segmenting by employment and income or age. Most organisations set their own segments and names for lifestyle segmentation. Here are a couple of common examples.

- The Bake Bean family has a low household income and usually more than one child. Although it is a low spending-power segment, it is also a large segment and therefore has products targeted at it, e.g. holiday camps and package holidays. The segment is very price sensitive but also has child provision needs such as 'kids clubs'.
- The Dinkies are a professional couple (socio-economic groups 1 and 2). They have a high purchasing power as both partners work. Although they might be 'cash rich' they can be 'time poor' (unable to take long periods of time off work) due to the responsibility of their careers. There have been a large number of developments in the tourism provision for this segment including all-inclusive, long-haul holiday resorts and also city breaks and weekend breaks. The Dinkies' needs include a stress relieving time on holiday but they also choose their destination for the status attached to it.

School and other organised groups

This is a specific market segment. Although schools are cost-sensitive groups, they tend to have a large number of customers so it is possible to produce a product tailored to their needs. Other groups could include clubs and organisations. Kuoni (the tour operator) has a department that specialises in producing tailor-made trips for these groups, which includes organising sports tours, etc.

ACTIVITY

Choose a type of customer (see pages 138–142). Identify travel and tourism products that have been created with this type of customer in mind. What needs are these products fulfilling?

Ethnic groups

Although this might seem a good way to segment a market, it creates some issues. People of the same ethnic group do not necessarily share the same needs and wants. However, there are organisations that segment their market on ethnic grounds. There are also some cultural-based holidays, which have more appeal to one ethnic group than another, for example tours around 'Bollywood' locations in the UK have brought over 200,000 Indian tourists to the UK.

Religious groups

There are a large number of organisations that provide holidays and travel arrangements for different faith groups, whether it is a pilgrimage, a retreat to contemplate on a person's faith, or simply a holiday that has provisions for a particular faith. For example, Mastersun provides family package holidays that also have provision for practising Christians.

Single-sex groups

Some people prefer to go on holiday with people of their own sex. This may have nothing to do with sexual preference but because they feel more comfortable and relaxed in a single-sex environment. American Round Up provides hiking and horse-riding holidays; it also runs women-only trips.

KEY POINTS

You segment the market in order to provide a product to a group that has similar needs.

Special interests

This is a major growth area in travel and tourism. As people are getting better educated about holiday destinations, more people are deciding to have holidays that cater for a particular interest. This could be to follow a sports team or a particular activity or to develop or gain a new skill. There are, for example, a number of hotels and bed and breakfast places throughout the UK that specialise in accommodation for bikers, with secure parking for their motorbikes, drying rooms and easy access to main routes.

Bikers on a special interest holiday

Source: Motorcycle Rider, the BMF magazine

Geographical location

Another method used to segment the market is the customer's geographical location (where they are from). This is used by independent travel agencies which may put together holidays, tour and travel arrangements focused on the needs of the local population. Most large towns will have a few independent travel agents.

CASE STUDY

Ian's balloon rides

Ian McCoy has been running his balloon-ride company for about four years. He has decided to open a second centre in your area which will specialise in running local balloon rides (weather permitting).

Until now, Ian's business has been targeted at the 'holiday makers market' in his local town, but he would like to find out what other markets he could target.

Ian has asked you to help him research the best target markets for his business in your area so that he can develop products for these markets.

Conduct a survey to find out about the people that would use Ian's services. You might like to focus on:

- **the age of the people**
- **whether they would use the service**
- **their reasons for using Ian's service**
- **the price they would pay for the service.**

In summary

- Methods of segmenting a market include: social economic groups, age, religious groups, ethnic groups, single gender groups, location, gender, lifestyle and family circumstances.
- Whichever method of segmentation the organisation uses, its aim is to identify a group of individuals that have similar needs and expectations of a product, so that it can produce a product that addresses those needs.
- The needs and expectations of customers will change over time, so organisations will review their products regularly, especially if they use customer feedback to develop their products.

ACTIVITY

Visit a local travel agency to find out what products they offer targeted at local people.

PRACTICE ASSESSMENT ACTIVITY

Level ✔

P4.2/M4.1 Explain how the two organisations you are researching have adapted their products to meet the needs of different types of customer needs.

D4.1 Analyse the effectiveness of each attempt to meet the needs of different types of customers.

D4.1 Make suggestions for new or adapted products for these different types of customers.

4.3 Market research

Market research involves finding out information about your market. This could be about what a particular group's needs are, or changes in needs, or about the market's perception of a product (what customers think about the product).

KEY POINTS

The more you know about a customer's needs and wants, the more likely your product or service will suit the customer's needs.

Why do market research?

You learnt above that marketing is focused on the customer and their needs, so one of the main functions of research is to find out what those needs are. Market research can also be used for the following reasons:

- Identify repeat business.
- Identify a need for new products and modification to existing products.
- **Gauge** customer satisfaction.

KEY POINTS

Gauge means to estimate or determine the amount or level of something.

Unless an organisation knows what the customer's wants or needs are, how can it develop products and services to address those needs? Without research an organisation will not know what customers desire and can only guess at what the customer wants. The more information an organisation has about its market, the better it will be able to segment the market, develop products, etc.

However, market research costs time and money, so a lot of thought needs to go into how much market research is required and what an organisation really needs to know.

ACTIVITY

Make a list of the different ways that you could get information about your customers and their needs, expectations and satisfaction. Compare your list with others in your group.

Types of market research

There are two main types of research:

- desk, or secondary research
- field, or primary research.

Secondary (desk) research

This is research that has already been done for another reason (so it is the second use of the information). It is sometimes known as desk research, as this is where the research takes place.

Secondary research could be information that an organisation has collected such as sales figures or customer comment forms, or it could be information from outside the organisation, for example from the government or a specialist research organisation (for more details of government reports, see the Office for National Statistics website: www.statistics.gov.uk).

KEY POINTS

Information can go out of date.

When looking at secondary research it is important to note how relevant the research is. You will need to consider the following issues:

- When was the research done? (Time affects how valid the results are.)
- Why was it done? (Most research is done for a specific reason and this will dictate what questions were asked.)
- How big was the sample group? (How many people were questioned?)
- Who was included in the sample group and where was it taken?

Benefits of secondary research

The main benefit of secondary research is the speed with which an organisation can gather the results. Secondary research is usually relatively cheap to obtain, although research reports may have to be bought, which in some cases could be expensive. However, these costs are small compared to the expense of employing people or commissioning a research organisation to carry out primary research and analyse the information.

Deciding on the type of research – secondary or primary – involves a balancing act between the time and cost of the research and the relevance of the information.

ACTIVITY

Can you think what the disadvantages of secondary research might be?

Primary (field) research

This research is being done for the first time and is purposely designed to meet an organisation's needs. There are four main methods of conducting primary research:

- questionnaires
- observation
- focus groups
- surveys.

Questionnaires

Questionnaires are commonly used in customer service to obtain customer feedback. The important thing to remember when designing a questionnaire is that it should be objective and not cause bias.

KEY POINTS

Quantitative data is data that can be used statistically to make charts and graphs showing trends.

Questionnaires may be designed to obtain information that is factual and which can be turned into numbers, or statistics. For example, 20 people were asked to give a yes or no answer to the following question: Was your flight on time? Fourteen people answered yes, six answered no.

You might want an answer that gives a range of opinion. For example, on a scale of 1–10, how did you rate the service (10 being good, 1 being bad)? This type of data is called **quantitative data**. It is useful for identifying trends but does not go into the customer's personal opinions or feelings in depth.

- *How did the service provided by Avis measure up to your expectations?*

☐ Greatly exceeded	☐ Somewhat less than expected
☐ Somewhat exceeded	☐ A lot less than expected
☐ Met my expectations	☐ Not applicable

- *Did you feel you were treated as an individual with very specific needs?*

☐ Definitely	☐ Not really
☐ Somewhat	☐ Definitely not
☐ Neutral	☐ Not applicable

- *How responsive were Avis personnel to your needs?*

☐ Very responsive	☐ Somewhat unresponsive
☐ Somewhat responsive	☐ Definitely not
☐ Neutral	☐ Not applicable

- *How effective was Avis in reducing your overall stress while traveling?*

☐ Very effective	☐ Somewhat ineffective
☐ Somewhat effective	☐ Very ineffective
☐ Neutral	☐ Not applicable

Source: Avis Rent A Car System, Inc.

The car rental company Avis uses a questionnaire to obtain feedback from its customers

Advantages of questionnaires

- Questionnaires are a good method of obtaining customer feedback.
- The data is easy to manipulate and is used to work out trends.
- They are relatively cheap to use, after the initial time invested in developing the questionnaire and the printing cost.
- Customers can see that the organisation is interested in their opinion.

Disadvantages of questionnaires

- Questionnaires tend to give polarised viewpoints. In other words, people tend only to fill in questionnaires if they either had a very good or bad experience.
- Unless the questionnaire and data are rigorously collected and acted on, it tends to become less useful.
- Data collected can be only quantitative. It often does not give details of customers' feelings or how customers would like to see the product or service developed or improved.

ACTIVITY

Choose an organisation in the travel and tourism industry. Select one of the reasons for performing market research given in the bullet list on page 144 (or think of another one).

Create a questionnaire that your chosen organisation could use, keeping the reason for the research in mind.

Observation

This method of research involves observing customers. It is good for monitoring how customers use a facility and how they interact with a product. For example, the managers of an international airport might observe the ways passengers move around the check-in area. They might wish to understand how space is used in order to decide the best places to put facilities, to speed up customer flow around the area, etc.

Advantages of observation

- The main advantage is that you are not interacting with the customer; you are watching how they behave naturally rather than asking what they think. People's behaviour can differ a lot from what they think their behaviour is.

Disadvantages of observation

- You are only monitoring the customer's behaviour. You do not have any insight into why this behaviour is happening.

Focus groups

A focus group involves bringing together a small group of product users. It can be used to test products or give detailed opinions and information about feelings. This is known as **qualitative data**. It cannot be used to show trends but shows consumers' perception of products and their feelings about different products.

Tour operators may use focus groups when considering developing new package holidays, especially if the product is targeted at a particular type of customer.

KEY POINTS

Qualitative data is data that gives people's opinions and feelings.

Advantages of focus groups

- Focus groups offer a detailed insight into what the customer feels about the product and service.
- This is the only method of primary research that really gives an understanding of the customer perception of the product/service.

Disadvantage of focus groups

- As the data is qualitative, the focus group has to be small enough to allow you to manage all the data. However, a small sample group might lead to a misleading or non-representative sample (the people in the focus group do not truly reflect the market).
- Focus groups can be quite expensive in time and money to run and organise.

Surveys

A survey is a targeted way of collecting data. To find out general trends or the average opinion, an organisation could ask everyone in the market their view. However, this would be too expensive and time consuming, so to save time and money, a sample is chosen that represents the market to be questioned.

Sometimes on your local high street, you may see researchers stopping people to ask them questions. You might notice that they do not stop everyone but select people to ask. This is because they are only looking for a particular type of person for the sample.

Surveys can be carried out in three different ways:

- telephone survey
- postal survey
- person-to-person survey.

Telephone survey

As the name suggests, this is a survey that is conducted on the telephone. Although this can be carried out in-house (using the organisation's own staff), there are many companies that specialise in this type of research.

Advantages of a telephone survey:

- Data can be obtained quickly, especially as it can be entered straight into a database while the questions are being answered.
- For primary research, this is relatively inexpensive as the number of interviews conducted by one member of staff can be quite high.
- As you are speaking to the customer you can ask supplementary questions if you do not understand the customer's response.

Disadvantages of a telephone survey:

- The survey can have a low response rate, especially if you are cold calling (calling a person that has had no previous contact with your organisation).
- As you are speaking to the customer in person, they may tone down their reply so as not to cause offence. Although this is pleasant, it will not give you the customer's true feelings, which can affect the validity of your research.

Postal survey

This is a survey that is conducted by post. It has quite a low response rate. A number of companies offer entry into a prize draw or discounts off products so as to increase the response rate.

The travel agency Thomas Cook sends a postal survey to every customer on their return from holiday to judge customer satisfaction and also to help the company develop its products to suit customers' needs.

Advantages of a postal survey:

- Customers have time to consider their response so the data will be less likely to be tainted by emotion.
- It is cheap to run as limited staff time is used.
- Customers are more likely to be honest than in a one-to-one situation.

Disadvantages of a postal survey:

- It is time consuming as it takes a long time for letters to be delivered and replies to be returned.
- It has a low response rate (especially if the survey is unsolicited).
- The organisation needs to decide how long it will wait for responses. Unlike the other two methods of survey, the organisation does not know if the customer is going to respond.
- Supplementary questions cannot be asked.
- There might be problems understanding customer responses or even their handwriting.

A market researcher interviews a shopper on the high street to find out their views

Person-to-person survey

This is a survey that you carry out in person. You might see this sort of market researcher in your high street.

Advantages of a person-to-person survey:

- This type of survey has a higher response rate compared to the other methods of research, as it is harder to refuse a person face to face rather than over the telephone when you can just hang up.
- Supplementary questions can be asked if answers are not understood.
- The researcher can choose who they survey. This is particularly important if you are trying to target a market segment. For example, there is little point asking a 50-year-old man about package holidays for the under-30s.

Disadvantages of a person-to-person survey:

- It is a very expensive method of researching as the organisation has to pay for researchers to collect the information.
- People will not consider their answer as much as with a postal survey, possibly just telling the researcher what they want to hear in order to get away as quickly as possible.

In summary

- Market research supplies managers with information to help them make more informed decisions.
- There are two types of research: primary (new research) and secondary (information that has previously been collected).
- Methods of primary research include: questionnaires, surveys, observation, focus groups.

Level ✔

PRACTICE ASSESSMENT ACTIVITY

P4.3 Explain how different market research methods are used in the travel and tourism industry. Include information about different market research methods and give examples of how they are used.

M4.2 Describe the advantages and disadvantages of the different market research methods you identified above.

4.4 Promotional methods

Promotional methods vary as much as companies do, from the common to the bizarre. This section looks at the most commonly used techniques and media.

Promotion is an important part of the product delivery system. After all, if customers do not know what an organisation is offering, how can they purchase its goods and services?

Promotional techniques

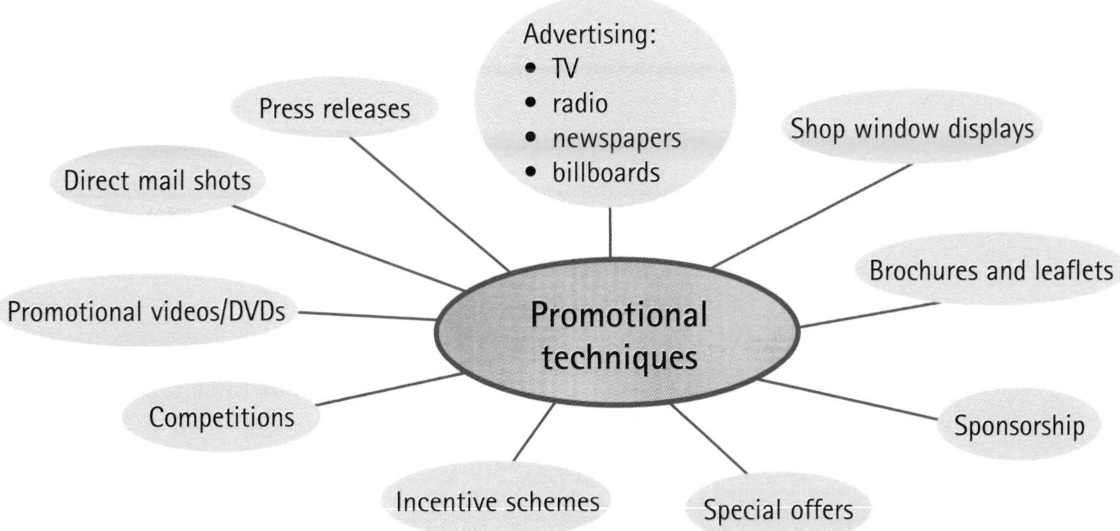

Promotional techniques are designed to encourage consumers to buy products

ACTIVITY

Produce a list of all the different places where you might see an advert. For example, bill board posters at bus stops.

Advertising

Advertising is any promotion that you pay a third party for in order to promote your product through their medium.

Promotional design is discussed later in this section. First, let's look at the advantages and disadvantages of each of the main media.

Television advertisements

These are advertisements that an organisation pays to appear on television. They are commonly known as commercials.

Advantages of TV advertisements

- Television is an active medium – you do not have to make any effort to watch a television commercial whereas most other media take some effort on your part. This means that people take notice of television adverts even when they are not taking any notice of the television.
- A TV advertisement does not only have images but also sound, so the advertisement can be stimulating and changing.
- Most commercial television channels in the UK are either regionalised or tend to specialise in a particular area of interest. This means that the organisation can target selected interest groups by advertising on a particular channel. For example, Legar Holidays advertises battlefield tours on the History Channel.

Disadvantages of TV advertisements

- The main disadvantage is the cost of not only showing the advertisement but also producing the advertisement in the first place. Only large local and national travel and tourism organisations can afford to advertise in this way.
- Television is an active medium – the customer does not have any information except what they can remember from the advertisement (compared to a newspaper advertisement that they can keep referring to).
- Only a minimum amount of information can be put across in each commercial.
- Although TV advertising is very good at getting the customers to be aware of a product, it is not very good at converting that awareness to sales.
- For a TV advertisement to be memorable, it has to be repeated many times, so increasing the cost.

Radio commercials

Like television, this is another mass-market form of advertising. The obvious difference is there are no pictures on radio, so the whole of the message needs to be put across in sound.

PRACTICE ASSESSMENT ACTIVITY

Level ✓

P4.3 Explain how different market research methods are used in the travel and tourism industry. Include information about different market research methods and give examples of how they are used.

M4.2 Describe the advantages and disadvantages of the different market research methods you identified above.

4.4 Promotional methods

Promotional methods vary as much as companies do, from the common to the bizarre. This section looks at the most commonly used techniques and media.

Promotion is an important part of the product delivery system. After all, if customers do not know what an organisation is offering, how can they purchase its goods and services?

Promotional techniques

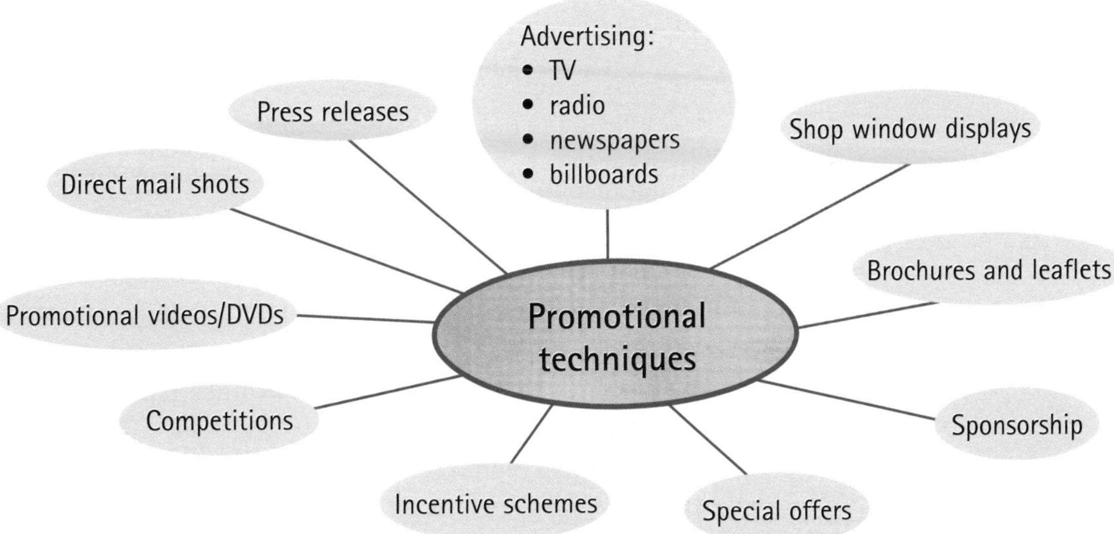

Promotional techniques are designed to encourage consumers to buy products

ACTIVITY

Produce a list of all the different places where you might see an advert. For example, bill board posters at bus stops.

Advertising

Advertising is any promotion that you pay a third party for in order to promote your product through their medium.

Promotional design is discussed later in this section. First, let's look at the advantages and disadvantages of each of the main media.

Television advertisements

These are advertisements that an organisation pays to appear on television. They are commonly known as commercials.

Advantages of TV advertisements

- Television is an active medium – you do not have to make any effort to watch a television commercial whereas most other media take some effort on your part. This means that people take notice of television adverts even when they are not taking any notice of the television.
- A TV advertisement does not only have images but also sound, so the advertisement can be stimulating and changing.
- Most commercial television channels in the UK are either regionalised or tend to specialise in a particular area of interest. This means that the organisation can target selected interest groups by advertising on a particular channel. For example, Legar Holidays advertises battlefield tours on the History Channel.

Disadvantages of TV advertisements

- The main disadvantage is the cost of not only showing the advertisement but also producing the advertisement in the first place. Only large local and national travel and tourism organisations can afford to advertise in this way.
- Television is an active medium – the customer does not have any information except what they can remember from the advertisement (compared to a newspaper advertisement that they can keep referring to).
- Only a minimum amount of information can be put across in each commercial.
- Although TV advertising is very good at getting the customers to be aware of a product, it is not very good at converting that awareness to sales.
- For a TV advertisement to be memorable, it has to be repeated many times, so increasing the cost.

Radio commercials

Like television, this is another mass-market form of advertising. The obvious difference is there are no pictures on radio, so the whole of the message needs to be put across in sound.

Advantages of radio commercials

- Radio is the most popular entertainment medium with the average person listening to more hours of radio a day than hours watching television.
- Radio commercials are cheaper to produce and also to air than TV advertisements.
- Radio stations tend to be more regionalised so that small or medium-size organisations can afford to promote on this medium to their own local market.

Disadvantages of radio commercials

- Although there are special interest radio stations, they tend not to be as subject specific as television stations but to reflect musical taste. However, musical taste can be linked with socio-economic groups, with groups 1 and 2 more likely to listen to classical music than groups 7 or 8.
- As with television there is no hard copy of the information. This means that the message has to be very clear or the advertisement has to be repeated regularly.

Billboards (advertising hoardings)

These are the posters that you might see around any town or city. They tend to be set beside main roads so that they have a high number of people passing them each day. The average person will look at a billboard for between five and 13 seconds which means that the message has to be very clear.

Advantages of billboards

- They are relatively cheap, compared to TV or radio commercials.
- Advertisements can be targeted at a particular area, e.g. a travel agency could have a billboard giving information about the location of its local branch in that town and different information in a different town.

Disadvantages of billboards

- Due to the huge amount of advertising and street furniture on the streets in the UK, advertising hoardings can be lost in the clutter.
- As there is no movement in most hoardings, this means that it can be quite difficult to attract people's attention.
- The message has to be simple, as people tend not to spend very long looking at a hoarding.

Newspaper adverts

Newspapers, both local and national, run advertising throughout their pages. Local papers, especially local free papers that are delivered to every house in an area, have a high readership and this can be an effective method of promotion for a small business.

National newspapers tend to target different types of readerships.

ACTIVITY

1 Make a list of all the national newspapers that you can think of.
2 Next to each, write down what type of person is likely to read that paper.
3 What type of travel or tourism product would appeal to each type of customer?

Holiday advert in a newspaper

Weekend papers are especially popular for advertising travel products. Some weekend papers contain special travel sections.

Advantages of newspaper advertising

- Compared with other advertising media, this is a relatively cheap form of advertising.
- Customers have a hard copy of the advertisement which they can refer to, unlike television, radio or billboards.
- Effectiveness of a newspaper's adverts can be assessed more accurately.

Disadvantages of newspaper advertising

- As this is a popular and effective method of advertising that is used extensively by travel and tourism organisations, individual advertisements may easily be 'lost' among all the others.
- Due to the popularity of advertising holidays in newspapers, customers can easily compare offers.

Displays

A brochure display

A display is any collection of material put together to promote a particular product or service. Travel agencies, especially independents, have eye-catching displays in their shop windows to encourage people to enter the shop. These displays could be a general one or for a particular destination that the agency is trying to promote.

Holiday representatives also use display boards in resort hotels to tell customers of facilities and excursions available while on holiday.

Brochures and leaflets

Brochures and leaflets are one of the most popular methods of promotion in travel and tourism.

Leaflets are used by most tourist attractions as an essential way to communicate information about the attraction. If you went into your local tourist information centre (TIC), you would notice the number of leaflets on display. Leaflets are a useful method of communication because of the amount of information that can be put across to the customer.

Unlike a leaflet that tends to be a sheet or two of paper, a brochure is a booklet. The main users of brochures are tour operators and travel agents. Brochures are a very good way for a tour operator to display its products and for travel agents to sell them. The main disadvantage of brochures is that they cannot be updated after printing so any important changes to the product would mean the brochure was out of date. Reprinting the brochure would add to its expense.

Sponsorship

In the past, you have probably been asked to sponsor someone or to get involved in a sponsorship event. An organisation may sponsor a cause or event to gain as much media exposure as possible for itself or its product and to give the organisation a better social image. On a small scale, this might involve sponsoring an individual to take part in a charitable event. On a large scale, it could involve the sponsorship of an entire sporting event. The organisation will want to make sure that customers and potential customers know that it is sponsoring the event or cause. It is important that the event or person sponsored enhances the organisation's product image and does not offend current customers.

Special offers

A special offer is when an organisation offers a particular product or service for a short period of time. This could be a reduction in the cost or some extra component to the product. Travel agents often offer discounts of free child places if you book your holiday early. Hotels often offer special weekend breaks in the quieter time of the week for room sales.

Special offers can be used to:

- encourage people to buy products early
- increase sales at slow trading times
- promote a new product or service.

The disadvantage of special offers is that they can undermine the consumer's view of the value for money of the product when the offer finishes and also reduces the amount of profit that the organisation is making on the sale.

Incentives

Incentive schemes are used to encourage customers to repeat purchase a product. Many hotel groups and airlines offer customer loyalty schemes, which give customers free or discounted use of a product as a reward for their loyalty.

The other main type of incentive is offered by tour operators to travel agents, for example free familiarisation trips to resorts or an increased percentage commission if a specific sales level is reached.

KEY POINTS

Promotion is about getting a message across to a customer. The method you use will depend on who you are trying to communicate with.

Competition

Competitions are another method used to promote a product. They help increase product awareness and give the organisation a way to communicate to potential customers.

Videos/DVDs

These are increasingly being used as a method of promotion. A number of holiday resorts offer potential customers free videos. Although they can be expensive to produce, a video or DVD gives a more detailed description of the resort than a brochure can.

ACTIVITY

Collect examples of advertising produced by travel and tourism organisations. If the advert is something that you cannot collect (like a radio advert or a billboard), make a note of it instead. In small groups, talk about the advertising you have all collected. What do you like/dislike about it? Who is it aimed at? Do you think it will work?

Direct mail shots

Most organisations keep a database of current and previous customers and enquiries. This can be used to send information about products to those customers. For example, a theatre preparing to put on a particular drama can use its database to send out information to customers who have expressed an interest in that type of play in the past.

Direct mail is most effective if it is addressed and directed to a person by name rather than to 'Dear customer'. As the computer is used to generate the mail shot, it is the design of the letter that is most important so that each customer feels it is a personal invitation rather than just another circular.

Press releases

A press release is when an organisation provides the press (newspapers) with information about itself or its products. A press release is usually written in the form of a newspaper story. It must contain a release date (date after which it can be used) and a contact name and details in case journalists require more details.

ACTIVITY

Write a press release for your local newspaper promoting your course.

You might like to focus on some event or trip that you have been involved in.

Advantages of press releases

- Most people will read a newspaper story and are more likely to believe it than an advertisement.
- It is a cheap method of promotion as the only cost is the time to write the article.

Disadvantages of press releases

- Newspapers have no obligation to use the story.
- The story can be changed or edited by the newspaper.

Shows and events

Shows and events tend to be used for trade promotion rather than for customers in the travel and tourism industry. One of the major ones is the World Travel Market. This is a great opportunity for organisations to communicate with trade customers and explain and promote their products. However, as it is such an important show, organisations have to expect that their competitors will also be at the event promoting their products.

Level

PRACTICE ASSESSMENT ACTIVITY

P4.4 Describe the different types of promotional methods used by travel and tourism organisations to promote their products and services.

M4.2 Describe the advantages and disadvantages of each promotion technique.

Planning promotional activities

Promotional activities need to be planned. The travel and tourism industry is a very competitive market place with a large number of organisations offering similar products and services. If you do not plan your promotion well, your message risks coming across as confused, and its effectiveness will be reduced.

Purpose of promotion and marketing objectives

There are many different reasons why an organisation may decide to run a promotional campaign. Some of the most common ones are:

- to increase repeat sales
- to increase product awareness among customers
- to encourage new customers to use products

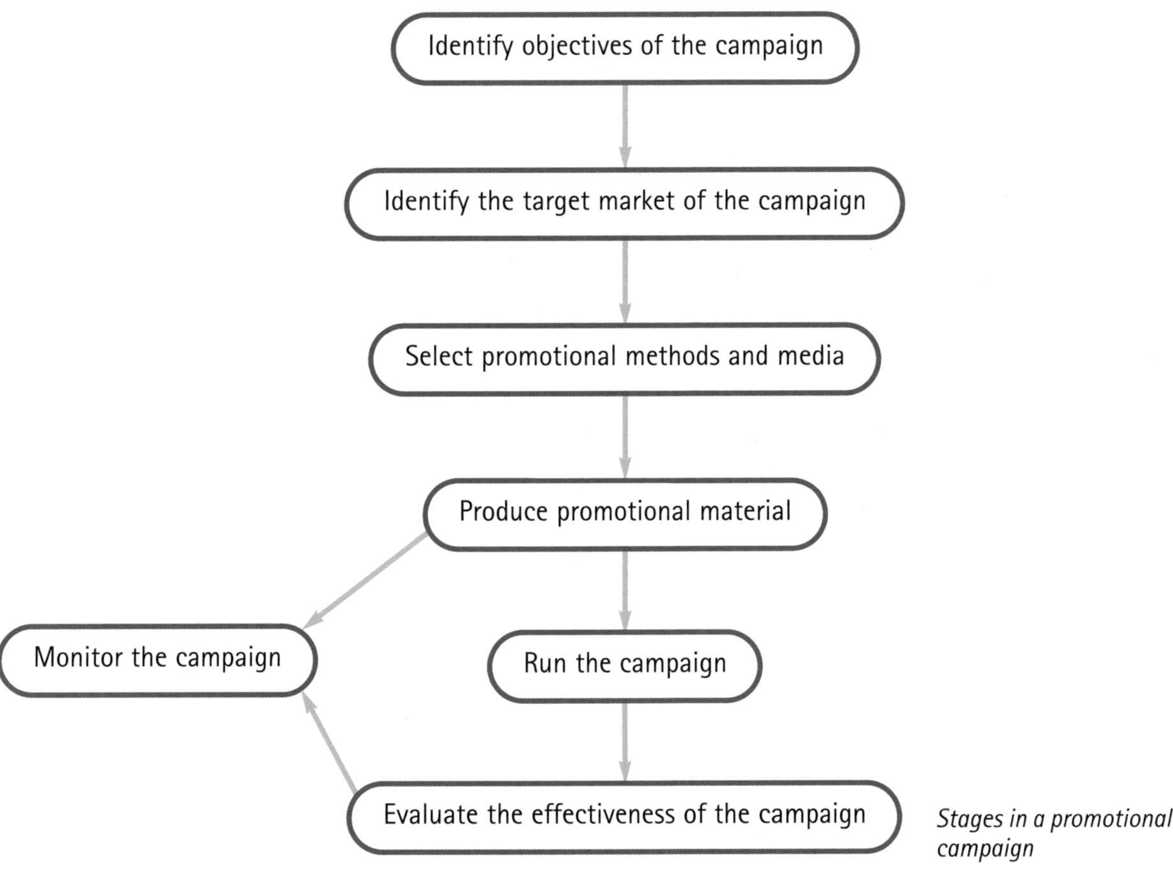

Stages in a promotional campaign

- to inform the market of a new product or changes to products
- because competitors are advertising and the organisation needs to defend its market share
- to counter rumours about the organisation or product.

Before beginning a promotional campaign you will first need to set your objectives.

KEY POINTS

Objectives must be SMART.

Identifying the target market

Once you have identified your marketing objectives, you will need to identify your target market. It is important that you know who your customers are before you communicate with them to ensure that the methods and media you choose will be appropriate.

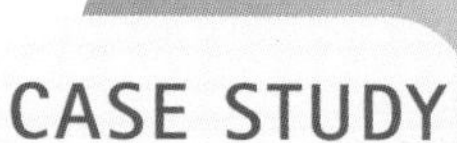

CASE STUDY

International airline Emirates and the Airbus A380

Emirates has played a central role in the development of the Airbus A380 'superjumbo', which was unveiled in January 2005.

The Chairman of Emirates said: 'I am very proud that Emirates was the first airline to sign for the A380 – and that today we are its largest customer.'

He added: 'This aircraft is a key element in Emirates' future growth. Air travel is forecast to double in the next 14 years. There are continued constraints on traffic rights and the availability of landing slots – and therefore, large capacity aircraft will be vital to Emirates' need to meet the increasing passenger demand. The A380 is the future of air travel.'

The Dubai-based international airline was not only the first customer for this next generation aircraft, but is also now its biggest customer, with 45 A380 aircraft on order, amounting to a cost of US$19 billion, something that astounded the airline world as the largest in civil aviation history.

Emirates has worked closely with Airbus in the design and development of the A380, as the airframe has moved from concept to the drawing board and on to the production line.

While some observers have arched their brows at the optimism of Emirates, the airline's faith in the future of air transportation and its own potential is rooted in a rock-solid record of consistent profitability for the past 17 years, and a doubling in size every four years on average.

Indeed, in Emirates' meticulous long-term planning, A380 operations have already been charted from October 2006, when the airline is scheduled to take delivery of the first of those aircraft.

In a first hint of what facilities might be found onboard, Emirates began finalising its commitments for the interior equipment at the Farnborough Air Show in 2004, placing a groundbreaking US$1 billion deal for an in-flight entertainment system for the Airbus A380. The carrier also committed US$80m to the purchase of First Class suites from B/E Aerospace for its A380 fleet.

The airline's global hub at Dubai International Airport will be ready to receive the double-decker at its newly opened Terminal 3, which will have a total of 23 departure gates and aerobridges specifically designed for the superjumbo.

The arrival of the first Emirates Airbus A380–800 in October 2006 will be a major milestone for the airline. It will signify its first step in the gradual build-up towards becoming the world's largest operator of the superjumbo. For the first time, Emirates will be able to transport more than 500 passengers in a single aircraft, with a quality of airline product and comfort that is Emirates' trademark and has helped it win more than 250 customer service awards during its less than 20 years in business.

CASE STUDY

International airline Emirates and the Airbus A380 (Contd.)

The airline's superior standard of product delivery to the customer that all carriers aspire to but few actually offer, is Emirates' hallmark philosophy since its inception in 1985 – and is as alive today as it was then.

Source: Adapted from Emirates news, 'Emirates, the world's first buyer of the airbus A380 will be its largest operator', 18 January 2005 (www.emirates.com/uk)

What is the message that the airline is trying to put across? Do you think that the message is clear?

Choice of promotional methods

The method of promotion you choose will depend on the target market. The trick is to adapt your promotion to target your intended market. If you were trying to promote weekend breaks, advertising on the London Underground where thousands of commuters pass every day would be an effective method, for example.

Over to you

How do you spend your time during commercial breaks when you are watching TV? Write down your answer and keep it safe.

Designing effective promotional material

On average, you see over 1200 advertising messages a day! How then do you get people to take notice of yours? The AIDA approach is used as a method of designing advertising so that people will take notice and remember it:

Attention Interest Desire Action

A is for Attention

Unless you can attract people's attention, there is little likelihood of your advertising campaign being successful. Different methods are used to attract people's attention.

Colour

Every colour has an association:

- Blue and yellow tend to be used by holiday brochures and tourism companies as they conjure up images of sea and sand.

- Green is often associated with natural food and is regularly used in the packaging of organic food.
- Red is usually associated with danger and excitement and tends to be used where a lively image is wanted.

Fonts and print style

Different fonts are used to symbolise different images.

AN ART-DECO FONT MAY BE USED TO EXPRESS AN IMAGE OF STYLE OR CLASS...

...whereas a fun font might be used for a children's menu...

...and a more rounded font to express friendliness.

Pictures and drawings

A good picture can sum up what could only be said in a detailed description.

'A picture speaks a thousand words' (old Chinese proverb). What does this picture 'say' to you?

Humour

This is used widely in promotional material as it helps attract attention and put customers at ease. Humour involving animals and small children can generally raise a smile in the majority of the population.

You have to be careful when using humour as not everyone's sense of humour is the same. What one person finds funny, someone else may find offensive.

I is for Interest

After you have attracted someone's attention you need to keep them interested in your product or service. This is the second part of the AIDA approach. The most common way that a customer's interest is gained is by slowly developing their interest in a product rather than bombarding them with facts. Fun can be used as a way of keeping people interested. Adverts with a simple ongoing story line encourage people to watch them just to see what happens next.

D is for Desire

After a promotion has created attention and interest, you will need to create desire in the customer to visit or purchase the attraction or product. The three main ways that desire is created in travel and tourism are as follows:

- By making the customer feel that they are already there. This can be done by the use of language in the promotional material. Adjectives like 'dangerous', 'exciting' and 'thrilling' are commonly used to create an air of anticipation, as are verbs such as 'experience', 'taste', 'join in', 'be a part of' and 'don't miss'. This can also be used to make the customer feel that they need the product or service.
- Personalising the information so that the customer feels that they are the ones who the product or service was created for.
- Through showing the customer the benefits of the product – how the product will fulfil the customers' needs and expectations. For example, you buy a seat on an airline not to fly but *to get to your destination.* If there were a quicker more comfortable method of getting to your destination, then you would find that the airline industry would become obsolete.

A is for Action

When you have persuaded a customer to buy a product or service you need them to take action. Research shows that the longer someone waits after deciding to buy a product, the more likely they are to change their minds. Therefore, promotional material needs to enable the customer to take action to buy the product. For point-of-sales promotion this is easy – the customer can purchase instantly. However, other forms of promotion need a method by which the customer can contact the organisation, for example through any one or all of the following:

- freephone number
- telephone number
- location map
- website
- email address
- address
- fax number.

KEY POINTS

The method should match the customers' preferred methods of communication. Some companies have started to use phone texting as the communication method to target younger people.

ACTIVITY

1 Select a few brochures and list the methods that they use so that customers can take action to gain further information on the product.

2 Select one brochure and analyse how the AIDA approach has been used in the production of the brochure.

Timing

Thinking about a holiday?

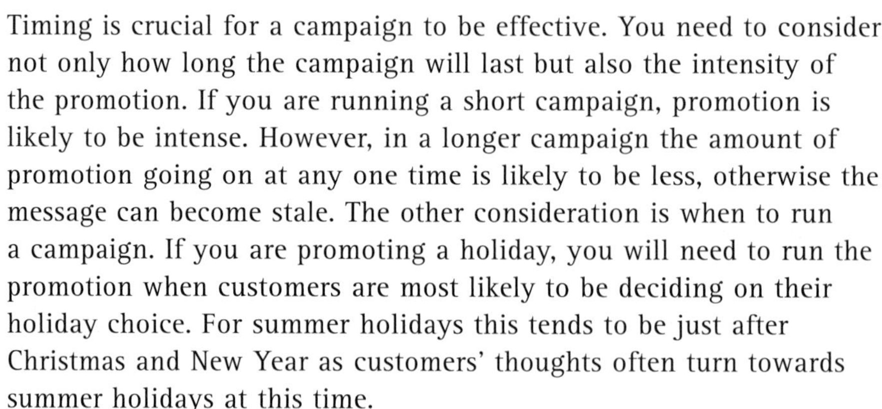

Timing is crucial for a campaign to be effective. You need to consider not only how long the campaign will last but also the intensity of the promotion. If you are running a short campaign, promotion is likely to be intense. However, in a longer campaign the amount of promotion going on at any one time is likely to be less, otherwise the message can become stale. The other consideration is when to run a campaign. If you are promoting a holiday, you will need to run the promotion when customers are most likely to be deciding on their holiday choice. For summer holidays this tends to be just after Christmas and New Year as customers' thoughts often turn towards summer holidays at this time.

KEY POINTS

The budget is set before you start the campaign and is monitored continually throughout the process.

Budget

The amount of money available to spend on a promotion campaign will affect what methods of promotion you can employ. A small business is unlikely to be able to afford a nationwide television campaign whereas a large multiple travel agency will. If you have a limited budget, you might have to be more inventive about your promotion and also more targeted. Remember that effective promotion increases business, which in turn increases profit. For small businesses the use of press releases, word of mouth and public relations will be both cheap and effective.

PRACTICE ASSESSMENT ACTIVITY

Level ✔

P4.5/M4.3 Produce two promotional materials to promote a travel and tourism product for a specified organisation and target market. Agree with your tutor what you are going to look at before you start.

D4.2 For each of the promotional materials you produced above, justify the choice of promotional methods used.

Evaluation

After a promotional campaign has run its course, it needs to be evaluated.

KEY POINTS

The evaluation is where you gauge success.

Purpose of evaluating

The purpose of this evaluation is twofold:

- To gauge the level of the promotion's success. It is worth taking time to evaluate if the initial objectives of the campaign have been fulfilled. This is why it is important to have SMART objectives so that the level of success can be evaluated.
- You also need to evaluate the effectiveness of each promotional method used. This is important regardless of the success of the campaign. If large amounts are being spent on promotion, you will need to find out how effective each method is. This is so that you can use this information to make future campaigns more efficient.

Methods of evaluating

It is very important to consider evaluation while you are designing a campaign. Although it can be relatively easy to identify how effective a campaign is compared to its overall goal, it is harder to evaluate the effectiveness of each type of promotion that you have used. This is because you may not be involved in just one form of promotion at any one time but be using a number of different channels. For example, you might be running a TV advertising campaign alongside billboard adverts and special offers.

An effective method of evaluating each type of promotion is to build in some way of identifying how the customer has heard of your product or service. This might be by giving a small discount if a code is quoted (the code being different for each form of promotion). This is used particularly with newspaper and magazine advertisements.

The other main method of evaluation is to use market research which you looked at earlier in this unit. This is a less effective method. However, you might notice that when you book a holiday with a travel agent you could be asked how you heard of the company. This could be built into a booking form as an additional question.

The evaluation is as important as the promotion as this helps the organisation to consider its promotional methods, media and design to better target that market segment in the future.

ASSESSMENT ACTIVITY

Level ✓

D4.2 Evaluate each of the promotional materials you produced earlier.

CASE STUDY

The farmers' market

There has been a growth in the number of people who want to buy low-intensity produced, locally grown and reared food.

A number of market towns in the UK have grown and thrived through the development of locally produced food and restaurants. Padstow in Devon is one such example, where Rick Stein's seafood restaurant has helped increase the prosperity in the local area through tourism. Ludlow, Shropshire, has four restaurants in the Michelin guide and has become a 'mecca to foodies' all over the UK.

A market town near you has decided that it would like to have a farmers' market to show and sell the best quality local produce. The organisers know that you are studying travel and tourism and have asked your group to come up with a promotional campaign to help promote awareness of the market among your area's tourists. They only have a limited budget that can pay for your materials but cannot afford to pay for promotion.

In a small group, using the skills that you have learnt in this unit, design a promotional campaign for the local farmers' market. Explain which techniques you are going to use and how you would focus on the target market.

In summary

- Methods of promotion include: advertising, displays, brochures and leaflets, sponsorship, special offers, incentives, competitions, DVDs/videos, direct mail, press releases, shows and events.
- The six stages of a promotional campaign are: (1) Identify objectives of the campaign, (2) Identify the target market of the campaign, (3) Choose promotional methods and medium, (4) Produce promotional material, (5) Run and monitor the campaign, (6) Evaluate the effectiveness of the campaign.
- When planning a promotional campaign, consider: target market, objective of campaign, timing of campaign, budget, evaluation methods.

TEST YOUR KNOWLEDGE

1. What are the 4Ps of the marketing mix?
2. What is a unique selling point (USP)?
3. What is a brand?
4. What is meant by the term 'target market'?
5. Why do we segment markets?
6. What are the SMART objectives?
7. Why do we set objectives?
8. Identify three different travel and tourism products.
9. List four different ways that we can segment a market.
10. From your answer to question 9, explain how you would use each method of segmentation and why you would use it.
11. What are the drawbacks of each method identified in question 9?
12. Give three reasons for carrying out market research.
13. Name the two different types of data that you can collect.
14. What are the two main types of market research?
15. What are the three methods of primary research used in the travel and tourism industry?
16. Give three types of survey that you could carry out.
17. Identify five different promotional methods.
18. Give three reasons for carrying out a promotional campaign.
19. What does the term 'advertising medium' mean?
20. What does AIDA stand for?
21. Explain the term 'target audience'.
22. Why is it important to evaluate the success of a promotional campaign?

Unit 5 Introduction to the Business of Travel and Tourism

Introduction

The travel and tourism industry is a large and diverse industry consisting of many different organisations catering for a wide range of customer needs. This unit introduces you to some of the organisational and operational aspects of the industry. You will learn about the different types of organisations, their objectives and their administrative and financial systems. The unit also looks at another important aspect of the industry – health, safety and security.

How you will be assessed

This unit is assessed internally, so the centre delivering the qualification will assess you against the criteria.

In this unit you will learn about:

① the types of organisation

② administrative and financial functions and systems

③ administration and financial documentation

④ health, safety and security.

5.1 Types of organisation

Overview of the travel and tourism industry

The industry can be divided into five main components, or parts:

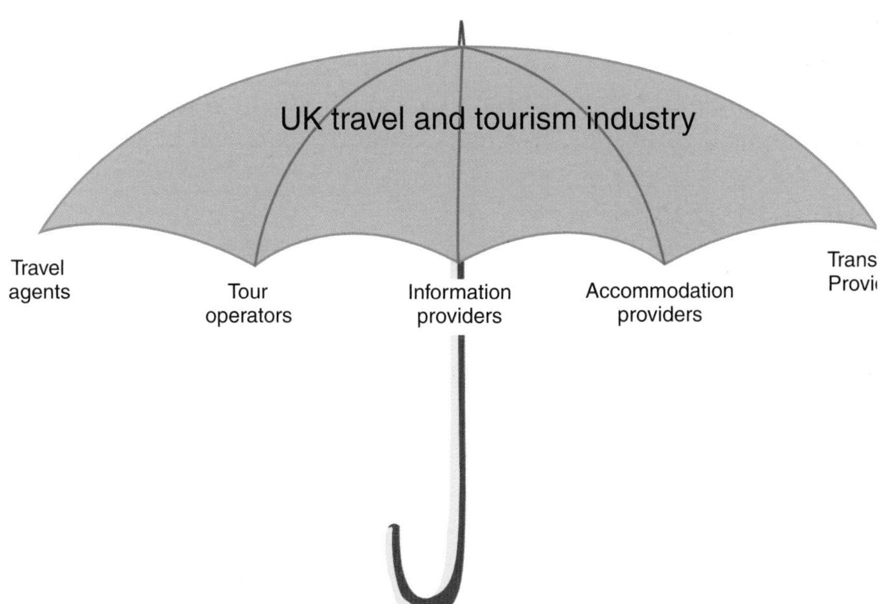

The travel and tourism industry

KEY POINTS

Key components of the UK travel and tourism industry:

- Accommodation providers
- Transport providers
- Tour operators
- Travel agents
- Information providers.

Accommodation providers

These are organisations that provide accommodation for people who are away from home. There is a huge range of accommodation providers ranging from a simple campsite to the world-famous, seven-star Burj Al Arab hotel in Dubai.

ACTIVITY

1 Make a list of as many different types of accommodation providers as you can think of.
2 Compare your list with others in your group and see how many your class can come up with.
3 Using a telephone directory or the Internet, find out what range of accommodation providers there are in your local area. Add any types of providers that you hadn't thought of to your list.

Transport providers

Transport providers are organisations that get you to your destination. They can be divided into three main categories: air, land or sea transport.

Air transport

The two forms of air transport commercially available to transport customers are aircraft and helicopters. There are two types of flight:

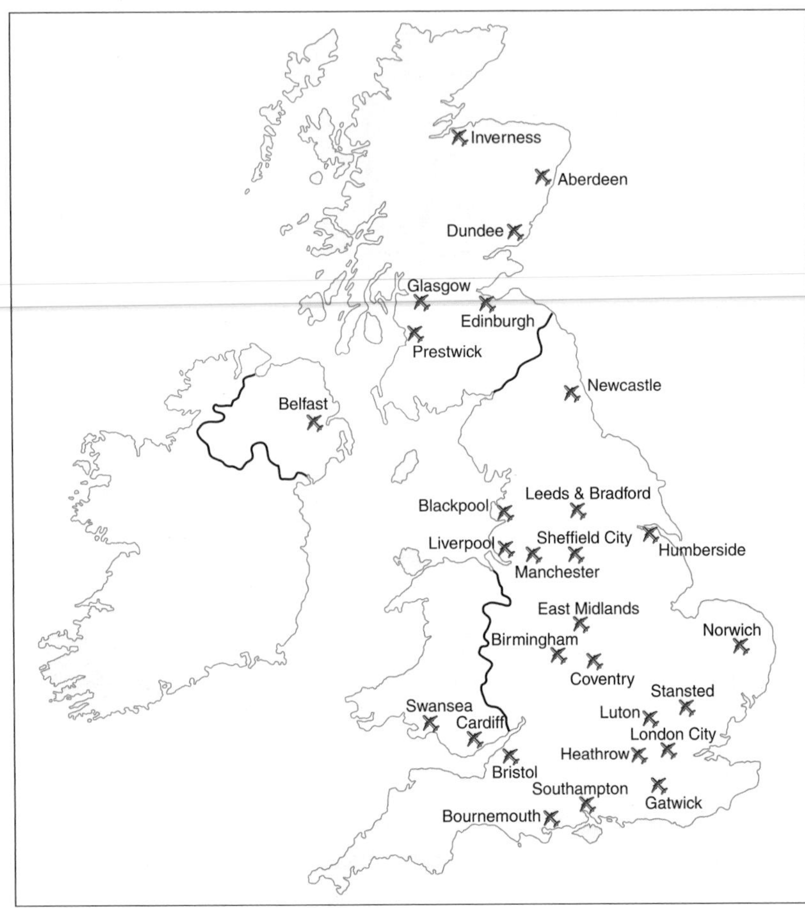

The UK's main national and international airports

- **Chartered flights.** This is where an airplane or helicopter is booked for a particular trip. These are used mainly by tour operators to transport customers to a holiday destination. The UK has a number of companies that specialise in chartered flights such as Air 2000.
- **Scheduled flights.** These are flights run to a schedule or timetable to destinations all over the world. The UK has a number of airlines providing scheduled flights, including British Airways and Virgin Atlantic.

Land transport

There is a wide range of land transport available. The main ones are covered below. There are also many other methods including taxis and hire bikes.

Trains

Trains were the first mass transportation system which could move people over long distances in a short period of time. Britain has a railway system that runs the length and breadth of the country and which connects to mainland Europe via the Channel tunnel.

Coaches

As with air transport, there are scheduled and chartered coach companies. The main provider of scheduled coaches in the UK is National Express, which runs a network of coaches from most major towns and cities, with local bus companies providing the same service on a local level. Most major towns also have chartered coach companies that provide coaches for hire to go to a destination of your choice.

Eurostar is the high-speed passenger train connecting Britain and the Continent

Hire cars

The other main form of land transport linked to travel and tourism is the hire car. Companies like Avis and Hertz offer tourists the chance to rent a car for the duration of their holiday.

Sea transport

The three main types of sea transport – ferry, hovercraft and catamaran – are operated by companies such as Sea France and P&O. They run scheduled sailings from UK ports around the coastline to other parts of the UK and to ports in mainland Europe. They are an important transport link.

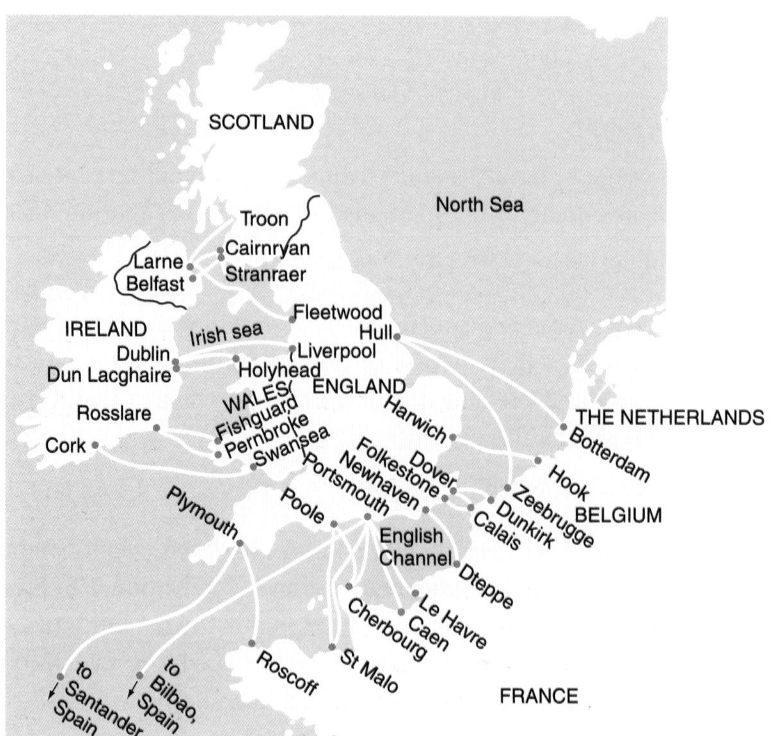

The UK's main ferry ports and routes

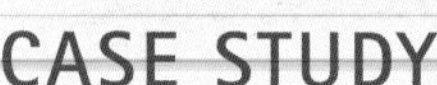

CASE STUDY

Heritage has a price

'I single to Stonehenge, over the plain and some . . . great hills . . . worth going this journey to see.' How to restore Samuel Pepys' view of Stonehenge has been discomfiting transport ministers for a generation, even though it is an uneven contest. On the one hand is Britain's equivalent of the Great Wall of China, one of the world's most important ancient monuments. On the other is one of the nation's most congested holiday routes, the A303 linking London and the south-west. This week, a public inquiry began into the latest scheme for a 2 km dual-carriageway tunnel which is the centrepiece of a much bigger project to whisk carloads of westward bound holidaymakers that little bit faster to their destinations while – far more importantly – finally freeing

Heritage has a price (Contd)

the awe-inspiring stones from the sight, the sound and the stink of bumper-to-bumper traffic.

It is more than 10 years since the government started trying to win public approval. Under sustained fire from a classy breed of protesters which did include English Heritage and still includes the National Trust, there has been retreat after retreat. First, a tunnel was conceded, then a longer one, finally a proper bored tunnel rather than the cut-and-cover option. Now the 12 km scheme will cost £200 million. Protesters still say this ancient landscape needs more protection. They insist the tunnel has to be a few hundred metres longer, to prevent traffic roaring into sunlight on a neolithic burial mound.

Stonehenge will only be a real victory if the highest possible standards are applied not only where the protesters come from the establishment, but wherever a new road is built.

Source: From the *Guardian*, 21 February 2004

There is currently a major debate about the impact of tourism on the local environment, with the building of a new terminal at Heathrow airport and the planned expansion of other UK airports, and increased pressure on the UK road network. These transport links are vital to the travel and tourism industry but the environment is as vital as the attraction.

In a group, discuss how these different pressures might be balanced.

Tour operators

Tour operators put together the services of the transport and accommodation providers to produce package holidays. They can also provide tailor-made holidays for their customers, but these tend to be expensive due to the time and effort involved. Internet tour operators like expedia.co.uk are reducing this cost through the use of computer software.

Travel agents

A travel agent sells the products of tour operators, accommodation and transport providers. They also provide a range of other travel products including help with visa applications, money exchange and travel insurance. Travel agents are regulated by a professional body called ABTA (Association of British Travel Agents).

The VisitBritain logo

Information providers

Information providers give information to travellers. Most towns will have a tourist information centre. These tend to be run by one of four national tourist boards – the Welsh, Northern Irish and Scottish tourist boards and VisitBritain, which is the national tourist board in England. VisitBritain is divided into six regional tourist boards. Tourist information centres not only give information about local visitor attractions, they will help tourists find accommodation and sell tickets to local events.

Organisation types

So far you have looked at the industry in terms of the functions it provides. Within each of these functions are a number of different types of organisation. These are discussed below.

KEY POINTS

Types of organisation:

- Sole trader
- Partnership
- Private limited company
- Public limited company
- Non-profit making.

Sole trader

A sole trader is a person who has started up a business on their own and has sole responsibility for the company. Sole traders tend to be small businesses. They are totally liable for their businesses and for any debt that the business may have.

Partnership

This is an organisation that has 2–20 partners who jointly own the business. Each partner is liable for the business and its debt. Partnerships tend to be small to medium-size companies. As more people are investing in the organisation, they tend to have more capital (money) invested in them.

Private limited company

Shareholders own a private limited company; a shareholder is someone who has purchased a share (part) of the company by investing money in the company. A private limited company has limited liability so that shareholders are not liable for any debts that the company has. A private limited company must register with Companies House in London and produce annual accounts. The 'private' refers to the fact that the shares are not floated on the stock exchange. The company will have 'Limited' after its name. The size of private limited companies can range from small to large organisations.

Public limited company

A public limited company (plc) also has limited liability. The difference between a private and a public limited company is that anyone can buy a share of a plc and the shares are traded on the stock exchange. Most large organisations in the private sector tend to be plc's. A plc has to follow strict financial reporting regulations.

Non-profit making organisation

Unlike the other types of organisation looked at above, these organisations do not try to make a profit for owners or shareholders. If a profit is made, this is reinvested into the organisation. Non-profit making organisations tend to have charitable status and most tend to be in the public sector, for example the National Trust.

The Youth Hostels Association is a non-profit making organisation

Sectors

All organisations in the UK can be divided into three main sectors:

- public
- private
- voluntary.

KEY POINTS

Sectors:

- Public
- Private
- Voluntary.

The public sector

The public sector is owned by the state. This sector is funded by grants paid for through local and national taxation. It includes state schools, hospitals, fire stations, etc. However, in the travel and tourism industry the only public sector organisations are concerned with promoting the UK aboard and information providing services, such as VisitBritain, or are a part of the national infrastructure, that is the road network.

The private sector

Most organisations in the travel and tourism industry fall into this sector. Private sector businesses are owned by individuals, either as sole traders, partnerships or limited companies. Their main aim is to make a profit to pay to the owners or shareholders who invested their money into the organisation. Examples in travel and tourism would include the airline Virgin Atlantic and the tour operator Thomas Cook. This sector is usually funded by loans, investments and government grants.

Voluntary sector

The voluntary sector is sometimes known as the charity sector. These organisations are non-profit making and aim to protect or help individuals or a particular site. Examples include the YMCA and the National Trust. Voluntary organisations tend to source their funds through donations and through membership. However, they might run commercial ventures on their site in order to increase the organisation's income, for example through the sale of gift items or a café.

Objectives

For an organisation to be successful it needs to have direction and a goal.

Mission statement

An organisation's overall goal is called a mission or vision statement (see Unit 3 Introduction to Customer Service in Travel and Tourism for more information on mission statements). This tends to be a general statement of the organisation's intent – what it aims to do. For example:

> *'Holidaybreak plc is the UK's leading operator of specialist holiday businesses. The companies within Holidaybreak retain a distinctive identity while sharing expertise and exploiting opportunities in areas of common interest. Holidaybreak's aim is to achieve continuing profitable growth by developing its existing businesses and market leading brands in the UK and European holiday markets and through acquisitions within the travel sector. (Holidaybreak plc)'*

Aims and objectives

From the mission statement the organisation knows what its general aim is. However, by itself, this is not enough. For the organisation to achieve its aim it needs to develop a set of SMART objectives – these will help to drive the organisation forward (see Unit 4 Introduction to Marketing in Travel and Tourism, page 134, for more information on SMART objectives).

Most organisations have three types of objectives:

- Short-term objectives tend to be set from a month to a year.
- Medium-term objectives tend to be set over a year to five years.
- Long-term objectives are any length of time over five years.

KEY POINTS

Objectives must be SMART:

- Specific
- Measurable
- Achievable
- Realistic
- Timed.

Level ✔

PRACTICE ASSESSMENT ACTIVITY

For this activity, you will research *two* different types of travel and tourism organisations. First, agree with your tutor the organisations you plan to look at.

P5.1 Describe two different types of travel and tourism organisation in terms of their objectives.

M5.1 Compare and contrast two different organisations in terms of their objectives.

In summary

- The key components of travel and tourism are: travel agents, tour operators, information providers, transport providers and accommodation providers.
- Types of organisations in travel and tourism are: sole traders, partnerships, private limited companies, public limited companies and non-profit making organisations.
- There are three business sectors: public, private and voluntary.
- Organisations set goals, called objectives, which give the business direction and help them to achieve their plans.

5.2 Administrative and financial functions and systems

All organisations have to carry out a number of different functions to be competitive and successful.

KEY POINTS

Key business functions:

- Management information
- Customer service information
- Performance targets
- Administrative systems
- Financial systems.

Management information

All management decisions have a level of risk involved. However, the level of risk can be reduced if a more informed decision is made. This makes management information vital to the success of the business. With computer systems, the amount of information that managers have to help them make decisions gives them a better control over the success of the business and informs them of problems early on. The more relevant information that managers have, the more informed decisions they will be able to make (see below for the systems available to help this function).

Customer service information

Customers are the lifeblood of any business. Unit 3 Introduction to Customer Service in Travel and Tourism looked at the importance of customer service and customer service techniques. However, without accurate and up-to-date customer service information, it is difficult to provide good customer service. In service industries like travel and tourism, customer service is a vital part of the product that the customer is paying for.

Performance targets

All organisations, regardless of sector, have targets to meet. These include performance or financial targets. Monitoring performance is a vital function

Customer service information must be accurate and up to date

of any business. Most organisations work within a budget, a budget being a projection of futures sales and expenses. Most organisations set annual budgets to control costs and to set sales targets. These can be broken down into monthly, weekly or even daily targets. This function helps monitor business success over the short term and, if communicated to staff correctly, helps motivate. Targets help an organisation move in the direction that management has decided upon.

Bonus payments to staff

Many travel and tourism organisations offer staff bonus payments. These are designed not only to motivate staff but also to reward them for their hard work and to help staff share in the success of the organisation.

Performance-related pay

This is where an element of the staff pay depends on their performance. Performance-related pay aims to motivate staff to perform. However, staff in the travel and tourism industry tend to work as part of a team so the performance of an individual often depends on others who work with them. It can also be difficult to assess the level of performance in some job roles.

Commissions

This form of bonus payment is widely used in travel and tourism. In some organisations holiday representatives and travel agents can earn commissions for selling excursions and trips to a customer. This is done to encourage staff to sell.

Christmas bonuses

Many organisations in travel and tourism reward staff with some sort of Christmas bonus. This might be in the form of a party, present or even financial reward. It is a tradition in the hospitality sector for staff who work on Christmas day to be served Christmas dinner by the management.

KEY POINTS

Rewards can help motivate staff to achieve targets.

Price alterations

Travel and tourism products are perishable products, rather like a pre-packed sandwich. They have a sell-by date. You cannot sell a seat on an aircraft after the aircraft has taken off! A hotel room left empty last night is a lost sale. Demand for travel and tourism products is not the same all year round.

ACTIVITY

1 Look through a holiday brochure and choose a holiday to a resort you would like to visit.
2 On graph paper plot the different prices of the holiday from month to month (months on the *x* axis and price on the *y* axis).
3 When the price is highest, the demand for the holiday is highest. Why do you think that peak demand happens? When is it?

Keep this safe – it could be used as evidence for Application of Number.

Administrative systems

A travel and tourism organisation may have thousands of customers a year. To make sure that every customer receives what they want and pay for, the organisation needs to make sure it has well-designed and structured administrative systems. Let's now look at some of the administrative functions and some of the systems that are currently in use in the industry.

KEY POINTS

Administration is required to maintain the smooth running of an organisation.

Customer enquiries

Every customer enquiry is a potential booking of the organisation's product and service. It is important for the organisation to record every enquiry as it can be followed up to try to convert the enquiry into a sale. To this end, the organisation needs to record some customer details. This can be done either on a standardised form or on a computer database.

ACTIVITY

Design a standardised customer enquiry form for a travel agency. Consider what information you will need to help you follow up the enquiry. Compare your form with others in your group.

Bookings and reservations

When a customer books a product or service, this information also needs to be recorded. You will need to record not only the customer's personal information (name, address, phone number, etc.) but also the details of the product that the customer has booked (product details, cost, special requirements, etc.). You should also inform the customer of the organisation's cancellation policy and record any deposit that has been paid. A copy of this information needs to be given to the customer so that they know what they have paid for and to give them peace of mind.

Manual and computerised systems

Every organisation has its own way of managing its administration. The method it uses is called the administration system.

Manual systems

Thirty years ago all organisations used manual systems. A manual system means that the whole of the booking process is done on paper. These days only small businesses use manual systems. This is mainly due to the growth in power of computers and also the way that the cost of computer systems has fallen over time. Examples of manual systems still in use today:

- The density chart is designed to map occupancy and is used by a number of hotels for their room bookings. The system is quite time consuming and takes up a lot of space, which is why it has largely been superseded by computerised systems.
- A booking diary records bookings on a day-by-day basis and is used mainly by smaller hotels, restaurants and organisations that have limited numbers of bookings each day such as charter coach companies. Each booking is recorded in the diary, rather like a density chart but on a smaller scale.

Computerised systems

Travel and tourism uses a large number of computerised systems. These have aided the administration of organisations but have also increased the range of products available to customers.

Computerised reservation systems (CRS) such as Worldspan, Galileo and Amadeus are used to book hotels, flights and other tourism products. They enable a local travel agent to book a seat on any flight on the system anywhere in the world. Hotel groups also use CRS to manage room bookings. Best Western Hotels uses a system called Hornet which books rooms in any Best Western hotel worldwide. These systems have not only helped in managing bookings and occupancy but also can be used to maximise income.

The main advantages of computerised systems compared to manual systems are as follows:

- Data retrieval is much quicker.
- Less space is required to store information.
- Information can be sent to service providers quicker and more cheaply.
- They produce more accurate management information.
- Information can be filed in many different fields rather than just the one offered by a manual system.

However, there can be concerns about computer viruses and security of data.

Processing data

Although there is a huge range of software available to fulfil the administrative functions, it largely divides into two main categories or a combination of both.

Databases

A database is a computerised filing system. Unlike a file, a database can be rearranged so that the information can be found in a variety of ways. Databases have some important advantages for an organisation. The information can be used to inform customers of special offers and products that they might be interested in. They can also be used to retrieve customer information to help with customer service situations.

Spreadsheets

These are used to give a picture of occupancy similar to a density chart. The difference is that a computerised spreadsheet will be able to update itself and each booking will automatically update the spreadsheet. This means that the organisation always has a real-time image of the current state of bookings.

Financial systems

Recording

All businesses have a legal obligation to keep some sort of financial records as they have a responsibility to pay tax. However, without keeping accurate accounts it is hard for a business to keep control of all the money flowing through the business. A plc must publish annual accounts. Keeping a number of accounts books, known as ledgers, usually does this (the ledgers might be computerised). These accounts are a summary of the trading profit or loss of the organisation and also a record of the company's assets. Assets are what belongs to or is owed to the company. This includes buildings, stock, etc.

KEY POINTS

Financial records are needed to control assets and funds and also for legal reasons such as paying taxes.

Invoicing

Invoices are sent out with every item that is purchased on credit. Credit is where a company lets you have goods to be paid for later. At the end of each month a final statement will be sent to the company that has received the goods. This final statement will contain a list of all the invoices sent out that month and a final balance that needs to be paid. The final statement will also include a copy of the terms and conditions of payment. This is commonly within 30 days of the final statement.

Payment processing

Credits/refunds

Not all goods will reach the customer in perfect condition. For example, a wine merchant might deliver a large number of bottles of wine to a hotel. When the hotel checks the delivery one of the bottles is damaged. After the hotel has informed the wine merchant that the goods are damaged, the wine merchant sends the hotel a credit note. As a purchaser of goods, a credit note means that the final statement value will be reduced by the amount that the account has been credited.

Payment security

All forms of payment must be secure. This is not only for the company's benefit but also for its suppliers and customers. The security of each method of payment is looked at later in this unit.

There are four main ways to make a manual payment:

- cash
- cheque
- postal order
- banker's draft.

Cash

Cash transactions are a secure form of transaction. However, there are risks involved in having large amounts of cash on a company's premises, leading to the expense of installing a safe or strong room on site. There is also the issue of fake currency, but notes can be checked with the use of ultraviolet detection systems or detection pens.

Cheques

A cheque is a promissory note that either an individual or an organisation writes. A cheque cannot be transferred but can be paid into a bank account like cash. Cheques from individuals should always be accompanied by a cheque guarantee card. This is a plastic card that validates a cheque up to the value stated on the card. Banks can be contacted during working hours to validate cheques of higher amounts.

A cheque and cheque guarantee card

Postal orders

A postal order is similar to a cheque but unlike a cheque, it is purchased from a post office and is valued for the face amount. Postal orders are mainly used for small amounts to be sent through the post. There is a cost involved in the purchasing of a postal order. However, this is more secure than sending cash through the postal system.

COUNTERFOIL £50
TO BE DETACHED AND KEPT BY THE SENDER
FIFTY POUNDS
SEE OVER FOR CONDITIONS OF USE
POSTAL ORDER
PLEASE PAY
THOMAS COOK TRAVEL LTD.
FIFTY POUNDS
RECEIVED/SIGNATURE
£50
NOT NEGOTIABLE
POSTAGE STAMPS
ISSUING OFFICE DATE STAMP
PAYING OFFICE DATE STAMP
06. MY 05
Post Office
DO NOT WRITE OR MARK BELOW THIS LINE
5466 192993
5466 192993

A postal order

Banker's draft

A banker's draft is similar to a cheque but is written and guaranteed by the bank, the amount being on the face of the draft. Banker's drafts can be transferred like cash. They tend to be used for large amounts of money when for security reasons you do not want to carry the amount in cash.

KEY POINTS

Manual methods of payment:

- Cash
- Cheques
- Postal orders
- Banker's draft.

Computerised payment systems

The growing need for security, the growth of the Internet and increased access to credit and debit cards mean that computerised payment systems account for the largest amount of transactions. Below are some of the different methods that you might come across.

PDQ 'swipe' machines

Today, 95 per cent of electronic purchases are made by credit card. A PDQ 'swipe' machine is used to record credit and debit card transactions. It is connected directly to the financial provider through a telephone line. This has been an area of major fraud; the change to 'chip and PIN' cards should help reduce this.

A PDQ 'swipe' machine records credit and debit card transactions

Payment service provider (PSP)

This is an Internet version of a PDQ machine. It collects payments on the Internet from orders on a website. A PSP might take payments in several currencies. There are also companies that run PSP as a service for organisations to use – these are called payment bureaux and are similar to a bureau de change at an airport.

BACS

BACS is used for business-to-business transactions and is a popular system for companies that make a large number of transactions each day. It involves the electronic wiring of payment from one bank account to another.

KEY POINTS

Electronic methods of payment:

- PDQ (credit and debit cards)
- Payment service provider
- Payment bureaux
- BACS.

CASE STUDY

Castle Cars Taxi Company

Simon Foster has run his taxi company for the past 20 years in the town of Oldcastle. He started the company as a single-person operation and has developed it so that he now runs up to six cars on a busy evening. Most of his business during the week comes from corporate customers who have accounts with Castle Cars.

In the evening most customers pay in cash as Castle Cars does not have other payment facilities. Simon is keen to look into different methods of payment to help him run his business more efficiently. He is particularly concerned to reduce the amount of cash sales as he feels that his drivers are at risk from attack if they are carrying a lot of money on them.

He is also interested in any payment methods that can help speed up his account customers' payments as he finds receiving cheques through the post and banking them very time consuming.

Simon knows that you are studying travel and tourism and has asked you for advice on the different methods of payment that he could utilise in his business. Write a report outlining each method and their advantages/disadvantages.

Data processing

Financial systems have benefited from data processing. It has led to huge increases in the speed that financial data can be changed into useful financial information. This aids management decision-making and also accounting.

Spreadsheet

Spreadsheets are a popular tool for processing accounting data. They can be used to present accounts in a useable way and are capable of performing thousands of calculations correctly. They can also be used to generate graphs, charts and diagrams to show trends and changes in the organisation's financial data.

Databases

The use of databases has helped improved financial reporting by speeding up the recording, payment and billing processes and ensuring a greater level of accuracy. Databases have also assisted the cost and debt control functions.

ACTIVITY

Using the information on manual and electronic methods of payment given above, produce a chart like the one below and describe the advantages and disadvantages of each method.

Payment method	Advantages	Disadvantages
Manual systems		
Cash		
Cheques		
Postal orders		
Banker's draft		
Electronic systems		
PDQ machines		
Payment service provider (PSP)		
Payment bureaux		
BACS		

Level

PRACTICE ASSESSMENT ACTIVITY

P5.2 Describe the administrative and financial functions and systems of the two travel and tourism organisations you looked at earlier.

D5.1 Assess how the administrative and financial functions and systems of a travel and tourism business contribute to meeting its objectives.

In summary

- To achieve its objectives, an organisation is divided into functions.
- Each function is responsible for a number of systems, which enables the business to work efficiently and effectively and to meet the needs of its customers, employees, legal requirements, etc.
- These systems can be either manual or computerised.

5.3 Administration and financial documentation

CASE STUDY

Tracy's beach chairs

Tracy Ely started up the Big Bournemouth Beach Chair Company, renting out chairs to the public on the beach at Bournemouth where she lives. Her business is doing really well and during the summer months Tracy can hardly keep up with the demand for her chairs.

However, she has become concerned about the administrative and financial side of the business. She was never very interested in maths at school and finds paperwork boring.

Tracy has asked you for help knowing that you are studying travel and tourism. Draw up a two-column table using the headings 'Problems due to poor administration' and 'Problems due to poor accounting'. List all the issues you think might arise as a result of Tracy's poor administration and accounting. Your aim is to show Tracy the importance of keeping records!

At the end of this section look back at your table and add any more problems that you may have come up with.

Administrative documentation

Documentation is crucial to the successful running of an organisation as it helps to prevent fraud, maintain a high standard of service and aids the smooth running of the operation. With the use of modern computer systems administrative functions are far more effective than they used to be. Below is a flow chart of the sale and purchase of an item between two companies, for example a tour operator and a travel agent, and the flow of documentation.

The diagram on page 190 shows the purchase cycle which begins when Company A orders stock from Company B using a purchase order. Company B sends the stock to Company A with a delivery note. Company A and Company B send copies of the purchase order and the delivery note to their accounts departments. Company B sends an invoice and statement to Company A. Company A then sends payment to Company B and informs the purchasing department of Company A that this has been done.

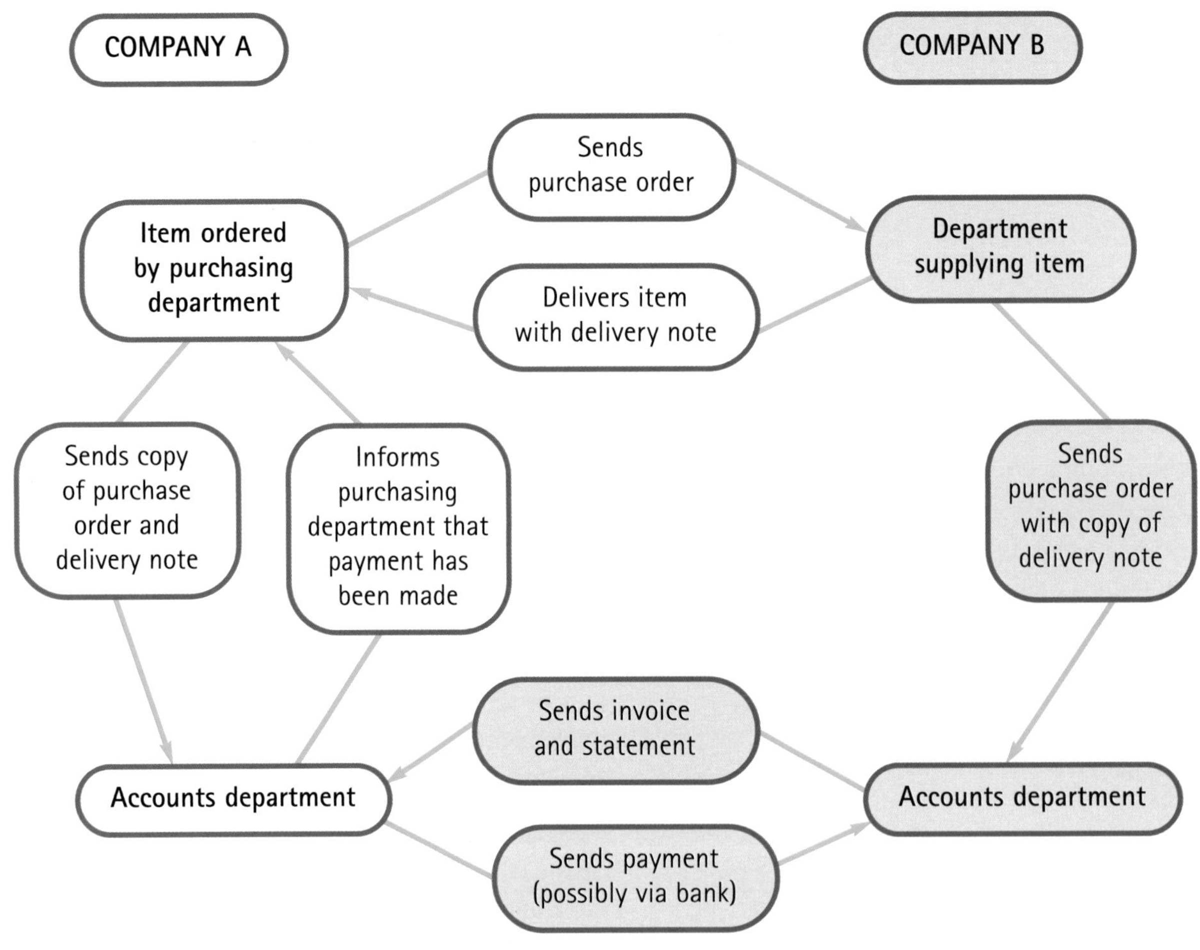

The purchase cycle

KEY POINTS

The purchase cycle is a step-by-step process used to buy stock from suppliers.

Purchase orders

A purchase order is a document which is used to order stock or items from either another department in a company or an outside company. Today, these tend to be computer generated and can be sent by email, fax or post. Orders may also be made over the phone.

Delivery note

This is the note that accompanies any incoming goods from another department or company. It will usually include an inventory of the goods and a record of who sent the order.

The goods should be checked against this note to make sure that the delivery is correct and not damaged. The delivery note, in turn, should

PURCHASE ORDER

Lazyfly Holidays Ltd
6 Market Square
Guildford
Surrey
GU31 1ED

Tel: 01483 1234567
email: lazyflyhols@isp.co.uk

VAT REG GB 0745 8485 56

Purchase order no:

Date:

To:

Product code	Quantity	Description

Authorised Signature . . . .

Date . . . .

DELIVERY NOTE

www.Doggyflights.com
Tel: 01876 9876543
VAT REG GB 0678 9876 54

Delivery note no:
Delivery method:
Your order code:
Date:

To:

Product code	Quantity	Description

Received:

Signature . . . .

Name (in capitals) . . . .

Date . . . .

KEY POINTS

Delivered stock should be checked off against the delivery note to make sure that what was ordered has been delivered.

be checked against the purchase order to make sure that the right goods were ordered and delivered.

After this, the delivery note should be recorded in the delivery log and sent to the accounts department to be checked against the invoice.

Goods received note

The department which has received the goods will produce a goods received note, copies of which are sent to the buyer, accounts department and stock room.

GOODS RECEIVED NOTE

Lazyfly Holidays Ltd
6 Market Square
Guildford
Surrey
GU31 1ED

Tel: 01483 1234567
email: lazyflyhols@isp.co.uk

VAT REG GB 0745 8485 56

Supplier: Date:

Order Number	Quantity	Description

Carrier: Consignment no:

Received by: Checked by:

Condition of goods: good/damaged/shortages (circle)

Copies to:

Buyer ☐ Accounts ☐ Stock room ☐

Invoice

The invoice is posted to the company which received the goods. This should be checked off against the delivery note. At this point, any defects should be reported. Prices and amounts should be checked on the invoice. Invoices are recorded and stored to be checked against monthly accounts.

INVOICE

www.Doggyflights.com
Tel: 01876 9876543

VAT REG GB 0678 9876 54

Invoice no:

Account:

Your reference:

Date:

Invoice to	Deliver to

Product code	Description	Quantity	Price	Unit	Total	Discount (%)	Net

Goods total	
Cash discount	
Subtotal	
VAT	
Grand total	

Terms

Net monthly

Carriage paid

Banking

Today, most banking is carried out electronically. However, in some travel and tourism organisations there are still many cash transactions. These cash transactions should be kept in a safe and later deposited into a bank. Cash transactions need to be recorded, as the records will be needed later to check against the bank statement.

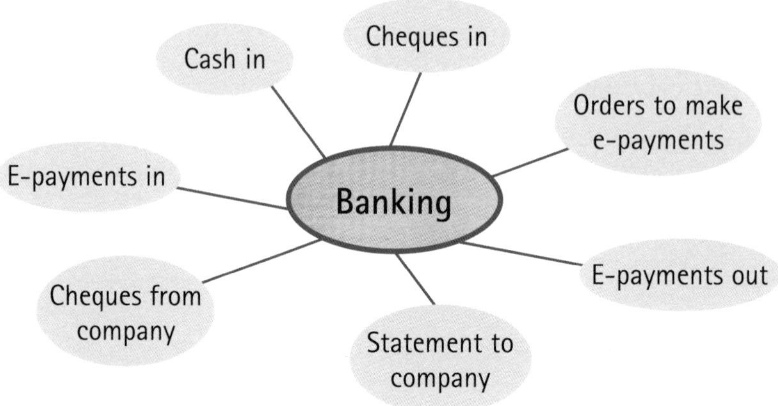

The different aspects of business banking

Chequebooks

Cheques are used to make small to medium-size, one-off payments. They are sometimes still used to pay wages. Once written, cheques must be signed by a named signature. Private cheques should be accompanied with a check guarantee card.

All written cheques have to be recorded in the chequebook with the amount, who the cheque was made payable to and for what. This information is very important as it will be checked later against the bank statement.

KEY POINTS

The bank statement needs to be checked to make sure that all money going in and out of the account is recorded and authorised.

Statements

At the end of each month the business will receive and send out a number of statements.

Bank statement

Once a month the business will receive a bank statement, which is a list of all the bank transactions it carried out in the last trading period.
The statement will show each individual transaction, identify its type, the

amount of the transaction and also the date of each transaction. The business will keep the statement as part of its records.

Supplier's statement

The business's suppliers will each send it a monthly statement. This is a statement of the business's account with them. It will include an opening balance – how much the business owed them at the beginning of the month – and list all the payments made and goods ordered during the month. It will also include a statement of how much the business is expected to pay off the account and by what date. This also forms part of the business's records.

STATEMENT OF ACCOUNT

www.Doggyflights.com

Tel 01876 9876543

VAT REG GB 0678 9876 54

Account no:

Date:

To:

Date	Details	Debit	Credit	Balance
		Amount now due		

Statement sent to customers

At the end of each month the business will send a statement to all its credit customers (people or businesses who owe it money for goods or services). This is a statement of their account and a reminder of payment terms. It will state their opening balance (how much the customers owed at the beginning of the month) and might include their credit limit with the company if they had one. It will also include all the invoice numbers of all the goods that they have purchased and a list of any credit notes issued.

Reconciliation of statements

This is the final important step in the monthly statement process. Reconciliation involves checking that everything balances. To reconcile its records the business will compare its accounts with the bank statement and its suppliers and customers accounts to make sure they agree. The diagrams below show which records are checked against each other for two of the statements you have just looked at.

BANK STATEMENT	*is checked against*:	Chequebook
		Banking (cash, etc. paid in)
		Standing orders (in and out)
		Closing balance from last month
		E-commerce

Bank statement reconciliation

SUPPLIER'S STATEMENT	*is checked against*:	Purchase order sent Invoice received
		Credit notes received
		Last month's statment Closing balance from last month
		Payments made

Supplier's statement reconciliation

P5.3 Complete simple administration and financial documentation. This activity involves practical skills – your tutor will explain what you need to do. It can be carried out through role-plays, interactive task days, simulations, presentations or even during work experience (if organised).

ACTIVITY

Tim runs a travel agency, Lazyfly Holidays Ltd. It specialises in top quality relaxing holidays. His supplier of flights is www.Doggyflights.com.

1 Tim orders a flight from Glasgow Airport to Paris Charles de Gaulle on 30 April. He will be travelling by GoFaster Airlines. The ticket is economy class and excludes VAT. The flight number is GF1011. What documents will be used during the purchase procedure? Explain the reason for each.
2 Fill in the forms required to complete this purchase.
3 What would be the advantages and disadvantages of using a spreadsheet program to generate these documents?
4 What would be the effect of an error in the information in these documents?
5 How would you check for errors in these documents?

In summary

An organisation must keep records of all its transactions. This enables it to control finances and to maintain the smooth running of the organisation. All records need to be checked against other records.

5.4 Health, safety and security

Legislation

Legislation refers to the laws passed by Parliament to govern the country. Working in the travel and tourism industry, you will need to be aware of health, safety and security at work legislation.

Health and Safety at Work Act (1974)

The Health and Safety at Work Act and its amendments are the basis of health and safety regulations in England and Wales. The Act states that both employers and employees are responsible for health and safety. However, it is the employer's responsibility to keep the building safe and adjust working practices wherever reasonable. This includes using safety guards, but also training to use specialist equipment, as well as health and safety training in some specialist areas.

The Act also identifies the need to carry out risk assessments when carrying out activities and when using equipment (see below).

KEY POINTS

Health and safety at work is the responsibility of everyone.

Children Act (1989)

This Act gives all children under the age of 18 years rights regarding length of working hours and conditions in which they are allowed to work. It also states the length of time that children are allowed to work in the evening.

Health and Safety (First Aid) Regulations (1981)

These regulations state that health and safety risk assessments must be carried out before a new item of equipment is used. Risk assessments should be reviewed regularly.

It also covers the provision of staff trained in first aid and provision of first aid kits.

Control of Substances Hazardous to Health (COSHH) Regulations (1999)

Using chemicals or other dangerous substances at work can put people's health at risk, so the Control of Substances Hazardous to Health regulations are designed to ensure the safe use and storage of chemicals and other hazardous substances. They include the following provisions:

- All chemicals must be stored in clean, clearly marked, labelled and sealed bottles.
- Chemicals should be locked away from the public.
- Chemicals should not be mixed unless they are specifically designed to do so.
- Safety equipment must be worn when using chemicals.
- Staff must be trained before being allowed to use chemicals.

Workplace (Health, Safety and Welfare) Regulations (1992)

This is a comprehensive piece of legislation that covers the conditions in which an employee can expect to work, including:

- lighting
- room temperature
- ventilation
- washing facilities
- eating and rest areas.

PRACTICE ASSESSMENT ACTIVITY

Level

P5.4 Describe the health, safety and security legislation with which organisations have to comply.

D5.2 Analyse the implications of failing to deal appropriately with health, safety and security issues.

How safe do you think it would be to work in this travel agency? How many hazards can you spot?

Documentation

To make sure that every organisation abides by health and safety legislation, there are two government bodies responsible for inspecting work places: the Health & Safety Executive (HSE) and environmental health officers (EHOs). EHOs are largely responsible for food production areas and service industries whereas the HSE is concerned more with manufacturing and heavy industry, construction, etc. However, the HSE may also be involved when accidents of any type occur.

Audit records

These are records kept by an organisation for health and safety audits. They include:

- the time of fire systems checks
- any health and safety incidents
- how and where the incidents were dealt with
- location of first aid boxes
- dates when first aid boxes were checked and replenished
- dates of fire extinguisher checks.

Records also need to be kept of:

- compliance testing of all electrical equipment
- the health and safety training of staff, including dates of health and safety training sessions
- staff fire safety training
- staff induction.

These audit records can and will be checked by the HSE or EHO when they make inspection visits. It is also a term of most insurance policies that the organisation maintains up-to-date audit records.

Risk assessments

Risks – the likelihood whether something is going to happen – have to be assessed. Without a standard form, you would find it difficult to evaluate the risk in a sensible order. When your school or college goes on a trip your tutor will carry out a risk assessment. This is a form where they will write down all the risks that they can see that are likely to be involved in the running of the trip. These risks will then be assessed for:

- the likelihood of the risk happening
- the likely seriousness of an accident
- the prevention methods in place
- the likely number of people getting hurt for each risk.

KEY POINTS

A risk assessment must be carried out before an activity.

Risk assessment forms

To reduce the risk of accidents and also to simplify the reporting of risks and their assessment, most organisations use a standard risk assessment form. This form has been designed so that the person either assessing the item or event can take into account every risk involved.

It is best to complete a risk assessment form as if you were taking a journey and you highlight every possible risk that you meet along the way. Most large organisations will already have produced a risk assessment of their site, for example.

ACTIVITY

1 Using the Internet, search for copies of risk assessments undertaken by well-known visitor attractions.
2 Use these risk assessments to help you design your own risk assessment form.
3 Before you next go on a trip with your school or college, try assessing the risk involved. Compare your risk assessment with your tutor's risk assessment.

Level

PRACTICE ASSESSMENT ACTIVITY

P5.5 Devise a simple risk assessment form for use within travel and tourism working environments.

High-risk activity

Some activities that you may do are high risk. This means that there is a likelihood of either yourself or someone else getting injured, possibly seriously. If you still decide to run a high-risk activity, you need to inform those involved. You might also need to make sure that special precautions are taken before the event. For example, at motorbike races ambulances are available on site in case an accident happens.

RISK ASSESSMENT FORM

Each assessment must take into account and record any specific hazards arising from the activity or a particular site, before the assessment is complete.

	Manager:	
Activity/workplace assessed:	Assessor:	Assessment date:

HAZARD potential for harm	Will affect	PRECAUTIONS/CONTROLS already in place to remove hazard, reduce risk level	RISK (with controls)			✔ Additional controls needed. Details over
			L	S	R	

The three columns (L, S, R) are for assessing the level or degree of risk. The first (L) is for an assessment of the likelihood of the hazard taking place, the second (S) for the severity of the hazard, both based on the following:

(L) LIKELIHOOD

1 Hazard exists very infrequently; limited numbers exposed
2 Likely to occur; hazard exists intermittently or occurs occasionally
3 Likely to occur soon; permanent hazard or occurs daily/repeatedly; many may be exposed

(S) SEVERITY OF HAZARD

1 Could cause minor injury only
2 Could cause major injury/3 days or more absence
3 Could cause fatality/severe injury

(R) RISK LEVEL is product of Likelihood and Severity (L × S)

Very high risks score 6 or 9
Moderate risks score 3 or 4
Low priority risks score 1 or 2

VERY HIGH RISKS NEED IMMEDIATE ACTION

Source: Guildford College of Further and Higher Education

In some cases you will decide that the trip or event should not take place due to the risk involved. If an organisation runs an event, then it has a duty of care to the customers at that event.

Vulnerable people

Some people are more vulnerable than others – the old, young, people with disabilities, pregnant women, etc. These vulnerabilities need to be considered when organising an activity and also as part of the risk assessment. For special cases you might need to do a separate risk assessment for the vulnerable person. This is called a vulnerable person's risk assessment and will cover the individual's needs. It is not intended to be discriminatory but is designed to highlight the risks involved so that a vulnerable person can be included.

However, there may be activities that are just not suited for everyone. If this is the case, you will need to explain carefully and discreetly to the person concerned that it is not safe for them to carry out the activity.

Over to you!

Health and safety issues are not a reason to discriminate against people with disabilities. The law does expect reasonable adjustments to be made for them, with regards to modifying equipment, activities and even buildings.

KEY POINTS

All accidents must be reported:

- to prevent a more serious incident happening
- in case someone has hurt themselves and it only comes to light later.

Accident report forms

Whenever there is an accident at work, it must be reported, even if no one appears to be hurt. After all, a near miss this time does not mean that next time it will be a near miss. Remember, it is everyone's responsibility to report accidents. Accident reporting is vital for a number of reasons:

- To make sure that the person who has had an accident gets the right treatment, and after treatment the accident is followed up to evaluate if the risk could be reduced.
- To highlight high-risk activities so that risk can be managed and reduced, or staff can be trained better, or the risk can be managed in a more appropriate way. Another option is to change or modify machinery or use a different process.
- To help record best working practices so that these can be shared with other departments and companies, making a safer working environment.
- To help provide the right medical support should the accident happen again.

ACCIDENT REPORT FORM

This form must be completed in all cases of accident, injury or dangerous occurrence.

Name of person reporting incident: ______________________

Position in organisation: ______________________

Name of injured person: ______________________

Date of birth: __________

Position in organisation: ______________________

Date and time of accident: ______________________

Details of injury/accident:

Activity at time of injury/accident:

Place of injury/accident:

Details of injury/accident:

First aid treatment (if any) given:

Was the injured person taken to hospital? If so, where?

Name(s) and position(s) of person(s) present when the accident occurred:

Signature of person reporting incident: ______________________

Date: __________

Accident report form

ACTIVITY

Try planning your own accident report form. This is a document that could be used to follow up an incident so you will need to make sure that your design gives enough information.

Roles and responsibilities

Although the safety of the activity is the responsibility of the organiser, it is also the responsibility of everyone involved in the event. This is in keeping with the Health and Safety at Work Act (1974) discussed earlier.

Legal requirements

Not only can an organisation be fined for being in breach of health and safety regulations but it can also be forced to stop operations until the problem is solved or, in the case of an accident, until the investigation is complete. In the most extreme cases, the management of the organisation can be tried for corporate manslaughter. For example, Network Rail and Balfour Beatty were charged with corporate manslaughter over the Hatfield rail crash of October 2000.

CASE STUDY

Daniella's bungee jump

'At the age of 21, I went on holiday with friends to South America. My dad nagged me to buy travel insurance, which I did, but I didn't bother with "extreme sports" cover because I wasn't planning to do any.

Right at the end of the holiday I had the chance to do a bungee jump. I just thought, "Great, let's do it!". Afterwards I felt very sick and dizzy. My friends got really scared and took me to the hospital where a scan showed that my brain had swollen due to the pressure.

The hospital treated me and then said I would need to rest for a few days and mustn't travel, which meant I had to delay my flight home. I had to buy another plane ticket – my original ticket wasn't transferable – which cost me around £700. I wish now I had taken out extra travel insurance to cover extreme sports.'

A number of travel agents have made it their policy that passengers must show proof of travel insurance before boarding the flight.

Do you think this policy is a good thing? Discuss this in your group.

Policies and procedures

Some policies and procedures that need to be followed have been discussed above, including:

- keeping all auditable records up to date
- recording and reporting accidents

- the organisation and recording of risk assessments on both equipment and activities
- ensuring the availability of first aid equipment and staff first aid training.

Organisations should always have a disaster policy. In the travel and tourism industry there have been a number of disasters, both natural and man-made. An organised and managed disaster recovery plan which involves the rescue services – police, fire services, coastal rescue and ambulance – can save lives in the event of a major incident such as an air crash or ferry disaster.

The Zeebrugge disaster

In March 1987, a British-owned car ferry, the *Herald of Free Enterprise*, sank off the coast of Belgium. The ferry's car loading doors were left open when the ferry set sail, and water flooded the car decks. More than 190 people died in the Zeebrugge disaster, as it came to be known.

The article below describes the findings of the coroner's inquest to the disaster:

'A coroner's inquest jury into the capsizing of the *Herald of Free Enterprise* has returned verdicts of unlawful killing. The outcome into the ferry disaster has now opened the possibility of a criminal prosecution by the Director of Public Prosecutions (DPP).

In summing up, the coroner said the verdicts could be returned only if the jury believed a criminal act had been committed and that there had been gross negligence.

The coroner had stressed that the purpose of the inquest was to establish facts not blame, but insisted only the actions of three crewmen could have led to the deaths.

But many of the victims' families have made it clear they wish to see the Townsend-Thoresen company directors (now part of P&O) face prosecution, and not individual employees.

After a public inquiry into the disaster, Lord Justice Sheen published a report which identified a "disease of sloppiness", and negligence at every level of the company's hierarchy.

The Transport Secretary said no one was immune from prosecution but that any decision was the DPP's alone. And in a judicial review, the Divisional Court judged future prosecutions for corporate manslaughter might be feasible.'

Source: From 'On this day 8 October – 1987: Zeebrugge disaster was no accident', http//news.bbc.co.uk/onthisday

In your group, discuss the importance of health and safety policies and procedures.

Comfort of employees and customers

There is another important reason for ensuring the health and safety of customers and employees – their comfort and security. In a service sector industry an organisation is only as successful as its last trip or event – the safety and comfort of customers and employees contribute greatly to that success.

KEY POINTS

The happier the staff are at work, the better service they will give the customer.

PRACTICE ASSESSMENT ACTIVITY

Level ✔

M5.2 For this activity, you need to research at least one travel and tourism organisation. First, agree with your tutor the organisation you plan to look at.

Explain the roles of the employee and employer in ensuring the health, safety and security of self, colleagues and customers within *one* specified organisation.

M5.3 Using the risk assessment that you devised earlier, complete the risk assessment for *two* different travel and tourism working environments. (This does not need to be two different organisations. It could be two different environments in the same organisation, for example a reception area in a hotel and a hotel bedroom).

In summary

- Health and safety is the responsibility of everyone within an organisation.
- The organisation is responsible for health and safety policies and procedures: to reduce the risk of incidents and in the event of an incident, how to respond.
- Risk assessments need to be carried out on all activities and equipment to assess safety and to identify training needs and safety requirements.
- Accidents must be recorded.

TEST YOUR KNOWLEDGE

1. Name the five main components that make up the travel and tourism industry.
2. Name three types of organisation, other than a sole trader, that you might be involved in.
3. What are the three different funding sectors that all organisations can be divided into?
4. Name the funding sources of each of the three sectors.
5. What are each of the SMART objectives?
6. What is a mission statement?
7. Why do organisations have objectives?
8. Give three functions of administrative and financial systems.
9. Give two examples of administrative systems.
10. Why do organisations keep financial records?
11. What are the benefits of a computerised system for recording either financial or administrative functions?
12. What is the purpose of a risk assessment?
13. Who is responsible for health and safety in the workplace (under the Health and Safety at Work Act, 1974)?
14. Why is it important to have health and safety policies and procedures?

Unit 6 Organising a Travel and Tourism Event

Introduction

Now it's time for you to plan, run and evaluate an actual travel and tourism event. This unit will take you through the stages of objective setting, planning, running and evaluating the event, and will enable you to practise the skills and techniques described. You will discover a lot about event management and yourself – what particularly interested you, what your strengths are, what skills you learned and what you can do to tackle your weaknesses.

This unit is a practical one. You will be working on a live project. You will work individually and as a member of a team. Part of the assessment is based upon an evaluation of the event, of the team and of the individual team members, including you. As there will be a lot of activity over several weeks, it is vital that each team member keeps a personal diary/log, recording events, problems, strengths and weaknesses of the project, the team and the individuals, including you. This diary should be completed throughout the study of this unit. Allocate a few minutes at the end of each session to record your thoughts.

Throughout this unit you will read about the experiences of some students at Oak College as they planned, operated and reviewed an event. Think about their experiences and what you can learn from them as you progress through the unit.

How you will be assessed

This unit is assessed internally, so the centre delivering the qualification will assess you against the criteria.

In this unit you will learn about:

① the planning and objective setting processes

② a team plan

③ working individually and as part of a team

④ evaluating the event.

6.1 Planning and objective setting processes

Over to you!

Think about your objectives for doing this travel and tourism course.

Objective setting

An objective is an aim or goal. It answers the question 'What are the desired benefits of doing this, and who will benefit?'.

You do it every day! You decide what your objectives are and you plan to meet them. You may not do it in a very conscious, organised way, but you do it. You decide you want to meet friends in the evening to exchange news and enjoy each other's company. They are your objectives. Then you plan how to meet those objectives. Do your friends want to meet you and are they available tonight? What time shall you meet and where? Do you need to book anything? How will you get to and from the venue? What will you wear? Do you need money? If so, how much? What do you want to talk about?

Even the biggest event goes through the same process, although on a much larger and longer scale. The objectives of the event have to be decided and planning is needed to meet those objectives.

CASE STUDY

The Olympic Games are planned many years in advance. First, cities clearly establish what their objectives would be if they were to host the Olympics. These are likely to include political issues such as providing employment and attracting international businesses and tourists in the long term. Then there is the preparation of applications to become the nominated host city. The International Olympics Committee considers these applications and announces the candidate host cities eight years before the event. In May 2004, Paris, New York, Moscow, London and Madrid were announced as the candidate host cities for the 2012 games. The final decision on the host city was made in July 2005 – it was London! The London Olympics may well become the biggest single travel and tourism event for the UK for decades.

Once selected, there are seven years of intensive preparation, including huge developments of

CASE STUDY

sporting venues, transportation and communication systems, building of accommodation and planning of events and entertainment, along with all of the marketing contracts which need to be established. Each of these will require objectives to be set before the planning starts. Planning and preparing for the Olympics requires many resources, for example funding, staffing, expertise, equipment, and liaison with governments, sporting bodies, participants, transport organisations and the media. All this has to be achieved by a set deadline – the date cannot be changed! Imagine the hard work and headaches, but also satisfaction and pride, in being involved in such a venture!

Years of objective setting and planning ensure the success of the Olympic Games

If you do not set objectives, how will you know what event to stage, or if that event has been successful? Objective setting results in all the team members knowing what the team is aiming to achieve so that they work together with a purpose. Objectives might include: increasing membership of a club; making a profit; gaining or improving skills; passing a course; having an enjoyable day, etc. Once objectives have been set, decisions can be made about what event you want to stage.

A useful technique to encourage ideas is to brainstorm. Each person in a group offers an idea on what the event could be. This is written on a flipchart. No explanation, justification or comment is made. The process continues around the group until everyone has run out of ideas. By then, some obvious and some far-out ideas will have been offered. This creates discussion, analysis and development until a feasible idea is selected.

Before running a brainstorming session, some boundaries or constraints may need to be set. For example, who are the 'customers'; is there a cost constraint, is there a date on or by which the event must be held, etc? You will read more about such issues as you progress through this unit.

ACTIVITY

In pairs, write down all the events you can think of which happen locally, e.g. craft fayre, Christmas bazaar, and nationally, e.g. Edinburgh Festival.

Once you have your objectives, you can brainstorm event ideas

Who are the stakeholders?

Stakeholders are people or organisations that may be affected by your objectives. They might include the following:

KEY POINTS

Stakeholders include:

- your customers
- your organisation
- parents/guardians
- sponsors.

- **Your customers.** Who will come to the event? It may be other students going on a day trip, or visitors to an exhibition you are organising. Why would they want to come to your event? What would they want to do? Unit 3 Introduction to Customer Service in Travel and Tourism looked at ways which will tell you what your customers want. You might talk informally with potential customers or distribute a questionnaire with proposals or gather a group of customer representatives to discuss their wishes.
- **Your organisation.** This might be your school or college, because what you are planning may impact upon the curriculum, or availability of school/college time or resources, or the image of the school/college.
- **Parents/guardians.** They will have an interest in what their children are going to do. They may also be financial stakeholders.
- **Sponsors.** You may have individuals or organisations that have agreed to provide you with funds or resources or accommodation or advertising space, etc.

You will need to identify all of your stakeholders and ensure your objectives and plans are designed to meet their needs.

There might be additional occasions during your event planning when brainstorming sessions would be useful.

Your objectives will need to be SMART (see Unit 4 Introduction to Marketing in Travel and Tourism, page 134, for information on SMART objectives). Too many plans fail because not enough care was taken to create objectives that can pass the SMART test. People are eager to get on with the outcomes rather than concentrating on creating SMART objectives and putting careful planning into place. Failure to do so results in tasks being missed or duplicated, deadlines being missed and resources such as money and people being wasted. Team members are not clear about what the team and individuals in the team are supposed to be doing. People become demotivated and the results are varying degrees of failure!

Later in this unit, you will evaluate the success of your event. You will only be able to do this effectively if you started with a set of SMART objectives.

KEY POINTS

Objectives must be SMART:

- Specific
- Measurable
- Achievable
- Realistic
- Timed.

ACTIVITY

1 Hold a brainstorming session to suggest objectives for a one-off event you would like to organise and operate. At this stage do not think about what that event will be.

2 In your team, consider each of the objectives suggested in the brainstorming session. Do they match the SMART criteria?

ACTIVITY

Once you have discussed the objectives, hold another brainstorming session to generate ideas for an event, e.g. a day out, a fundraising event. The event should require a significant amount and range of planning across several weeks. Your tutor may give you guidance.

Decide which ideas do not meet your objectives, e.g. would it cost too much, would it be too late? Then agree on which ideas are worth discussing further. Having discussed them, agree on your event.

Now that you know what event you will stage, look again at your overall objectives and make a list of your stakeholders. Are the objectives still suitable? Do more objectives need to be added?

ACTIVITY (CONTD)

In your team, write down the SMART objectives for your chosen event. Make sure that each person has a copy of your final objectives so that they can be referred to before, during and after the event.

Oak College – objective setting

As part of their course, six Travel and Tourism students were tasked with planning and running a four-day overseas event for their college. Their tutor established where they had been before, as one of her objectives was for the students to experience a different country and culture. She also measured the proposed destinations against the learning value to the course. The students were given a choice of destinations and they chose Prague.

The Oak College Travel and Tourism team chose Prague as the destination for their event

The students individually created objectives and discussed them. They were pleased to find they had many common ones, but also some which others had not thought of. They agreed their objectives were to:

- enable each student on the project to pass the course
- use the skills and techniques described in the course
- develop team skills
- learn about another country
- promote the college image
- financially break even (neither make a profit or a loss)
- meet the needs of all stakeholders
- have fun!

They checked each of their objectives against the SMART criteria and the event for feasibility. They felt it would require a substantial amount of planning, but this could be achieved within the ten weeks available.

ACTIVITY

In your team, write down the SMART objectives for your chosen event. Remember to recognise the needs of each type of stakeholder. Record the agreed objectives so that they can be referred to before, during and after the event.

Ensure each person in the team has a copy of the objectives.

Is the event feasible?

Once your team has decided on the objectives and the event, do a reality check. Does the proposed event meet the objectives? If not, can the event be adjusted, or is a different event needed to meet the objectives? Alternatively, should your objectives be adjusted? It is also worth checking on the competition. Is anyone else planning a similar event around the same time? (Think how many Christmas fayres there are!)

In summary

- Brainstorming is a useful technique to generate ideas.
- It is vital to create a SMART set of objectives.
- The interests of all stakeholders must be met throughout the project.
- A feasibility check must be done to ensure the event meets the objectives.

Level ✓

PRACTICE ASSESSMENT ACTIVITY

P6.2 Identify the objectives of your event and explain why they were selected.

P6.2 Explain which objectives apply to which stakeholders.

P6.2 Explain how *each* objective meets *each* of the SMART criteria.

Planning processes

Once you have decided upon the event and have designed and tested your objectives, you will start to think about what needs to be planned.

The more you think about the task, the more complex it seems to become. There seems to be so much to do and it is difficult to 'see the wood for the trees'. How can you make sense of it all?

People's minds work in different ways. Some people like making lists of tasks to be done. Others like to create a picture and look for links between tasks.

One way to generate thoughts on what tasks need to be done and get them into some kind of logical grouping is to use a **mind mapping** technique. Draw an oval in the middle of the page. In the oval, write the name of the problem or task. Put the main issues which you think need to be considered on branches coming out of the oval. As you do so, more thoughts will stem from your main ideas, so attach them as twigs to the branches. For example, you may feel that Finance should be a main branch. As you think about Finance, your thoughts might turn to having financial sponsors, charging an entrance fee, cost of hiring equipment, keeping financial records, storing cash in a safe place. All of these would be shown as twigs coming from the Finance branch. You might show hiring equipment as a twig off the Finance branch, and also have equipment shown as a twig on your Resources branch. That is an obvious link, so draw a dotted line between those two issues.

When you have finished, you will find that you have written down a comprehensive set of planning tasks and have grouped them in a logical fashion, linked to other areas as appropriate (see mind map, right).

ACTIVITY

1 Individually, prepare a list or mind map for your event.
2 As a team, agree whether you are going to complete activity 3 as a list or as a mind map.
3 Once the team has agreed, decide on the main headings (branches). Have one person act as scribe and coordinator and write/draw the main headings on a large board, using the items offered by team members. Then move to the subheadings (twigs).

At the end of the above activity, you should have a display of the tasks which the team, at this stage, believes needs to be done for the event to be successful.

Identifying roles

In order for a team to function well, everybody needs to know what their contribution to the event is. Now that you have some idea of the main areas of activity, this will help you to decide who will undertake what roles. It is important that you allocate a role(s) to each person in

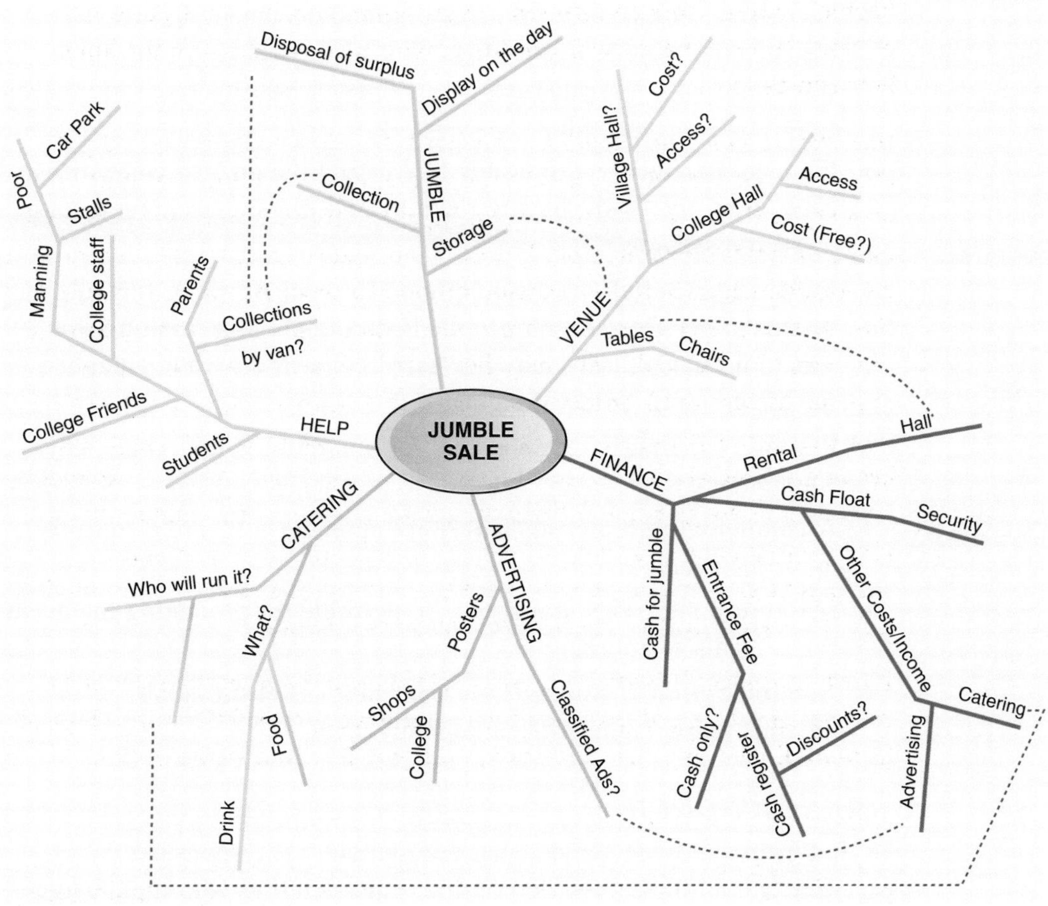

A mind map for a jumble sale

the team, and that you develop effective team working skills. Every task needs an 'owner' who will make sure it is actioned. The project will fail unless team members work together. They must know what each of the team is doing, and how that might affect what others are doing, so that everyone can help each other, otherwise tasks will get overlooked or done twice, conflict will arise and the team will become demotivated and inefficient.

Once the objectives and project have been decided upon, roles need to be allocated. These will depend upon the project, but your list or mind map will indicate most of the key functions. Roles typically include:

- **Project leader** – responsible for the coordination, control and leadership of the project. This might be the tutor's role. Alternatively, if one of the team members is project leader, it should be in addition to a 'task' role.
- **Chairperson** – responsible for controlling and ensuring effective meetings. It is a better learning experience if all team members take it in turns to be chairperson in addition to their 'task' role.

- **Secretary** – responsible for arranging and documenting meetings, e.g. agenda, minutes of meetings. This also could be a role which rotates through all team members. Whoever has this role should also have another 'task' role.
- **Finance manager** – responsible for costing the project, collecting and controlling the funds, paying the bills and keeping accurate records of all transactions.
- **Event organiser(s)** – depending upon the type of event, this role may be shared between several people. For example, if a fashion show was to be staged, tasks may be shared between the choreographer, the director and the set designer.
- **Resources manager** – responsible for obtaining volunteers, equipment, etc.
- **Accommodation/Catering/Transport manager** – this role depends upon the event.
- **Marketing and sales manager** – responsible for promoting the event, sales, media relations.
- **Administration/IT manager** – responsible for ensuring all administration is undertaken, possibly using IT.

Job description

So that everyone understands what the jobholder is responsible for, everyone should have a job description. This identifies who the jobholder reports to, who reports to the jobholder, and the responsibilities of the jobholder.

Job title: Events manager
Jobholder: Dave
Reports to: Project leader
Reporting to jobholder: Events support organiser
Responsible for:

- establishing students' interests, through liaison with students and their tutors
- research into suitable events and venues
- booking of events and venues
- liaison with transport manager for transportation
- liaison with finance manager to acquire funds and pay charges
- liaison with administration manager to create and maintain names of attendees and all other records
- liaison with marketing manager to promote events
- communication with all team members regarding actions taken
- ensuring all legal requirements are met during these events, including the health, safety and security of participants.

A typical job description

To ensure legal requirements are covered adequately, each team member must have legal responsibility identified as one of the responsibilities detailed in their job description.

Over to you!

Think about your tutor. Who is his or her manager? Does your tutor have any staff reporting to him or her? What are your tutor's main responsibilities?

Job share

It can be a good idea to cover each job by a lead person and a support person. This ensures that if the lead person has a problem or is absent, support is available to ensure the task is completed on time. However, this does mean that the job sharers must keep each other up to date. It is no help at all for a support person to tell a team meeting, 'I don't know what the lead person has done, and he took all the paperwork home with him!'

Working in pairs also gives each person experience of being in lead and support roles.

ACTIVITY

In your team, decide what roles need to be allocated. Then design a job description for each role, listing the responsibilities of the job holder.

Ensure each team member has a written copy of every job description.

Meetings

Meetings offer opportunities to create and discuss ideas, resolve problems, make decisions and communicate progress. They must be frequent enough to ensure the team can operate in an integrated, efficient and effective way. Unstructured meetings waste time and will not produce the outcomes that are needed.

Roles

Everyone at the meeting represents their own role, for example marketing manager, but will also be a team member, helping the team to come up with ideas, resolve problems and make decisions.

There are two additional roles at meetings:

- chairperson
- secretary.

The chairperson

The chairperson takes an impartial role, providing leadership and motivation to the team members to help them get results. The chairperson ensures the items on the agenda are properly discussed and keeps the meeting under control and focused. They ensure everyone has the opportunity to express their views. Some people are rather reserved and like to think about what is being discussed. They may need encouragement to contribute. Others tend to dominate meetings with their ideas and comments. The chairperson must ensure there is a balance and may need to resolve conflicts amicably.

The chairperson has responsibility for the structure of the meeting. They should:

- Ensure the meeting starts punctually and finishes within the allotted time.
- Note any apologies for absence.
- Ensure the team agrees that the minutes from the previous meeting are correct.
- Introduce the agenda – the items planned to be discussed at the meeting.

Fashion Show Committee Meeting
17 October 2005

AGENDA
1 Apologies for absence.
2 Acceptance of minutes of 10 October meeting.
3 Progress update from each member. Discussion of any problems arising.
4 Discussion and decision on catering.
5 Any other business.
6 Date of next meeting.

Agenda for a meeting

Over to you!

How would you feel if you went to a meeting, not knowing what was going to be discussed? How would it affect your effectiveness at and after the meeting?

The chairperson must also:

- ensure each item is properly discussed and that any necessary decisions are made
- ensure that all members give an update on their progress, and that any problems they have are discussed
- ensure that all members understand what actions they must take before the next meeting – it is a good idea to have a column on the minutes which records who has the responsibility to action each item
- ask if there are any other items to discuss – this is usually under the heading Any Other Business (usually shortened to AOB) on the agenda
- agree the time, date and venue for the next meeting.

The secretary

The secretary records what was discussed at the meeting. They need to listen carefully and be able to summarise accurately. In advance of the meeting, they should circulate the minutes of the previous meeting and the agenda for the coming meeting, so that everyone comes prepared. This information should go to all team members, including those who were absent from the previous meeting, and also to others who may have an interest. The Secretary is also responsible for booking and preparing the meeting room.

Fashion Show Committee Meeting
17 October 2005

MINUTES OF MEETING
Distribution: All team members plus tutor and college principal
Chairperson: Emma Wallis
Secretary: Nikita Patel

1 **Apologies for absence:** Hannah Brown, Joseph Jordan

2 **Acceptance of Minutes of 10 October meeting.** Read and accepted by the members.

3 **Progress update:**
Rachel said she had paid for the hire of a cash register and that £73 was left for other expenses. She will obtain 500 tickets for issue at the entrance, by the next meeting. **Rachel**

Cliff reported that posters had been displayed in college and in the local supermarket. He was meeting a reporter from the local newspaper next week to discuss an article about the charity which is being supported by the fashion show. **Cliff**

4 **Fashion show catering:**
Emma reminded everyone that there had been a proposal to have catering at the event. They needed to decide if there would be and, if so, what type and who would be responsible. The members agreed that there should be catering. A suggestion to offer wine was decided against because of the mix of ages and possible problems with legal requirements. It was agreed that tea, coffee, soft drinks and cakes would be offered. Claudette offered to be responsible for catering and said she would establish whether the college's Cookery School would provide the food and drink. She said she would also work out prices with Rachel and report on progress next week. **Claudette/Rachel**

5 AOB
Jamie suggested leaflets be handed out with the entrance ticket giving information on the charity they were supporting. The team agreed and Jamie said he would obtain the leaflets by 29 October. **Jamie**

Emma reminded everyone that they should be in the College Hall by 0930 on the day of the fashion show, 31 October.

6 **Next meeting:** 1000, 24 October 2005 in room F41.

Minutes of a meeting

Team members

As a team member you have responsibility for effective meetings. You must:

- attend punctually. If absence is unavoidable, tell the chairperson or secretary and update them on any issues which need to be discussed.

- share information, even if it is bad news! Tell those who will be affected if you cannot do something you previously agreed to do, including meeting a deadline. They may be able to help, but also they may need to adjust what they were going to do and when they were going to do it.
- be supportive to others. Respect their views even if you don't share them.
- take full part in the meeting, but don't hog it!

Meetings should be businesslike

ACTIVITY

Decide upon a meetings chairperson and secretary.

Agree and distribute an agenda for your first meeting to discuss your event.

Hold the meeting.

Produce and distribute the minutes.

Oak College – Nicky's diary/log

3 October: We had our first meeting today. Louise was the chairperson and Craig was the secretary. We weren't sure how to structure it, or what to discuss, but our tutor helped us and we were soon coming up with lots of ideas. We agreed a set of objectives. Michelle was a bit quiet, I must try to encourage her to take part when I am chairperson. Shaunne kept pushing his idea about going to a football museum and was a bit grumpy when the rest of us didn't support him. We agreed that each group would go to something which reflected the subjects they were studying. We realised that we needed to allocate jobs to individuals, so we agreed what jobs there would be. By the next meeting we will have prepared a set of job descriptions and will decide who does what role at that meeting. Shaunne will be chairperson and I will be secretary. I'm a bit nervous about that, as I have never done it before, but Shaunne and I met up today to put an agenda together, which I wrote up and sent to everyone, together with the minutes of today's meeting.

In summary

- Mind maps and lists are useful techniques for identifying the tasks that need to be done.
- Every task needs to have an 'owner' who is responsible for actioning it.
- The main areas of functional responsibility will depend upon the event but typically include: finance; event organisation; accommodation, catering and transport; resources; marketing and sales; administration and IT.
- Each team member should have a written job description stating their responsibilities.
- Projects require a project leader, meetings chairperson and meetings secretary.
- Meetings are important. They enable ideas to be created and discussed. Progress can be communicated, problems resolved and decisions made.
- Meetings must be frequent enough to ensure the team can operate in an integrated, efficient and effective way.
- Meetings must be structured, otherwise they will waste time and will not produce the required outcomes.
- Every meeting should have an agenda and minutes from the previous meeting.
- The minutes should record what is to be done, by when and by whom.
- The behaviours and skills of everyone at the meeting are important to the success of the meeting and the project.

Level ✔

PRACTICE ASSESSMENT ACTIVITY

P6.3/P6.4/M6.1 Write the agenda or minutes of at least one meeting.

D6.1 Analyse how you went about the writing of that agenda or minutes.

M6.1 Did you move away from the points on the agenda? If so, why?

M6.3/D6.1/D6.2 How successful was the meeting? What and who contributed to the success or otherwise of it, and how?

6.2 Team plan

Before writing your team plan, there are a number of planning issues you may need to think about, depending upon the event you have in mind.

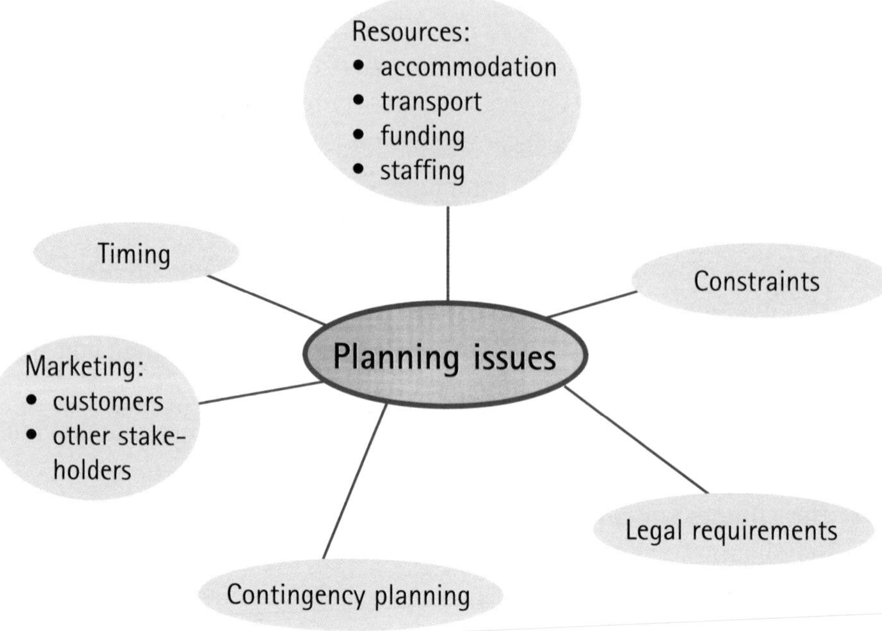

Planning issues you may need to consider

KEY POINTS

You must keep in mind:

- Your target audience – the customers
- Resources
- Constraints
- Legal requirements
- Contingencies
- Timing.

Resources

What resources do you need? They might include all or some of the following:

- **Accommodation.** Do you need a venue for a fashion show or jumble sale? Hiring can be expensive, so could it be staged for free in the college? Do you need overnight accommodation for a college trip? What is available, and at what cost?
- **Transport.** If people are coming to you, how will they get there? Do you need parking facilities? If you are taking people to the event, what transport is available? Which is the best choice, balancing cost and convenience?
- **Funding.** How will you fund your event? How much finance do you need? Do you need to get estimates from suppliers? Will you need to pay your costs before you have received the revenue? If so, how will you do so? What if your costs are greater than your income? How will that shortfall be resolved? What systems are needed to record the flow of money and to keep any money safe?
- **Staffing.** Is your event going to need extra staff? Will you need experts to assist, e.g. IT support, cooks, entertainers? How much help will you need before and during the event, and for what tasks?

Talking point

In your team, discuss what resources you think you will need for your event. Try to include additional resources to the ones given here.

Constraints

As you plan your event, you will hit constraints, for example the theatre is only available for three of the four nights that you wanted it, you can only take 30 people on a coach trip, there will only be £250 to support the event. For each constraint you will need to find a solution. Are there different ways of doing the task which will resolve the constraint? Do you need to compromise and stage a smaller event?

Legal requirements

All legal requirements, including the health, safety and security of the project team, its customers and the public, must be addressed for every aspect of the event. Examples of legal considerations could include the following:

- Are there any risks or limitations at the venue? Is there a maximum number of people that can legally be accommodated? Is the building or room, and all the equipment safe (and, if necessary, has it been tested and certificated)?

- Are food and drink preparation, storage and serving laws being met?
- Are procedures in place for the safety and security of all participants and their belongings?
- Are any licences or approvals required, e.g. public entertainment licence, performing rights permission, drinks licence?
- Is the event, and those involved in it, properly insured?
- Are fire regulations being met?
- Are you and the participants aware of the national laws, e.g. if travelling overseas, what are the laws about drinking and smoking?

Speak to your tutor, school or college management or other experts for advice. Seek out existing risk assessments that have been conducted, so that one can be produced for this event. Travel organisations will normally have conducted risk assessments on the holidays they offer, including the transportation and accommodation. If you are using a company for your event, ask them if they have done so for your transportation, accommodation, etc.

Contingencies

The weather may be something you will have to plan for

What will you do if the coach fails to arrive, or if it rains on the barbecue, or someone gets separated from the group? Always have written contingency plans for each part of your event and make them known to everyone who may need to know them.

Oak College – contingencies

The Oak College team discussed what to do if the flight home was delayed or cancelled. They decided on the following:

- If the participants would still arrive on the same flight on the same day, parents/guardians would be asked to use Teletext/Ceefax, the airline or airport websites or phone the airline to check the arrival time.
- If the flight was cancelled or delayed overnight, a cascade system would be used to tell the college and parents/guardians of the new arrangements. One person on the tour would call two college managers who would each contact three parents/guardians, and each of those parents/guardians would call two more. Anyone who did not wish to take part in the cascade system would receive a call from the college instead.

Talking point

When did you hit a constraint? What solution did you find?

In your team, discuss the contingency plans you are likely to need.

Roles and responsibilities

Each person in the team will have different interests, skills and abilities, so different roles appeal to different people. For example, a finance manager should be organised, accurate and good with figures; a marketing manager should be creative and a good communicator. Team members should be given a role which they can take on with enthusiasm!

ACTIVITY

Look again at the job descriptions you produced for each of the roles. Which roles do you think you would like to do?

In your team, discuss and agree who will take which roles. This may require some negotiation. Record and distribute the list of jobholders to every member of the team.

ACTIVITY

Make a list of your interests, skills and abilities. Look at the list of job roles that you produced earlier. Which job(s) do you think would suit you? Which jobs might you find more challenging and would give you some new skills?

Discuss your thoughts with a friend. Do they agree your views are right for you?

Marketing

How are you going to tell people about your event and encourage them to take part? Will it be through announcements within the college, posters, leaflets, letters to parents/guardians, articles in local newspapers, interviews on local radio?

You will need to make sure your marketing materials contain all the following information:

- WHAT is the event?
- WHERE is it?
- WHEN is it? (both day and time)
- WHO is running it?
- WHY is it happening?

Posters and leaflets will need to be eye-catching and colourful – you may have to compete with a lot of other events, so you need to make yours stand out.

Come to a

FASHION SHOW

Main Hall

24 February 2005
11 am–1 pm

Proceeds to British Heart Foundation
Organised by First Diploma Travel and Tourism
Clothes donated by Comfy Leisurewear Ltd

A poster marketing an event

ACTIVITY

Design a poster for a Christmas Fayre where the profits are going to The Save the Children Fund. The Fayre will be held on 14 November in the Main Hall at 11.00 am for two hours. It will be organised by the First Diploma in Travel and Tourism group.

Producing the team plan (timing)

Now it is time to produce your plan! You had to consider timing when you thought about the feasibility of the project. More work will need to be done on timing. Some tasks will have to be done before others. Some tasks can be done at the same time as others. Some tasks have to wait for other tasks to finish before they can start. If a task is not finished on time, it may delay another from starting, which might result in the task not being done in time for the event!

Schedule planning

Once planning starts, time schedules should be created. These will identify what has to be done, by when and by whom, and will help the team and all the members to keep track of what should be happening and will help them meet their deadlines.

There are two main types of plan that you could use:

- key events plan
- Gantt chart.

Key events plan

This type of plan specifies the overall framework so that everyone can fit in their work to meet the events shown on the key events plan. In the example below, the dates of some key events are shown in the planning of an overseas trip. Also shown are the main tasks which have to be done for those key events and who is responsible for each task.

Date	Key event	Tasks to be completed before specified key event
10 February	Overseas trip announced to college	Decision made on dates, destination, method of transport and outline costs Posters and explanatory leaflets prepared
24 February	Provisional bookings made with tour operator	Deposits received
10 March	Parents/students evening	Presentations prepared Information packs produced Invitations sent by 3 March Hall and equipment booked Refreshments arranged
17 March	Final balance paid to tour operator	All payments received
24 March	Meeting of those going on visit	Briefing packs produced Rooming arrangements agreed Tutors briefed
31 March	Visit begins	All planning completed

A key events plan for an overseas trip

A key events plan does not identify all of the tasks which need to be done. It only highlights key events along the way, and key tasks which need to be completed before them.

ACTIVITY

As a team, think about the event you have chosen. Agree the key events which need to be undertaken during the planning period.

Produce a key events plan to identify those events and the tasks needed to enable those events to happen. (At this early stage, you may not know all of the key events, but you can return to the plan later and amend it.)

Gantt chart

A rather more complex, but very useful technique is a Gantt chart. This lists tasks in more detail and shows the period when they need to be done. The length of the task line should also indicate how long that task will take.

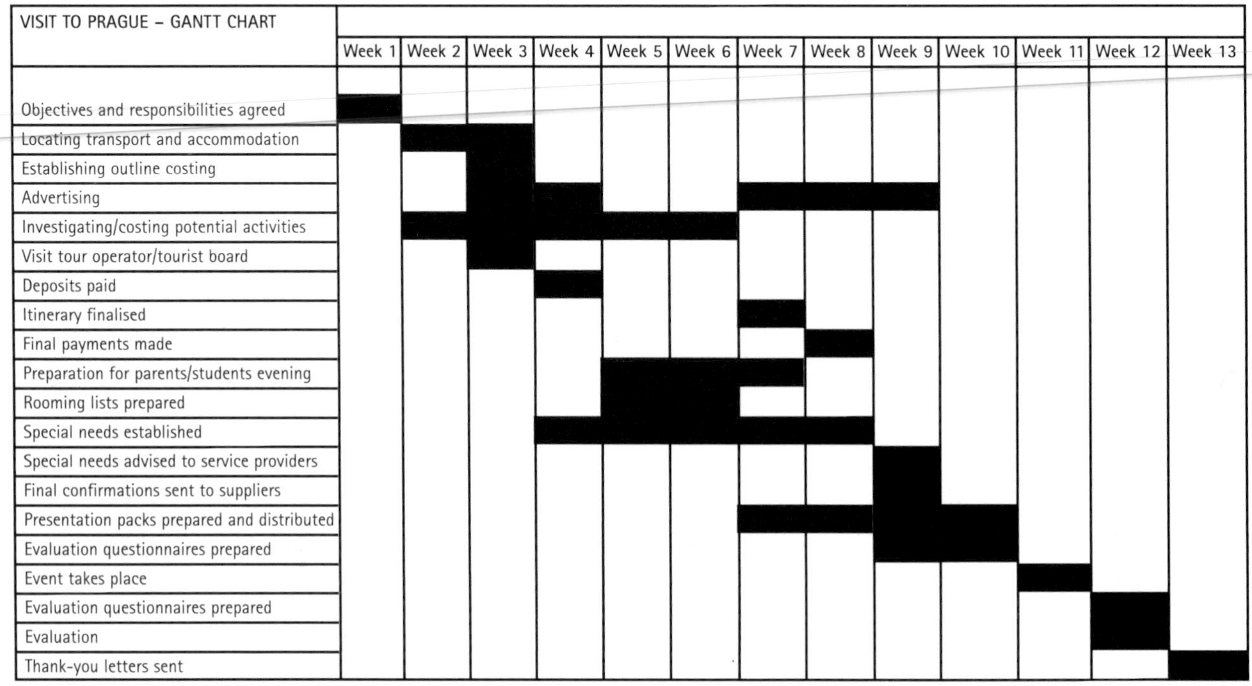

VISIT TO PRAGUE – GANTT CHART	Week 1	Week 2	Week 3	Week 4	Week 5	Week 6	Week 7	Week 8	Week 9	Week 10	Week 11	Week 12	Week 13
Objectives and responsibilities agreed													
Locating transport and accommodation													
Establishing outline costing													
Advertising													
Investigating/costing potential activities													
Visit tour operator/tourist board													
Deposits paid													
Itinerary finalised													
Final payments made													
Preparation for parents/students evening													
Rooming lists prepared													
Special needs established													
Special needs advised to service providers													
Final confirmations sent to suppliers													
Presentation packs prepared and distributed													
Evaluation questionnaires prepared													
Event takes place													
Evaluation questionnaires prepared													
Evaluation													
Thank-you letters sent													

A Gantt chart for an overseas trip

Keeping records

Your team will need to keep records to allow you to keep track of what you have done. Records are required for the efficient organisation and management of the project, for example a personal diary/log, job descriptions agendas, minutes. Other records must be kept about the planning, operation and evaluation of the event itself. The records needed will depend upon the event but might include:

- correspondence, such as letters, memos, emails to and from the venue and suppliers
- price quotations
- written records of verbal conversations, e.g. telephone conversations with suppliers
- event itinerary
- participants' names
- contact addresses and phone numbers of next of kin
- participants' personal information, e.g. special diets, passport details, medication, physical limitations.

Although each person should keep a record of what happens in their area of responsibility, the team may have an administration manager who can record and retain these records and chase up missing information. They may need to create computer records. All team members must treat information confidentially.

KEY POINTS

Keep records of:

- correspondence
- price quotations
- conversations
- event itinerary
- participants' names
- contact addresses and phone numbers of next of kin
- participants' personal information.

Over to you!

It is essential to keep personal information confidential. The Data Protection Act requires that such information should not be misused.

Oak College – the team plan

Here are some of the plans created by the Oak College team. Notice how they divided up the workload, came up with contingency plans to cope with unexpected events and helped each other.

The team created a mind map of the tasks. The mind map would help the team create their plan. Almost a whole classroom wall was covered in the team's map, but it detailed every aspect of the event and helped the team organise the tasks. Job descriptions for each task-group were agreed by the team and team members were selected to manage each of those areas.

The team designed a Gantt chart showing the tasks and the time frames. They displayed it on a wall so that the whole team could check it during the weeks of planning. Then each team member identified their own tasks that needed planning and created an individual Gantt chart for their tasks.

They decided to use a professional tour operator to provide the flights and accommodation but would arrange their own ground transport, catering and events. They agreed not to exceed £300 per person for the complete package. The team selected a tour operator and planned to meet with the company to discuss requirements. It was estimated that 30 students and 3 teachers would go.

- Louise was the team's marketing manager. She planned to advertise the trip by displaying posters and giving out flyers at college. Louise had thought about what might happen if more than 30 students applied for the trip. If this happened, the team would have to contact the tour operator and find out if the airline and hotel had extra space at the same price.
- Nicky was the transport manager. She had to arrange transport to and from the airports in London and Prague and also book any transport to the events being arranged by Dave the activities manager. Nicky couldn't book any of the events transport until Dave had arranged the events. She therefore had to work closely with Dave.
- Dave was the activities manager. His plan was to use the Internet and other sources of information to find suitable day and evening events and venues for the students and to book them. Because Nicky needed to arrange transport to and from any events, his plan had to allow enough time for her to do this. Dave had considered what might happen if students studying other subjects applied for the trip. He therefore looked into a few extra events and activities that he could keep to one side just in case this happened.
- Shaunne was the administration manager. He planned to create an IT system that would record each person's personal details and the amount of money they had paid.
- Michelle was the accommodation and catering manager. One of Michelle's tasks was to let students and parents/guardians know about the hotel. She planned to do this by putting photographs and information about the hotel into an information pack. Michelle couldn't organise the catering until she knew what events Dave had organised. Michelle planned to meet up with Dave when he had booked each event.

The team came up with a plan for helping each other if one member was having problems with their tasks. If someone was having any trouble, the team planned to hold a meeting and talk about who had some spare time to help out. This way there wouldn't be one team member overloaded with work whilst another team member's tasks were finished.

ACTIVITY

As a team, you have decided what the event will be, what the objectives are and what role you will be taking.

Now, individually, produce a written list of tasks you have to do, together with notes on who you will need to work with, or contact. Note the target dates for completion of each task. Once you have done this, discuss with the other team members, so that all plans are coordinated. For example:

Transportation

Task	How	By when
Contact coach companies	Speak to college administrator; search *Yellow Pages*	12 Oct
Obtain written quotes	Call selected companies	19 Oct
Recommend coach company to team	Talk to team at meeting	On 22 Oct
Book coach	Write to coach company; obtain funds from college	26 Oct

In summary

- Planning techniques should be used to organise tasks and set time frames.
- Contingency plans are needed for every element of the plan.
- Records need to be kept in an organised way.
- Legal requirements must be understood and met.

PRACTICE ASSESSMENT ACTIVITY

Level ✓

P6.3 Provide a job description for the role you are undertaking in your event.

P6.1/P6.3/P6.4/M6.1 What planning issues did your team decide needed addressing?

P6.1/P6.3/M6.2 Provide a simple Gantt chart for your part of the event plan.

M6.2/M6.3/D6.2 Assess and evaluate your involvement in defining the planning issues.

Over to you!

How's your diary/logbook coming along? It is most important that you have a comprehensive record of events and issues throughout the planning stages and of happenings during the actual event. You may want to design some check-sheets to help you and your team.

6.3 Working individually and as part of a team

Working individually

Your job description identifies your responsibilities for your part of the project. The success of the event depends upon you delivering.

Each member of the team will have prepared their own task list with deadlines. Remember to:

- complete the task on time
- record what you have done, who was involved and how you overcame any problems
- have a contingency plan
- keep others informed.

Don't leave things to the last minute! Some things will take longer than you expected. Perhaps somebody has not contacted you when they said they would. Perhaps your first choice supplier cannot meet your needs. Perhaps the project has to be adjusted, which means you need to finish a task earlier than expected. Perhaps you have to do more tasks than you expected. Get ahead of the game!

KEY POINTS

Keep a record of what you have done and keep others informed.

Oak College – working as part of a team

When a total of 40 people applied for the trip, everything was fine until the hotel suddenly said it could not accommodate the increased number of participants! Fortunately, the tour operator had an alternative hotel, but Nicky had to advise the coach company in Prague of the change; Michelle had to compile a new rooming list and rearrange the hotel catering; Shaunne had to agree new rates with the tour operator and change some of his records; Louise had to change the hotel details in the presentation packs she had prepared. Fortunately, the team worked well together and helped each other out with this extra work.

Problem-solving

There will be problems to overcome, so it is useful to have some planning techniques to help you. The diagram below demonstrates one problem-solving technique.

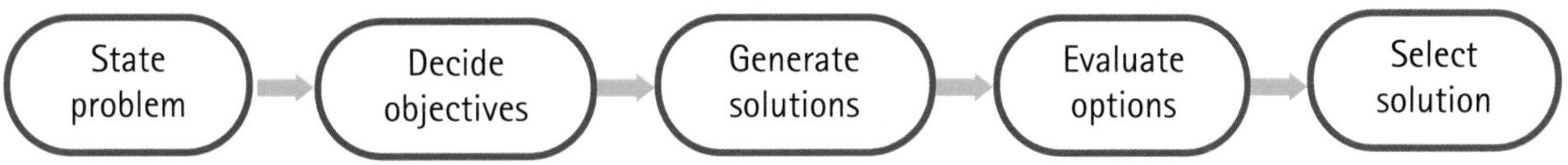

A problem-solving technique

The first step is to clearly identify the problem. In the Oak College scenario, that would be: 'Hotel unable to accommodate the extra participants'. The second step is to decide on your objectives. These could be:

1 to have sufficient suitable accommodation for all the participants
2 not to increase the cost per participant
3 to have everyone share all of the visit.

The third step is to generate various solutions. These might include:

- staying with the existing hotel and telling the additional participants that they cannot take part
- finding a hotel just for the additional participants
- finding a new hotel for all the participants.

The fourth step involves evaluating each option against the objectives.

The Oak College team rejected the option of refusing the extra participants, as this did not meet objective 1. They also rejected putting just the extra participants in the new hotel because that would not meet objectives 2 or 3. This left them with the option of moving all the participants to the new hotel. The price was acceptable, so all three objectives were met by this option, which enabled the team to move on to step 4 of this problem-solving technique. They decided to move everyone to the new hotel.

Communicating effectively

You are responsible for communicating needs and information to others, verbally and in writing. Refer back to Unit 3 Introduction to Customer Service in Travel and Tourism, page 86, which will remind you of some of the communication techniques.

You should keep a record of all communications, whether written or verbal.

You will need to influence people to agree with you and do things for you, so an approachable style is important.

Before you speak or write, organise your thoughts. Communicate in a clear and logical manner. If it is a verbal communication, summarise what you have said and perhaps confirm it in writing. Likewise, it is useful to confirm to someone that you have received a written communication from them and that you accept its contents.

Communicating in writing

We looked at how you set out an agenda and minutes earlier in the unit. You may also need to write to your colleagues using a memo (short for memorandum) or to outside organisations in a formal business letter.

Use a memo to inform another team member what you have done:

MEMO

To: Lee Sung
From: Anita Gray
Date: 21 January 2005
Subject: Advertising leaflets

I have been to R & B Printing and they have given me prices of:

200 black and white A5 fliers – £7.50

100 coloured A5 fliers – £7.50

This is more expensive than Boston Blueprint, so I suggest we order through them.

A memo

You do not need to sign a memo – it is only for people *within* your team (or organisation).

If you are writing to an organisation outside your team, you will need to do a formal business letter.

Anita Gray
c/o Boston Business School, Boston, Lincs BO14 1QP

20 February 2005

Mr Peter Mills
Boston Blueprint
150 High Street
Boston
Lincs
BO41 2PJ

Dear Mr Mills

Thank you for your quotation for A5 fliers. I would like to order the following:

400 black/white A5 fliers

The artwork is attached. Please could you confirm that these can be delivered by 14 March 2005.

Yours sincerely

Anita Gray

Anita Gray

A business letter

ACTIVITY

Write a memo to your finance manager asking for a cheque to be sent to Age Concern for £265.00.

Working as part of a team

Although you have been assigned a role with individual responsibilities, you cannot work on a project in isolation. Others depend on you.

Fulfilling your role

You accepted the role and responsibilities, so you must fulfil them. Some tasks may not be easy. Don't worry, others may be able to help you, for example other team members or your tutor. However, just as you would be grateful for help from your colleagues, they may be grateful for help from you. Watch for team members who may be having difficulties, and be ready to help them.

Over to you!

How would you feel if someone has promised to do something by a certain date but fails to warn you that they will miss that deadline? How would the situation be made easier if they gave you warning?

Meeting deadlines

Meeting deadlines is key. Others depend upon you to complete your task(s) on time, so that they can do theirs on time, and enable the event to be a success.

Some tasks may take longer than expected and your deadline might be in danger. Tell those who might be affected by you missing the deadline. They may be able to help you get back on target, or they may have to reorganise and reschedule the tasks they have to do.

You have a greater chance to meet your deadlines if you clearly identified your tasks, put a time frame on them and discussed them with those you will be depending upon to help you meet the deadlines. A Gantt chart as described on page 230 will help.

Meeting deadlines is also a frame of mind. Don't leave tasks to the last minute! Even if you did still finish on time, your work would not be of the same quality as it would have been if you had allowed more time for the task.

Team relationships

Together, you and your colleagues can achieve more than you can individually. Each of you has strengths which you can share, and weaknesses that you can help each other overcome. Every team member brings something to the team. In turn, this will enable the team to:

- create more ideas
- solve problems more creatively
- take better decisions
- provide a sense of belonging, which is motivating
- keep a focus on the team's objectives
- provide support to individual team members.

To be successful, team members have to behave responsibly, by fulfilling their individual responsibilities, communicating honestly with each other, playing an active part in team issues, and respecting and supporting other members.

Personality clashes

We are all different. Sometimes there are personality clashes with those we cannot get on with. Differences have to be put aside in the interests of the team and the project. Behaviour must be constructive, not destructive. Respect should be shown to each other and each others' views. Differences should be discussed openly, as this can remove any misunderstandings and may produce solutions.

The chairperson or project leader may need to intervene, either to ensure fairness or to arbitrate when there are disputes. The more individuals can get on with, and respect, each other, the more the team will be motivated and the more successful the project will be.

ACTIVITY

Nothing is solved by not facing up to unpleasant situations, like personality clashes. Think about someone you don't get on with. Use the problem-solving technique on page 235 to address the problem: 'I have a personality clash with . . .'

Write down:

- what objective you have (perhaps it is to work better with the person)
- that person's strengths
- that person's weaknesses
- what behaviours you don't like seeing in them – avoid emotive words
- your strengths
- *your weaknesses*
- *any of your own bad behaviours which you would like to stop.*

Think about the options open to you to improve the situation. For example, do either of you have any strengths which could help the other? Do either of you have any bad behaviours which can be stopped? Are there any types of tasks which you could work well on together? How would you discuss these issues with the other person?

Select one or more options, then do it! Remember to keep calm, and be constructive.

In summary

- You are responsible for completing the tasks allocated to you, on time, communicating honestly and telling others if you are having problems.
- You have a responsibility to record what you have done and to tell others.
- Problems will happen, but there are techniques to overcome them.
- Good preparation and not leaving things to the last minute will reduce problems and missed deadlines.

- There is strength in teamwork which creates better outcomes. Encourage that synergy!
- Personality clashes can occur and are demotivating to the whole team. They must be addressed.

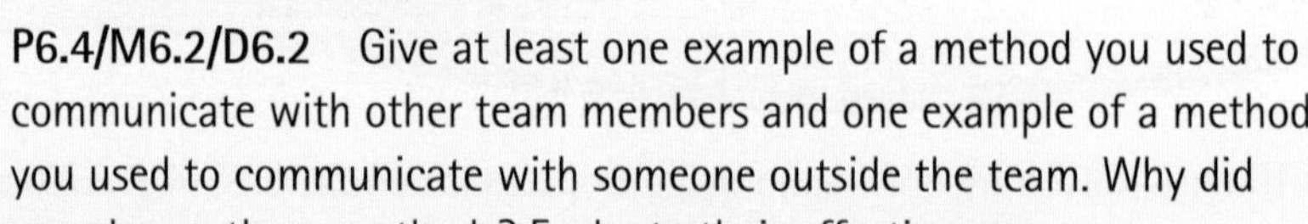

P6.4/M6.2/D6.2 Give at least one example of a method you used to communicate with other team members and one example of a method you used to communicate with someone outside the team. Why did you choose those methods? Evaluate their effectiveness.

M6.2/M6.3 Consider one of the tasks for which you had responsibility and which did not go according to plan. What was the problem? How did you overcome it?

P6.4 Describe at least three methods that assist good team working.

The big day!

The big day has arrived! It is a good idea to have a log sheet for recording what you did on the day – it will soon become a hazy memory otherwise!

ACTIVITY

Design a log sheet which suits your event – you can pre-print some of the detail on it and distribute it to your team. Your log sheet could look something like this:

EVENT LOG SHEET

Time	What happened?	Comment

You could also record the day through:

- photographs
- videos.

6.4 Evaluating the event

The event is over – almost! It is time for the all-important evaluation. A key stage of project work is reflecting on what happened, identifying what went well and what could be done better next time.

Gathering evidence

You have been gathering information throughout this unit on how the project, the team and you are developing. Your sources of evidence will include:

- **Your diary or log.** This will have recorded actual activities; your involvement in them; the involvement of others; any problems and how they were resolved; any other comments and observations you made, like how motivated you felt; your views on your performance and the performance of other individuals and the team as a whole.
- **Other written evidence.** Copies of all the correspondence (including emails) and records of conversations, agendas, minutes, risk assessments, check sheets, financial and other records.
- **Customer evaluation.** It is important that you get the customers' views on how you performed. After all, the project was for them! You can discover customers' views in many ways. It could be formal methods, for example a customer questionnaire or a witness statement. It could be informal, for example asking them verbally during or after the event, or having some project members in the audience listening to customers' comments. If possible, gather customer opinion by more than one method.

The Oak College team produced a questionnaire which they distributed to participants on the flight home, and collected it as the participants got off the aircraft – that way they hoped to get a higher response than if they asked participants to return questionnaires later.

PRAGUE VISIT, OCTOBER 2005

1 = Excellent 4 = Very poor

	1	2	3	4	n/a	Yes	No
Before the trip							
1 Rate the amount of information you received about the trip.							
2 How well did your class representatives keep you informed?							
3 Did you attend the parent/student evening? If yes, go to Q4, if no, go to Q5.							
4 How useful did you find the evening?							
5 Did your parent/guardian attend that evening? If yes, go to Q6, if no, go to Q7.							
6 How useful did they find the evening?							
Sunday							
7 How informative/enjoyable was the sightseeing tour with the Czech students?							
Monday							
8 How interesting/enjoyable was the Skoda car plant visit?							
9 How interesting/enjoyable was the film studios visit?							
10 Rate the service at the evening restaurant you chose:							
a Red Hot Blues							
b La Rostica.							
11 Rate the food/drink at the evening restaurant you chose:							
a Red Hot Blues							
b La Rostica.							
Tuesday							
12 How would you rate Prague Castle as a tourist attraction?							
13 To what degree do you think the Prague Castle visit was value for money?							
14 How informative/interesting was the study visit you made to either:							
a Prague Information Service							
b Cerge Institute?							
15 Rate the evening meal venue and service.							
16 Rate the evening meal food/drink.							
Wednesday							
17 How appropriate was the amount of shopping/sightseeing time you had?							
Hotel and transport							
18 Rate the hotel check-in/check-out arrangements.							
19 Rate your hotel bedroom.							
20 Rate the hotel catering (Sunday evening and breakfasts).							
21 Rate the hotel service.							
22 What overall rating would you give the hotel?							
23 Rate the Prague sightseeing transport.							
24 How smoothly did the flights and airport coach transfers run?							
25 Rate the airline service.							
General							
Rate the planning and organisation of the trip.							
Rate the trip overall.							
Would you consider returning to Prague?							
Would you recommend Prague to someone else?							

Please add any other comments here and continue overleaf. Thank you for your time.

Name (optional)

Oak College's feedback questionnaire for the Prague visit

ACTIVITY

1 As a team, design a customer feedback questionnaire for your event. Structure it so that you can measure the responses, but leave some space for freehand comments. Look at the example in Unit 3 Introduction to Customer Service in Travel and Tourism, page 113. Remember to ask questions which will give you feedback on whether your objectives were achieved.

Decide how and when you will distribute, collect and analyse this questionnaire.

2 Decide upon at least one other method of customer feedback you will use for your event.

There may be other stakeholders in the project such as your college, parents/guardians, sponsors. How will you get feedback from them? You will need someone to collect, analyse and distribute the responses, possibly with the aid of a simple IT programme. Perhaps your administration/IT manager would do it.

Evaluating the evidence

Project results

The team can now evaluate the information it has gathered. You need to compare the feedback with each of the objectives you created at the beginning of the project. These might include:

- Did you achieve the customer satisfaction level you wanted?
- Did you achieve the desired financial result?
- Did you obtain the required resources?
- Did you use the resources effectively and efficiently?
- Did you pass the course?
- Did all the participants have fun?

Note what went well in achieving these results, what proved difficult, how the difficulties were overcome, what did not go well and why.

KEY POINTS

Your evaluation must be honest!

Organisation

How well did the team organise themselves and the event? Were all the tasks and roles anticipated and covered well? Were there any that were missed or not prepared sufficiently well? How could the organisation have been better?

Planning

Did the plan run smoothly? Did everyone stick to it? What was difficult? What had not been planned or had to be rethought? What planning techniques were used and how effective were they? What other techniques could have been used?

Talking point

As a team, agree a set of questions to ask about team performance. Individually, spend 15 minutes writing down your own answers to the questions. When the team is ready, discuss your answers.

Team performance

This should be discussed by the team in an open and constructive way, by asking two questions:

- What did the team do well?
- What could the team have done better?

Avoid personalising the analysis. It is about the team, rather than individuals. Topics might include:

- Were we motivated? Why?
- Did we demonstrate enthusiasm?
- Did we meet deadlines?
- Did we support each other?
- Did we handle unplanned events well?
- Were we professional, demonstrating leadership inside and outside the team?

Feedback on peers' performance

How do you feel other individuals in the team performed? Your views should help them recognise their strengths and improve their performance.

We enjoy hearing feedback about our strengths. We may be less comfortable hearing of our weaknesses. Always give feedback in a positive and constructive way. Instead of being told, 'You were hopeless at communicating!', the person will be more receptive, and more likely to improve, if the comment was phrased positively, such as 'I would have welcomed more communication from you because I found I couldn't do some of my tasks without knowing how far you had got with yours'. Your colleagues will be helped best by giving them honest, useful feedback, in a positive manner.

One technique is to use a pro-forma which lists key performance indicators common to all the team members, such as the one shown below.

Team member's name ______________________
Role ______________________
Date ______________________

1. How many team meetings did he/she attend?
2. How many times was he/she chairperson?
3. How well did he/she perform that role? How could he/she do it better?
4. How many times was he/she secretary?
5. How well did he/she perform that role? How could he/she do it better?
6. Did he/she complete tasks on time?
7. Did he/she always act in a professional manner?
8. How punctual was he/she at meetings?
9. Did he/she assist others?
10. Did he/she have effective contingency plans?
11. Did he/she handle unplanned activities well?
12. Did he/she communicate well?
13. What were his/her particular strengths?
14. What areas would most benefit from improvement?

(Include examples to support each answer.)

A peer evaluation pro-forma

ACTIVITY

Produce a peer evaluation pro-forma.

ACTIVITY

In your team, decide on an appropriate method to provide feedback to each team member on their performance. Seek guidance from your tutor.

Agree what performance issue headings there should be (the same list for all members).

Agree when it will be done by.

Do it!

ACTIVITY

Complete a peer evaluation pro-forma about yourself, making sure you are being honest! Look at your peers' comments about you. Are they similar? Is there a theme?

Self-evaluation

Now is the time to be honest with yourself! You have an excellent opportunity to think about your own strengths and weaknesses, and what to do about them.

Self-improvement plan

With the evaluation completed, you can prepare an improvement plan for yourself – see the example below. This should identify weaknesses you want to improve. You will need to say how you will improve, to what level and by when. You will need to check that your objectives meet the SMART criteria.

ACTIVITY

Based upon your evaluation results, decide upon four areas you want to improve. Prepare a self-improvement plan, stating what you want to improve, to what level, how and by when.

Review your progress monthly.

I want to improve	The standard I want to achieve	How?	By when
Problem-solving skills	Resolve problems in a structured way	Reading on the subject	Complete by end June
Accountancy skills	Be able to keep accurate records of payments and receipts	Evening class	Start September
Speak French	Conversational GCSE to C grade	Evening class	Complete by end December

A SMART self-improvement plan

In summary

- The job is not done until the evaluation is completed!
- Evaluation is important to enable improvements for the future.
- There are many formal and informal, written and verbal ways to collect feedback.
- Always get feedback from your stakeholders, including your customers.
- Team and individual feedback needs to be given in a constructive manner.
- Development plans need to be SMART.

PRACTICE ASSESSMENT ACTIVITY

Level

All team members must participate in the preparation and presentation of this task.

Prepare a ten-minute presentation on the planning, operation and evaluation of the event. Each member must be responsible for part of the presentation, which should cover:

- the objectives of the event **(P6.2)**
- the process which identified what tasks there would be and who would be responsible for them **(P6.1/P6.4/D6.1)**

Level ✓

PRACTICE ASSESSMENT ACTIVITY (CONTD)

- what methods were used to communicate and discuss issues, both with other members of the team, and with those outside the team (**P6.4/M6.2/D6.1**)
- what problems arose and how they were overcome (**M6.2**)
- an evaluation of the event, using feedback from stakeholders and comparing with the specified objectives, using SMART criteria (**P6.4/M6.3/D6.2**).

ACTIVITY

You and your colleagues have worked hard on your project. Almost certainly you will have achieved much more as a team than you could have done as individuals.

Celebrate! Have a fun event together – and don't forget your tutor! (Of course, this will need an event plan!)

In summary

In this unit you had the opportunity to plan, organise operate and evaluate a real event. You learned more about the importance of SMART objectives. You were introduced to the concept of stakeholders. You will have appreciated the importance of identifying the tasks that need to be done, and of clearly stated roles and responsibilities. You discovered the issues that commonly have to be addressed when planning events and you learned some planning and problem solving techniques. You experienced the value of teamwork and learned how to hold effective meetings. You gained practice in gathering and using feedback.

TEST YOUR KNOWLEDGE

1. Why is objective setting important? Why must objectives be SMART?
2. Who might the stakeholders be if you planned to run a fashion show for a charity in the local college hall?
3. List six groups of planning issues that typically have to be considered when organising events.
4. What legal considerations might there be if you planned a disco with a band, wine, beer and pizzas in the local community centre hall?
5. What information does a Gantt chart provide which a key events plan does not?
6. Everyone comes to meetings with a functional role to play, but there are two members who have additional roles at meetings. Describe those roles.
7. Describe the stages of problem-solving.
8. Name six benefits that result from the additional strength created by teamwork.
9. You are organising a day visit for Travel and Tourism students to a tourist attraction. Who would you wish to gain feedback from, and how would you obtain it?
10. What two aspects of your own performance would you most want to improve if you were to arrange another event? What would you do differently?

Unit 7

Work-based Project within the Travel and Tourism Industry

Introduction

In the previous units you learned about various aspects of the travel and tourism industry; now you will have the chance to put your skills into practice, spending at least ten days in work-based experience which must be related to the travel and tourism industry.

You will be able to prepare yourself for a job application by practising the skills needed for application through to the interview.

You will also complete a travel and tourism project which should be creative, analytical, innovative and/or problem-solving.

Your work-based project might take you to a busy travel agency

How you will be assessed

This unit is assessed internally, so the centre delivering the qualification will assess you against the criteria.

In this unit you will:

① learn about related documents and interview skills

② plan and carry out a selected project during your work-based placement

③ monitor, review and present your project.

7.1 Documents and interview skills

Documents

Preparing your CV

A CV (curriculum vitae) is a document which has to 'sell' your skills to your future employer. For this reason, you should take trouble to make it eye-catching and accurate, and it should be word processed.

There are three main ways to set out a CV:

- a traditional CV
- a skills-based CV
- an individual CV.

Examples of each are shown on pages 251 and 252.

Talking point

In pairs, look at the three types of CV. Which do you prefer? Which do you think is the most effective, and why? Name two advantages and two disadvantages of each type of CV.

CURRICULUM VITAE

Name: Julie Smith
Date of Birth: 22 July 1982
Address: 36 Any Road
Anytown
Somewhere
ANY 1OW
Nationality: British
Email: smithj@hotmail.com

EDUCATION

2003/4–2005 Anytown College of Further and Higher Education, Somewhere, ANY 1OW

GCSEs

Business Studies D
Science Double DD
Maths D
Technology D

WORK EXPERIENCE

Date: March 99–present
Company: Cornhill Insurance
Position/skills used: Cleaner (2 hours daily Monday to Friday)
This job enabled me to further enhance my skills as an independent worker. As a key holder my main responsibilities included vacuuming and cleaning of a designated floor.

Achievements and leisure activities
December 1997
I achieved a high level of attainment in lifesaving and swimming, necessitating the successful completion of a first aid course.

Sports
I am a fairly sporty person, I enjoy water sorts such as swimming and canoeing. I also enjoy cycling.

Interests
Computing takes up a lot of my spare time, whether it be reading to expand previous knowledge or by practical approach.

Leisure
I am a sociable, outgoing person and enjoy meeting people and going out to pubs and clubs with friends.

A traditional CV

CURRICULUM VITAE

Name: Julie Smith

SKILLS

A confident, enthusiastic person who enjoys learning new skills, offering determination and commitment.

Customer service – experience gained at work placement at Eternity Travel where I received commendations on my interpersonal skills.

Teamwork – I am used to working in a team, as I work as part of a lifesaving team. I also take part in team canoe charity work.

IT – I am confident in the use of Word, Excel and PowerPoint. I have used these on my College course.

QUALIFICATIONS

GCSE Business Studies – D
I was part of a business competition team – we sold theatre tickets.

GCSE Science Double – DD
I was particularly interested in Biology and Nutrition.

GCSE Maths – D
I am currently re-sitting this.

PERSONAL DETAILS

36 Any Road
Anytown
Somewhere
ANY 1OW

Date of birth
22 July 1982

A skills-based CV – note the change in emphasis

CURRICULUM VITAE

Julie Smith

Address
36 Any Road
Anytown
Somewhere
ANY 1OW

Date of birth
22 July 1982

A confident, enthusiastic person with a variety of skills.

QUALIFICATIONS

GCSE Business Studies – D
I was part of a business competition team – we sold theatre tickets.

GCSE Science Double – DD
I was particularly interested in Biology and Nutrition.

GCSE Maths – D
I am currently re-sitting this.

SKILLS

I am good at customer service, and enjoy meeting people. I am used to working as part of a team to achieve my goal.

An individual CV

Research shows that people only read the top third of a page properly, so make this part of your CV stand out. Put the most interesting information at the top.

ACTIVITY

Write a CV and then swap with a partner. Give each other advice – what is good about it? How could you improve it?

KEY POINTS

Make several drafts of your CV in different styles. Ask friends and adults which one they prefer.

Always ask someone to proofread your documents. It is very easy to overlook errors if you proofread your own – you see what you expect to see!

Letters of application

You may want to apply for a particular job, or you may just want to work for a particular company. Either way, you will need to send a letter of application – and unless you know someone willing to take you (relatives and friends are very useful here!), you may need to send many applications in order to get a placement! Don't be discouraged if you receive a refusal – or indeed no reply at all. Don't take it personally and try again!

You will need to write a standard letter which can be adapted for different circumstances. These need to be word processed and should be set out in a

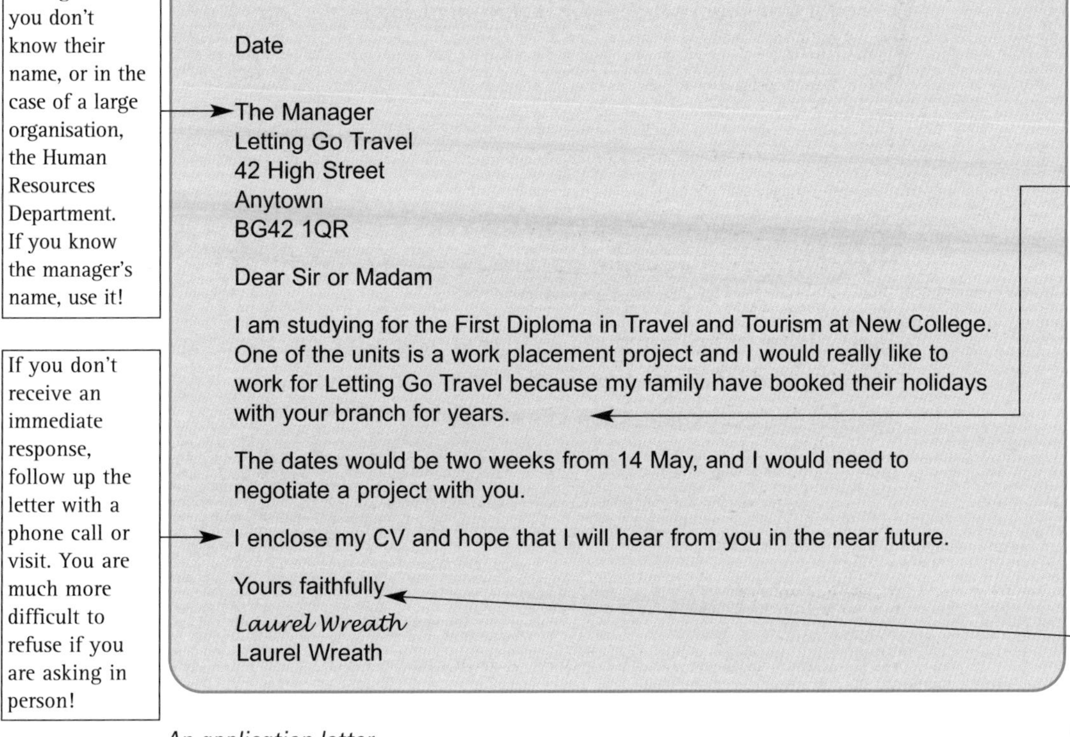

Your address

Date

The Manager
Letting Go Travel
42 High Street
Anytown
BG42 1QR

Dear Sir or Madam

I am studying for the First Diploma in Travel and Tourism at New College. One of the units is a work placement project and I would really like to work for Letting Go Travel because my family have booked their holidays with your branch for years.

The dates would be two weeks from 14 May, and I would need to negotiate a project with you.

I enclose my CV and hope that I will hear from you in the near future.

Yours faithfully

Laurel Wreath
Laurel Wreath

An application letter

formal business format. An example is shown on page 253. If you have a knowledge of mail-merge or similar systems, this will be quicker, but 'cutting and pasting' or deleting and re-typing can work just as well.

Ensure your letter has correct spelling, punctuation and grammar – read it through carefully to check for any mistakes. Remember to emphasise the skills you have which would allow you to do a job in that organisation.

ACTIVITY

Look in your local newspaper or in the *Travel Trade Gazette*. Choose a job and write a letter of application for that job.

Over to you!

Make sure that your letters are word-processed and correctly spelt and set out. Always ask your tutor to check them before sending. Some colleges and schools send out a covering letter explaining more about the project and endorsing your application. This is sometimes a good idea, and should stop many students in a class applying to the same company!

ACTIVITY

Draft a letter of application to a range of businesses, e.g. travel agent, tour operator, tourist information centre. Make sure you state your reasons for applying to each organisation in particular.

Letters of acceptance

Well done! You've been offered a placement. You need to accept this – see the example below – and ensure both you and the company understand what happens next!

Your address

Date

Mr H Smithers
Letting Go Travel
42 High Street
Anytown
BE42 1QR

Dear Mr Smithers

Thank you for your letter of 26 January offering me a placement for two weeks from 14 May.

I am very much looking forward to working with you and would like to arrange an interview to discuss a possible project during next month, if convenient. I will telephone you to arrange an appointment nearer the time.

Thank you very much for supporting my studies.

Yours sincerely
Laurel Wreath

A letter of acceptance

If, of course, you are lucky enough to be offered several placements, you will need to decline gracefully, or offer it to another student. An example of a letter declining a placement is shown below.

Your address

Date

Mrs C Bloomer
Hotel Saunders
The Esplanade
Anytown
BG42 1PJ

Dear Mrs Bloomer

Thank you for your letter of 31 January offering me a placement from 14 May.

Unfortunately, I have already accepted another placement, but I know that a fellow student, Lucy Fanshawe, is intending to apply to you and I hope you would be willing to accept her instead. She will write to you separately.

Thank you for supporting my studies.

Yours sincerely
Laurel Wreath

A letter declining a placement

ACTIVITY

Draft letters of acceptance and decline, ready for those offers coming in!

Over to you!

When turning down a placement you can recommend another student, but check to make sure that they apply!

Application forms

Sometimes organisations prefer applicants to complete a standard form. You need to make sure you write on these legibly, using capital letters and blue or black ink. Some applications can be completed online and emailed.

In either case, *make a copy* of the form and *practise* completing it.

Don't lie or exaggerate – remember what you are applying for and try to reflect the skills and personal qualities needed to do a job in that organisation.

ACTIVITY

Copy the application form and practise filling it in. Sell yourself, remember!

PRACTICE ASSESSMENT ACTIVITY

Level ✓

P7.1 Produce two different forms of documentation to be used to obtain work-based experience.

SUNNY TOURS APPLICATION FORM

Please complete form in block capitals

Mr/Mrs/Miss/Ms (delete)

First names:

Surname:

Address:	Age:	Date of birth:
	Tel. no:	

Education

Secondary school:	Dates	
	From	To

Post Secondary:	Full or part time	Dates	
		From	To

Qualifications

Awarding body	Subject	Qualification awarded	Date of award

Membership of voluntary organisations:

Employment and work experience

List in chronological order, starting with the earliest, all previous employment

Date		Full or part time	Employers	Nature of duties
From	To			

An application form

Preparing for interview

So now you have a placement, it may be subject to interview. Again, this is your chance to 'sell' yourself, but there are a few techniques which will help you fulfil your potential.

Know the organisation!

Make sure you know exactly what the organisation does, how big it is, what its image is, etc. Visit the organisation's website, find a copy of its company report in the local library and read the introduction, talk to people who have worked there or used their services. Interviewers are always impressed if the candidate has done some background research and it will make *you* feel more confident that you know what you are letting yourself in for!

Dress code and appearance

You will need to be clean and smart for the interview. Try to find out what the people who work there are wearing – if they wear smart suits, then you should aim for a similarly formal look. If you are going to an organisation which deals with student backpackers, then smart casual wear would do. Whatever you wear, you must make sure it – and you – are clean and tidy, with neat hair and clean nails and hands! Most organisations in the travel and tourism industry have a 'customer focus' and need to employ staff who would impress their customers.

KEY POINTS

Be confident, or at least look confident – you can do this by making sure you leave plenty of time, have done your research and look well presented and unhurried.

Do your research into the organisation. This will impress your interviewers and give you confidence.

Interview procedures

You will be going for a placement interview but you may later want to apply for a permanent job. You should keep this in mind.

When you go for an interview, a little preparation will make you appear more confident and will help to banish any nervousness:

- Telephone the organisation and confirm you will be attending the interview.
- Check the time and place and ask for travel directions.
- Check travel arrangements in advance, particularly if it involves a complicated journey by public transport. Do a 'dummy' run so you are sure.
- Write down questions you want to ask at the interview, particularly about the project or working conditions. Write down the answers as well!
- Arrive early! Even if you have to wait around for a while, it is better than arriving late and flustered.

Interview skills

Body language

You know when someone you are talking to is bored or not listening – so does the interviewer.

Sit up straight, with your arms comfortably placed at your side, not crossed, and look interested. Don't say you are only there because your tutor says you have to do a project!

ACTIVITY

In pairs, one of you try to convey a feeling by using body language, no words. Try to guess what each is feeling. Write a list of the most common ways of expressing emotion without words.

Social skills

An interview is a formal situation and you need to act formally:

- Wait to be asked to enter a room – knock if the door is closed and wait for an answer.
- Wait to be asked to sit down.
- You may be asked to shake hands. Make sure you offer your right hand and grip firmly (but don't overdo it!)
- Say thank you and goodbye on leaving – remember the organisation is doing you a favour, not the other way round.
- Remember to *smile* and look enthusiastic about working there.
- Respond to questions positively – if you don't understand, then say so. You can always say 'Do you mean . . . ?' and suggest alternatives.
- Repeat the question in your own words if you are not sure how to answer.
- Make sure you ask questions yourself. You should have written down some questions before arrival, and you may have thought of more during the interview. Jot these down in a notepad – it will jog your memory.

PRACTICE ASSESSMENT ACTIVITY

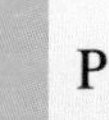

P7.2 Use appropriate interview skills for obtaining a work-based placement.

M7.1 Promote yourself positively throughout the interview and through documentation used to obtain work experience.

KEY POINTS

The whole of the job selection procedure is shown in the diagram (right).

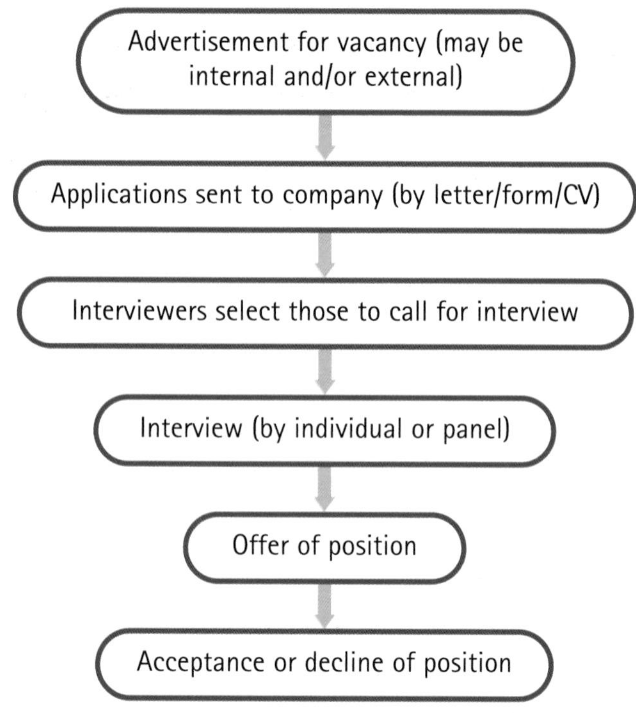

Job selection procedure

7.2 Your project

Planning your project

Each placement may have a particular project which is unique to that organisation. You may be just the person to help them with research they have wanted for years! However, you may need to think of a project yourself. Below are some suggestions.

Customer service

Does the organisation know how well (or badly!) customers rate their service?

- What monitoring methods does it use?
- What results does it get?
- What does it do with the results – who sees them?
- Does anything happen as a result of this information? If so, what?
- Do the employees think the results are important?
- What improvements could be made?

Marketing

- How does the organisation market its product?
- Is it aimed at a particular market segment?
- Does it advertise? Does it use promotions?
- Are there any markets not seeing this material?
- Can any improvements be made?
- Does it know if any particular strategy is better than another?
- Are there any statistics available?

A marketing tool you may be familiar with

Qualifications/experience

- What sorts of qualifications does the organisation look for?
- Do current employees have these skills?
- What staff development takes place?

ACTIVITY

Assume your group has found placements in different sectors of the industry. Find people within the same area, e.g. hotels, and brainstorm all the different kinds of projects you can think of for that sector. Produce a spider diagram.

- Do the employees see the benefit of this development?
- Do the current employees have any travel-specific qualifications (NVQs, BTEC diplomas, ABTAC, IATA, Fares and Ticketing)?
- Can any improvements be made?

There are many other kinds of projects and each organisation will be different. However, each project needs to have an **outcome**, for example 'to review the current qualifications within the Anytown Travel Agency branch and to compare these with the organisation's requirements'.

It should be quite clear to both the organisation and yourself what you hope to find out, and how you are going to do it.

Skills

So, now you have your title and outcome, how are you going to go about it? Tactfully would be one answer! Remember, you are a guest in the organisation and you don't want to be heard saying how amazed you are that nobody in the office has the right qualifications!

Practical research

Ask if you can keep copies of blank customer feedback forms, brochures, development session minutes, etc. Do not just take them; most organisations are happy for you to have them, but some information is sensitive. Use questionnaires – these will make analysing the answers much easier than a jumble of information. You can produce charts and graphs from the data you receive.

Make sure you ask permission if you want to use a questionnaire, particularly if the information may be sensitive.

Do not leave the project to the last day of the placement! Plan your time effectively so that if one method does not work, you have time to change. You can work on the presentation later!

Undertaking the project

Planning

This is essential, and should be done in advance. There are lots of ways to plan, but it is usually better to set down your plan formally. Two types of plan are shown below – the management time plan and the outcome action plan.

TASK / DATE	14/5	15/5	16/5	17/5	18/5	21/5, etc.
Decide on project title	→	→	→			
Draft questionnaire	→					
Ask permission of manager	→	→	→	→		
Ask questionnaire in marketing	→	→				
Sales	→	→	→	→	→	

A management time plan

OUTCOME	What do I have already?	What else do I need?	How?	When?	Completed
Completed questionnaire	Project brief	Word-processed questionnaire	Draft in pencil	Monday 14/4	Revision needed
	List of departments		Get tutor approval		Completed 17/4

An outcome action plan

Always review your plan regularly and update what needs to be done.

ACTIVITY

On your chosen project, draft an outline action plan of how and when you are going to complete it. It does not matter if it needs to be altered as you go along. This is a sign of good monitoring!

Keep records

You will forget! Always keep records of the interviews and conversations you have. If you are gathering examples of promotional campaigns, write down when and where you found them. This attention to detail will pay off in the end.

KEY POINTS

Plan effectively – **do** a plan, **refer** to it and **monitor** it.

Write down your experiences as you go!

Level

PRACTICE ASSESSMENT ACTIVITY

P7.3 Plan the work-based project, listing key objects, proposed outcomes, time scales and resources.

Presenting your findings

This will depend on the project and your tutor's instructions, but bear in mind you know more about this placement than anyone, so assume your audience/readers know nothing. Use photographs, pictures and products of the company to illustrate what you are saying.

Try to produce data which can be beautifully shown in charts and graphs. The more information, the better!

7.3 Monitor, review and present your project

Recording your progress

Keeping a log

You will need to make sure that you keep records of all that you are doing *as you go along* – don't imagine you will remember what you did, at the end! An example of a log is shown below.

Date	Activity	Notes	Initials of supervisor/tutor
17 May	Asked Marketing Department to complete my questionnaire	Sally and Ravi not in. To ask on 19/5	
18 May	Asked permission to give questionnaire to Ticketing Department	Manager agreed, but said to do next week	

A log

Research diary

Another way of recording your progress is to keep a research diary. Below is an example.

Don't forget to complete your action plan – in advance – and to monitor where you have achieved your planned activity. Remember too, to take notice of where you have identified that you need to find further information and make sure this appears later in your plan!

ACTIVITY

Draft a log sheet for your placement. You can fill in many of the boxes now, ready to complete on the day.

Recording methods

If you are going to interview one or more people, remember there are other ways of recording what they say other than taking notes!

Name: ____________________

Project: ____________________

Date	Topic	Comments
15 May	Look at customer service records in use	Mr Marti gave permission Collected blank form from reception

A research diary

You could use an audio or video tape – but ask permission first. Videos can be used to record work practices or marketing events – be creative! You can use clips or photographs in your presentation later.

You may also like to use a witness testimony to record a particular event. An example of a witness testimony is shown below. It could be used to support audio or visual evidence. If you do not have any audio or visual evidence, your witness testimony will have to show more detail of the event (an explanation of the situation, what each person said, the skills and knowledge used etc).

Name: Laura Bates
Project: Customer Service Methods
Activity: Role Play
Date: 21 May 2005

Laura took part in a training session during which she undertook a role play situation. Laura played a receptionist who had to explain an over-booking situation. She did this well, calming down the client and listening to his point of view before offering an alternative.

Signature: *Usha Patel*

Name: Usha Patel
Position: Training Manager

A witness testimony

Reviewing your project

You will need to review how well the project is going against the objectives you agreed at the beginning.

It is usually best to do this at regular intervals during the project (formative) as well as at the end (summative).

Look at what went well, and think about what did not go so well and what you would do next time to improve it. Be honest – a clear and objective review with sound suggestions for improvement is far better than saying everything went well and hope no one notices (they will!).

Always refer back to your original objectives – how well did you achieve what you set out to do?

Presentation

You will need to present the results of your project in the way requested by your tutor and/or the organisation.

You may be asked to do an oral presentation. Remember to dress smartly, stand up straight and talk enthusiastically to your audience. Use anything you have brought from your organisation as visual aids, for example brochures, menus, pictures, videos. Remember to use data from questionnaires in the form of graphs and charts. If you are able to use PowerPoint or slides for overhead projectors, then do so – this will give your presentation a professional look.

If you are required to write your project result, then think about how to make it interesting. Use pictures, examples of forms, photographs, charts, etc. to illustrate what you are reporting. Use the organisation's logo on the front – be creative!

Planning how you are going to write your report is really important. Make sure that you refer to the project's objectives and clearly organise your work. Leave enough time to produce a draft and then to proofread this before aiming at a final version.

Finally – enjoy it! You have spent a considerable amount of time and experienced the world of work. Anyone listening to you or reading your report should be able to understand what it was like and what you found out. Who knows? You might end up with a full-time job at one of these organisations!

Level

PRACTICE ASSESSMENT ACTIVITY

P7.4 Monitor and review your project against agreed outcomes and time scales.

M7.2 Use a range of sources of information and research skills to complete your work-based project.

P7.5 Present your work-based project in an agreed format.

M7.3 Clearly and coherently present an in-depth project that meets key objectives and proposed outcomes within planned time scales.

D7.1 Present your project which should show in-depth understanding with analysis of issues presented. Include and justify recommendations for future actions.

In summary

PREPARE for the placement:

- Produce a professional looking CV.
- Make sure your letters are business-like, correctly spelt and laid out.
- Photocopy application forms and practise completing them.
- Research the organisation you want to go to.
- Take pride in your appearance.
- Appear confident and enthusiastic during interviews.

PLAN your project:

- Ask the organisation if it needs research on a particular topic.
- Use your research to identify a project concerning customer service or marketing, etc. – subjects you have studied.
- Write a plan, read it and monitor it regularly – don't just write it and forget it!

RECORD what you do:

- Keep a log or diary.
- Gather leaflets, brochures, posters, etc. during your time at the organisation.
- Refer back to what you are trying to find out (your objectives).
- Be honest in your evaluation and what you have learnt from it.

TEST YOUR KNOWLEDGE

1. How should you begin and end a business letter?
2. What is the usual procedure for job applications?
3. What preparation should you make for interviews?
4. Name two kinds of plans you could use.
5. Why is it necessary to be truthful about your analysis of the issues?
6. Write a list of *four* possible projects which someone could undertake in a travel and tourism organisation.

Unit 8

Travel and Tourism Study Visit

Introduction

To achieve your BTEC First Diploma in Travel and Tourism, you will need to plan and take part in a study visit. This unit will enable you to do this and to experience how the many and varied components of the travel and tourism industry fit together.

You will need to plan an itinerary for a study visit, taking a variety of issues into consideration, as well as taking part positively in a specific visit. It is also important to be able to evaluate the visit from the curriculum and your own objectives.

How you will be assessed

This unit is assessed internally, so the centre delivering the qualification will assess you against the criteria.

In this unit you will:

① plan an itinerary for a study visit

② contribute to the planning of a study visit for an agreed destination

③ positively participate in a study visit

④ evaluate the study visit.

8.1 Planning an itinerary

Talking point

Decision 1: Within your group and with your tutor's advice, decide whether you are going to be looking at day or residential visits.

It would be great, wouldn't it, if you could arrange to go anywhere you wanted? Unfortunately, as for everyone, you may well have to take a number of things into consideration.

The first may well be *cost*. It is likely that you will have to pay the full cost of the visit(s), so a luxury cruise is likely to be out of the question!

So, will you be looking at a residential visit, where you stay overnight, or several nights, or a day visit somewhere? A residential visit may cost £200 or so; a day visit more like £20, depending on the destination and the number of participants.

Day visit costs

One of the biggest costs may be the transport. Your school or college may use several coach companies. To give you some idea of what a coach costs, you need to pay for the driver's time, the use of the coach, petrol and parking. All this is usually given as a total cost; but remember, they don't come cheaply!

Rail fares are often good value for students under 18, travelling together to and from the destination.

Minibuses are normally costed the same way as coaches and may be cheaper if the group is small.

Costings usually show both total cost and cost per participant. The cost needs to be clearly calculated, labelling all the items. For example:

Item	Cost	Total cost
Cost of coach	£250.00	£250.00
Entry price	18 @ £14.50	£261.00
wheelchair user	1 @ £10.50	£10.50
helper	Free	–
1 adult	£20.00	£20.00
1 adult (tutor)	Free	–
Car parking; tolls	£20.00	£20.00
		£561.50

Divided by 20 students = £28.08 per person

Destination

This is likely to be a difficult choice! It is unlikely your tutor will agree to an unsuitable destination, however potentially enjoyable! Be realistic –

this visit should add to your knowledge of travel and tourism. Suggestions might include:

- a theme park, e.g. Alton Towers
- a city, e.g. Edinburgh
- a castle, e.g. Warwick
- a large shopping mall, e.g. Bluewater
- a museum, e.g. Science Museum
- a seaside resort e.g. Brighton
- an outdoor museum, e.g. Ironbridge Gorge
- a theatre visit.

Where you visit is up to you!

KEY POINTS

To decide on a destination, think about:

- Why go?
- How do we get there?
- How much?
- Who is going and what are their needs?

Your choice will depend on where you are. A day trip by coach should not be more than two hours' drive in each direction.

Many attractions supply worksheets, talks, picnic areas, etc., or information sheets. This will give a focus to the day (for more information, see below).

Talking point

Decision 2: Where to?
Stage 1: In groups, use a flip chart sheet to brainstorm ideas about destinations. Just say whatever comes to mind.

Stage 2: In groups, take each of the suggestions and evaluate them for viability.

The following may help you to make your decision:

- What is our objective in going there?
- How long will it take to get there?
- Is it easy to access (train, coach parks, etc.)?
- What is the cost of (a) transport (b) entry?
- What is there to do when we get there?
- Are there worksheets, study rooms, speakers?
- Is the visit dependent on good weather?
- Are there facilities for food/drink/toilets?
- Is any special equipment needed?
- Do any of the group have particular needs which need to be taken into account?

If you are still left with too many options, try awarding points to each of the above.

Itinerary development

Itineraries are normally set out in chronological (time) order. For example:

Visit to Alton Towers, Tuesday 10 May 2005

0900	Meet outside college main gates
0915	Depart college
	Travel to Alton Towers
1045	Stop at motorway service station
1105	Depart motorway service station
1230	Arrive Alton Towers
	Picnic lunch
1800	Meet at main gates
1930	Stop at motorway service station
1950	Depart motorway service station
2130	Arrive back at college main gate

Don't try to make the itinerary too tight – allow time for traffic jams, roadworks, etc. Remember that coaches travel more slowly than cars – ask the coach company for advice.

You may wish also to explain what will be happening at the visit, so that everyone knows the arrangements. For example:

Please bring a picnic lunch. We will eat this on arrival at Alton Towers. If it is raining, there will be a room provided.

You will be free to go on the rides, but please stay in pairs or small groups. There will be a rendezvous point at 1530 at the main gates for assistance. Please contact the tutor on mobile 07 . . . in an emergency.

The cost will be £ . . . per person, payable by 6 May.

This means everybody knows exactly what is going on – when people are herded like sheep they tend to act like sheep and lose the ability to think!

Once you have drafted your itinerary, it might be helpful to present your ideas to the rest of the class, and really *sell* the visit. Obtain leaflets/brochures from the destination so you can explain exactly what it is like!

Level ✔

PRACTICE ASSESSMENT ACTIVITY

P8.1 Produce a travel itinerary for a study visit.

M8.1 Evaluate the itinerary for the visit, explaining how it takes into account a range of considerations. Using the research you have done so far, produce a clear itinerary for a proposed destination for a study visit.

Residential visit costs

These are more complex since you are adding a further component – the accommodation. This will add to the cost considerably, particularly if food is included. Be careful to calculate the cost of each night. For example:

Cost per twin room = £30	× 2 nights × 18 students =	£1080.00
Single room = £35	× 2 nights × 2 students =	£140.00
Evening meal = £3.50	× 2 nights × 20 staff =	£140.00
Room price includes breakfast		–
	Total	£1360.00
	Price per person	£68.00

You will need to include the hotel details in the itinerary as parents and the school or college will want to know these. For example:

> Accommodation will be in twin rooms at the Garden Hotel, 13 Park Road, Warwick CV99 1XX (Tel: 012345 24678) for two nights including breakfast and evening meal.

8.2 Planning the visit

Now for the real thing! You may be going on one or several day visits, or on a residential visit. You may be using one or more of your draft itineraries, but you will need to go into more detail before you will be ready to depart!

Aims and objectives

You may have a general aim for the whole group, for example:

- to gather information for Unit 4 Introduction to Marketing in Travel and Tourism
- to have an interesting day out
- to look at customer service at a hotel
- to see components of travel and tourism in action
- to get information from a theme park location.

You will also need to develop a set of SMART objectives (see Unit 4 Introduction to Marketing in Travel and Tourism, page 135, for information on SMART objectives).

Your objectives might be:

- to collect five leaflets for my marketing assignment from the shop
- to help to organise a day out which 90 per cent of respondents enjoy
- to complete a questionnaire for customer service at the Garden Hotel on Wednesday
- to complete a report on travel and tourism components by the end of March
- to take notes from Alton Towers' marketing officer during their presentation.

Over to you!

Well-written SMART objectives will enable you to do the evaluation at a later stage more easily.

KEY POINTS

Your objectives must be:

- Specific
- Measurable
- Achievable
- Realistic
- Timed.

You must be clear *why* the visit is taking place to these specific destinations. It may be so that you can assess possible destinations for work experience or to make sure that it will be possible to check whether the objectives have been met. This could be done by the completion of a questionnaire, for example, at the time or at a briefing.

Constraints

The participants

You must take the age of the participants into account. You may think a visit to a nightclub might be enjoyable, but the nightclub is unlikely to accept a group where any member is under the age of 18. Equally, a visit to a puppet theatre might not be appropriate for 17-year-olds!

If the group includes a participant with special needs, this must be taken into account. The Disability Discrimination Act requires destinations (unless exempt) to make 'reasonable adjustments', for example ground-floor rooms, flashing fire alarms, ramps, toilet facilities, etc.

KEY POINTS

You must consider the needs of the participants in terms of their age, needs and constraints.

You will need to:

- ask the participant exactly what needs they have
- inform everyone involved, e.g. coach company, railway, attraction, hotel, and *confirm in writing.*

Most organisations are only too happy to help. Wheelchairs may be available on loan, and many town centres have mobility centres where equipment is for hire.

You will need to make sure that you have written permission for the visit from the necessary college/school authorities and also parents/guardians. If participants are under 18 years, or older if 'vulnerable', the party leader has to be an adult and will be *in loco parentis* (taking the place of parents/guardians). This is even more important for residential visits and signatures of parents/guardians *must* be obtained. Below is an example of a parent/guardian consent form.

CONSENT FORM

I agree for ______________ to travel and take part in the visit.

I accept liability for full payment.

I understand that those supervising ____________________ are acting *in loco parentis* and will exercise a standard of care that would be expected of a reasonably prudent parent. I also understand that during any free time he/she will not be under direct supervision.

The College/School will not be responsible for personal injury or any other damage or loss unless due to negligence of the staff.

I agree to all the items above.

Signed: ______________________ Date: ______________
Name: ______________________________

Parent/guardian consent form

The destination

The destination of the visit is of central importance. If a visit to another country is suggested, remember that participants will require:

- a current passport – it is advisable to have a minimum of six months left to run on the passport from the date of return (inspect all passports at least a month in advance, and take a note of the number in case of loss)

and may also require:

- a visa (applies to some countries outside the European Union – check with the country's embassy)

- vaccinations and health advice, depending on the country you are planning to visit (check out the Department of Health website for health advice to travellers: www.dh.gov.uk).

The Foreign and Commonwealth Office has a useful travel advice section on its website: www.fco.gov.uk.

Visits within the UK also need careful thought. You may already have carried out the brainstorming exercise earlier in this unit. If you have not yet decided on a suitable destination, then a questionnaire might help you to make the final choice.

Budget

The budget is also important – you may have already paid some money and the budget is therefore set. You may be given a range of costs or you may have to just make it as cheap as possible!

It is always wise to add on £20 or so for contingencies such as tolls or car parking and you may also need some money to buy brochures, etc.

Check the formula in the first section above for assessing cost.

ACTIVITY

Draw up a questionnaire and ask people both within and outside your group for their thoughts on:

- how far they would be prepared to travel
- how much they would be prepared to pay
- the type of destination they would like to visit – give them a choice of five or so different destinations, e.g. city, seaside, etc.
- their own suggestions.

Health, safety and security

It is advisable for each participant to provide a list of medical conditions and/or prescribed medication, dietary needs, allergies, etc. when going on a residential visit. This means that should a participant fall ill or an accident happen, the tutor will have this information to hand over to a doctor. An example of a medical information form is shown on the next page.

MEDICAL INFORMATION FORM

Student's name: ______________________
Tutor: ______________________

Medical conditions/other	Delete as appropriate	
Medical condition (give details)	Yes	No
Allergies (give details)	Yes	No
Medication prescribed (give details)	Yes	No
Dietary needs (give details)	Yes	No
Asthma/medication	Yes	No

I declare this information to be correct.

Signed: ______________________
Name: ______________________
Date: ______________

A medical information form

Unless medically qualified, tutors are not allowed to dispense medicines, so participants should be encouraged to bring patent medicines such as paracetamol if they wish to!

You should also ensure you have a list of mobile telephone numbers so stray students can be contacted, as well as emergency numbers for parents/guardians. Remember to include the tutor's mobile number.

KEY POINTS

Health and safety must always be of prime importance and should override all other considerations.

Risk assessments

All transport providers/attractions should have their own risk assessment, but you will need to do a risk assessment for the trip.

A risk assessment looks at possible **hazards** and at the **controls** put in place to avoid them or minimise the effect. How the controls manage to offset the hazards will result in the risk assessment. An example of a risk assessment is shown below.

Hazard	Precautions	Risk
Travelling by coach	Comply with level of staff/student supervision Ensure students seated Ensure seat belts worn Ensure behaviour is appropriate	Low
Slipping/tripping/falling	Keep to pavements/footpaths Follow instructions	Low

A risk assessment for a day visit

Your school or college is likely to have a similar assessment which will need to be completed.

Time and location

You should make sure you set the date at a point in the year when you will have time to complete the preparations and also to evaluate effectively. It may need to be at a convenient time for other studies too, for example to research marketing. It is advisable to talk to everyone who might have an input into the timing.

KEY POINTS

You must consider the needs of the participants in terms of their age, needs and constraints.

The plan

Once you have decided on the time of year, you will need to decide on the best day of the week. This may depend on your tutor's availability, how many other classes it may affect, opening times of attractions, etc. It may be best to avoid days of heaviest traffic, which is often Monday morning and Friday afternoon.

Departure time is important – try not to leave in the middle of the rush hour; an hour earlier or later may save almost as much if you can avoid traffic jams. Always arrange a meeting time 15 minutes before you *must* depart, as there are bound to be people who arrive late!

Try not to cut transport times – be generous in your estimations. Ask for advice – it is far easier to arrive in good time rather than have to hurry at the last minute.

Try to ensure that you build in **comfort breaks** every couple of hours or so. Ask for advice about service stations, public toilets, etc.

Remember, if you are visiting a city or attraction by coach, you will need to check where the coach can drop-off/pick-up and then go to park. Check the cost of **parking**, too, and build it into the cost of the trip.

Make sure you allow plenty of time to get to your destination

ACTIVITY

In groups, go through *all* of the activities for each day and check that decisions have been recorded.

Make a file with plastic pockets containing each day's attractions and transport arrangements.

Ensure you have any confirmations, joining instructions, phone numbers, maps and any other correspondence in your file.

If you are arranging a residential visit, perhaps a group could provide a file for each day. If several day visits are planned, then a group could take responsibility for each visit.

Destination

You will need to make sure that for every destination you have a set timetable of activities.

If you are visiting a tourist information centre or other information source, it may be possible for them to arrange a talk. Many marketing departments are also happy to do this, and often supply information or task sheets linked to the curriculum.

Tourist information centres are a good source of information

If you are going to arrange a talk, you will need to ensure the speaker understands what information you need – send a copy of the assessment criteria or assignments.

If participants are going to an attraction without a set information session, a questionnaire or 'treasure hunt' might be helpful. Many attractions welcome a visit prior to the group arriving.

A set time and meeting point to gather all participants together at points throughout the day would be helpful to check that objectives were being met.

ACTIVITY

Choose a large attraction near you and find out if it has an education officer. Most English Heritage properties or those which belong to large groups like Madame Tussauds will have someone responsible for education.

Ask them to send you a pack so that you can see the kinds of services they offer.

Itinerary

Now for the final documents! You might like to produce a **formal itinerary** – similar to the one in the first section. On a residential visit you may need several sheets of daily schedules. For example:

Itinerary for Monday 9 May

0830	Breakfast
0930	Meet in foyer
0940	Depart for museum by foot
1015	Arrive at museum
1030	Talk by curator
1115	Visit to museum
1300	Lunch break
1400	Visit to cathedral – meet on front steps
1500	Talk by guide
1600	Free time – shopping
1800	Evening briefing – main lounge
1900	Evening meal

You might also like to do a **presentation**, either using your formal itinerary as a base, or using PowerPoint slides to give more details and photographs. Ensure the equipment is available to do this! Try to get leaflets/information sheets so that you can hand these round to your audience.

You could also do a **brochure** for your trip. Again, it could be based around the formal itinerary, but you could use pictures and photographs as well as colour and varied fonts to make it look really interesting – sell it!

Talking point

In a small group, collect three or four tour brochures.

Discuss how they encourage people to go on their holidays, e.g. added information/maps, etc.

What can you learn from these that you can use in your own brochure?

8.3 Participating in the visit

Positive participation

Code of conduct

Very often a code of conduct is more effective if the group agrees on what is acceptable behaviour. There are usually some negative instructions, but positive phrases are much more likely to have positive outcomes! Your group's code of conduct might include the following:

- Any participant found under the influence of or in possession of drugs or alcohol will be severely disciplined.
- All behaviour should benefit the reputation of the school/college.
- Dress should be appropriate on all occasions.
- All participants should arrive at all meeting points punctually.

There will be many more depending on the kind of visit you are considering.

As the organising group, you will need to make sure that you are always punctual, and encourage other groups to be as well. Your itinerary will be guaranteed to run late if several people always arrive late, to the great annoyance of everyone who has managed to get there on time.

Team work

Remember that you are part of a team – what you do will affect the reputation of the other participants. You will need to take care that everybody has the information they need and that their personal objectives will be met.

You will need to make sure you are organised yourself, with the correct information and paperwork at all times. You will need to have professional personal presentation, smart and clean as agreed by the group. You may like to dress as a professional tour guide when on duty, with a jacket and trousers or skirt. Name badges and logos would also add to the image.

Respect

Remember that you may be going among the public! Bear in mind there may be vulnerable people around and take account of the impact of a group of people on children and the elderly.

Over to you!

If you are taking responsibility for a visit, or part of a visit, it needs to be clear who is responsible for what. You will need to decide this in advance. For example:

Visit to 'Magma', Doncaster

Responsibility	**Who?**
Headcount at departure point	*Tom and Rajid*
Register on coach	*Abigail*
Headcount on coach after comfort break	*Darren*
Briefing on coach	*Kylie*
Brochure distribution	*Simone*
Tidy up coach	*Whole group*

You could add another column for comments on how well this went!

Your group may have people with particular needs – ensure these are met or report to someone in authority if they are not. These needs may be physical, emotional or religious.

ACTIVITY

Copy and complete the table below:

Need	Solution	Comments
Wheelchair user	Hire collapsible wheelchair	Can hire in shopping centre if necessary
Hearing impaired	Inform all destinations	
Lacking confidence/shy		
Devout Muslim		

Gathering evidence

This visit is not just for fun – it should also be contributing to your studies!

You may like to think about the following:

- collecting information (souvenirs, leaflets, brochures, guidebooks)
- notes or questionnaire completion (questionnaires/checklists)
- research completion (notes from talks, etc.).

You will also need to have evidence of your own involvement through, for example:

- photos/videos
- audio tapes (of briefings, etc.)
- log sheets (see below)
- statements from your tutor/group.

LOG SHEET		
Visit to: ______________________		Date: ______________
Activity	My contribution	Outcome
2 people late	I phoned on my mobile	We waited 3 minutes
Briefing	I handed out the resources	All had them

A log sheet

Make sure any changes to the itinerary are noted down at the time – you are likely to forget in all the excitement later!

Skills

It is important to remember that organising a visit is much harder than it looks! Tour guides go through a period of intensive training and possess many skills to deal with their group.

Remember to show positive body language – look alert and interested and don't put your hands in your pockets or slouch! Stand up straight and keep eye contact with your group; above all, *smile* and be positive and polite.

You will need to take responsibility for your own contribution to the visit – this might mean helping to solve any problems, from coach breakdown to loss of bags! You may well be judged on the kinds of skills shown in the example assessment on page 286.

Be positive and polite when dealing with problems

Visit to Magma

Student: ______________________

Demonstrated skills	Activity
Body language	Smiled and looked interested during briefing
Interpersonal skills	Ensured all participants paired/in a group
Personal effectiveness	Made file of all organised attractions available
Problem-solving	When student late, found phone number and called
Time management techniques	Always arrived 5 minutes early
Teamwork	Helped unwell colleague by typing booklet
Communication	Talked on microphone on coach effectively

Example of skills assessment

Above all – have a successful visit!

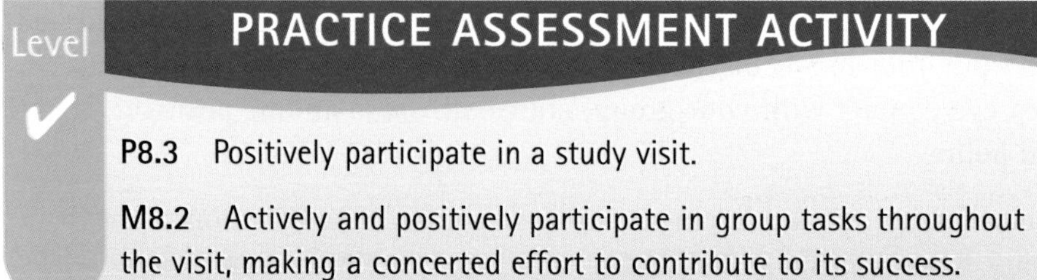

Level ✔

PRACTICE ASSESSMENT ACTIVITY

P8.3 Positively participate in a study visit.

M8.2 Actively and positively participate in group tasks throughout the visit, making a concerted effort to contribute to its success.

8.4 Evaluating the visit

The visit

This is where you can *honestly* evaluate how well the visit went – don't worry if it all went wrong, there will be much more to say!

It would be helpful if you had some data on which to base your evaluation. This can easily be done by asking participants to fill in a questionnaire about the visit or your part of the visit. It is best to ask them to do this at the time or at the end of the visit – if you leave it too long, people will forget! An example of an evaluation questionnaire is shown below.

EVALUATION QUESTIONNAIRE

1 How would you describe your trip overall?

❒ Excellent ❒ Good ❒ Average ❒ Poor

2 Would you return to this area/hotel in future?

❒ Yes ❒ No

3 Do any of the organisers/staff deserve a special mention?

____

4 Did you achieve your objectives?

❒ Yes ❒ No

5 How did you rate the food?

❒ Excellent ❒ Good ❒ Average ❒ Poor

6 How did you rate the transport?

❒ Excellent ❒ Good ❒ Average ❒ Poor

7 Do you have any further comments?

____

8 Is there anything you would like to improve?

____

An evaluation questionnaire

ACTIVITY

Produce a clear questionnaire – yes/no boxes plus comments are easiest – for areas such as:

- the journey – route/amendments/method of transport/time scales
- destination – attractions/features/entertainment/facilities
- extras – guest speaker/tours/packs
- value for money – what's included/overall cost.

KEY POINTS

Draft a questionnaire which can be easily completed and analysed.

When you have the results of your questionnaires, compare them with your own opinion and expand on why things worked out as they did. For instance, if many of the responses said the journey was too long, it may be that you can explain that this was as a result of emergency road works.

Level 

PRACTICE ASSESSMENT ACTIVITY

P8.4 Produce a basic evaluation of the study visit.

KEY POINTS

Be honest in your evaluation!

Personal evaluation

You may receive feedback from your tutor. However, you need also to evaluate how well you think you did and what you have learnt – be honest!

Assess whether you now know more about:

- the travel and tourism industry and how it works
- what you learnt 'on the job'
- how well you work in a team
- your own role in a group situation
- how effective you are at solving problems
- how organised you can be
- anything else, e.g. your ability to stay calm in a crisis.

Level

PRACTICE ASSESSMENT ACTIVITY

M8.3 Evaluate your own development during the planning process and study visit, describing strengths and weaknesses.

Talking point

In a small group, discuss your assessment of yourself and take notes on how the rest of the group sees your contribution and whether this agrees with your own viewpoint.

Feedback from suppliers

You may also be able to get feedback from the coach driver, attraction guide, hotel manager, etc. It is a good idea to produce a short questionnaire for them to complete at the time, but make sure it is related to the service they are providing.

Objectives

Remember the objectives you established at the beginning of this unit? How well did (a) you and (b) the group achieve them?

You will be asked to produce evidence of your evaluation either in the form of a presentation or as a discussion, or possibly a written report. Ensure you include all your sources of evidence and any visual aids such as photographs, leaflets, etc.

Talking point

In your group, discuss whether your objectives were achieved and how (or not) this was done.

If you needed to obtain a leaflet, make sure you have these available for evidence!

KEY POINTS

Remember to collect evidence as you go – it's too late when you come back!

Level

PRACTICE ASSESSMENT ACTIVITY

D8.1 Evaluate the study visit against personal and curriculum objectives, using input from a range of sources, making justified recommendations for improvement and personal development.

Talking point

In your group, discuss what you would do again in the same way and what you would change next time. Keep notes of your discussions.

This cycle of organisation, visit and evaluation is a pivotal part of travel and tourism.

Well done – you have now experienced what happens everyday in the travel and tourism industry!

In summary

RESEARCH:

- your visit options (destination, transport, cost)
- the needs and requirements of your group
- and produce a *viable* itinerary.

PLAN:

- your visit using SMART objectives
- your visit bearing in mind the health and safety of all participants
- your 'sales pitch' to the group!

PARTICIPATE:

- professionally, punctually and enthusiastically
- as part of a team
- responsibly, ensuring safety at all times.

RECORD:

- what the team did together
- what you contributed to the team effort
- on the appropriate form *at the time*
- formally both your evaluation and that of the group.

TEST YOUR KNOWLEDGE

1. What is a SMART objective?
2. Why does a party leader have to take particular care if a group contains people under 18 years of age?
3. Name three ways in which risks can be minimised on a study visit.
4. Name four things which need to be taken into account when planning a visit.
5. Name three advantages of working in a team.
6. What should *always* override any other consideration?
7. Name two ways in which you can prove you participated effectively in a study visit.
8. Should you write your log sheet and evaluation (a) during the visit, (b) the night before your assignment is due?!

Index